PREVENTING VIOLENCE IN SCHOOLS

A Challenge
to American Democracy

PREVENTING VIOLENCE IN SCHOOLS

A Challenge to American Democracy

Joan N. Burstyn, Syracuse University
Geoff Bender, Syracuse University
Ronnie Casella, Central Connecticut State University
Howard W. Gordon, State University of New York at Oswego
Domingo P. Guerra, Syracuse University
Kristen V. Luschen, Hampshire College
Rebecca Stevens, University of South Carolina Spartanburg
Kimberly M. Williams, State University of New York at Cortland

LAWRENCE ERLBAUM ASSOCIATES, PUBLISHERS
2001   Mahwah, New Jersey   London

Lawrence Erlbaum Associates, Inc., Publishers
10 Industrial Avenue
Mahwah, NJ 07430

Cover design by Kathryn Houghtaling Lacey

Library of Congress Cataloging-in-Publication Data
Preventing violence in schools : a challenge to American democracy / Joan N. Burstyn ...
[et al.]
    p. cm.
    Includes bibliographical references and index.
    ISBN 0-8058-3733-7 (cloth.: alk. paper)—0-8058-3734-5 (pbk.: alk. paper)
    1. School violence—United States—Prevention. I. Burstyn, Joan N.

LB3013.3.P757 2000
371.7'82'0973—dc21

                                                                    00-062252

Books published by Lawrence Erlbaum Associates are printed on acid-free paper, and their bindings
are chosen for strength and durability.

Printed in the United States of America
10   9   8   7   6   5   4   3   2   1

Contents

Preface

Gun violence among adults has long been endemic in the United States. In the 1990s, however, when highly publicized incidents of gun violence took place not only among adults, but among children in schools; in middle class suburbs and rural areas as well as in financially-strapped cities; and among children of the White majority as well as among minority populations, the public became outraged. The authors of this book believe that the outrage about violence in schools was long overdue. The use of guns, while the most lethal, is still the least likely form of violence in schools, but violence through bullying, extortion, name calling, sexual harassment, and suicide are prevalent nationally.

We have written this book to explain the cultural and psychological underpinnings of violence among youth; to assess the effect of programs already adopted by schools; and to galvanize professional educators and the public to act on their outrage by adopting a whole-school approach to preventing violence, an approach that will involve communities as well as schools in addressing the problem.

Young people of school age belong to a network of systems—family, community, and school. Each of these has its sub-systems. The community, for instance, includes federal, state, and local legislatures and executives, religious organizations, social service and law enforcement agencies, private corporations, and the media. Responsibility for the violence among young people today does not lie with any one system; all are complicit in it. Change in one system cannot end violence. While this book tackles the school as a location for change, families and communities must, also, change for violence to end.

How did we come to write this book? My own interest in violence prevention and conflict resolution has been long standing. In the 1990s, I and Neil Katz, of the Program for the Analysis and Resolution of Conflicts in the Maxwell School of Syracuse University, arranged day-long conferences for teachers and administrators in central New York on conflict resolution in schools. A grant from Syracuse university enabled me to design (with help from Rebecca Stevens) two courses for educators entitled: Infusing conflict resolution into the K–12 curriculum, and A whole school approach to conflict resolution. Teachers, counselors, and administrators who took those courses, and students who occasionally visited class to talk about their lives, increased our knowledge of the problems, as together we struggled to find ways to address them.

Through Syracuse University, I, Rebecca Stevens, and others gave workshops for teachers and administrators in central New York on ways to prevent violence in schools. Whether from rural, suburban, or city school districts, educators declared that violence, in one form or another, posed a threat to their schools. The chapter in this book on ways to implement a whole school approach to preventing violence, grows out of these years of work with schools.

Several authors—myself (as principal investigator), Ronnie Casella, Domingo Guerra, Rebecca Stevens, and Kim Williams — have worked on the Syracuse University Violence Prevention Project, funded since 1997 by the U.S. Department of Justice, Office of Juvenile Justice and Delinquency Prevention, as part of the Hamilton Fish National Institute on School and Community Violence. In its first year, the SUVP project examined efforts to prevent violence in one city school district, completed an assessment of the needs for a future intervention, and piloted a small-scale intervention. Several chapters in this book—by Ronnie Casella, Domingo Guerra, Rebecca Stevens, and Kim Williams and myself—draw upon that first year's work, as well as work conducted subsequently by the project. Ronnie Casella has been influenced by his subsequent work on violence prevention in Connecticut in schools and a prison, and Kim Williams by hers assessing the effectiveness of programs to prevent violence in rural and suburban school districts in central New York.

We are grateful for the opportunity the Federal funding has provided to engage in this research, and to present it at national meetings, such as the annual meetings of the American Educational Research Association. There, and in discussions with teachers, university faculty, and students, we came to understand that the literature lacked discussion that combined both the socio-economic and cultural dilemmas that lead to violence in our schools, and the effects of interventions already adopted.

My two chapters, which begin and end the book, focus on the social, cultural, and emotional contexts of violence in schools. To help readers understand those contexts more clearly, other authors examine how boys and girls are socialized to deal with violence. Howard W. Gordon and Geoff Bender discuss African American and White boys respectively. Kristen Luschen writes about the socialization of girls.

While most chapters are based on ethnographic research, where the voices of students, as well as teachers and administrators, are highlighted, Gordon's chapter breaks the mold with a piece of fiction: a short story about a fight, followed by an interview between Gordon and me about his intentions in writing the story and his views on the pressures faced today by African American males as they grow up.

As well as thanking the U.S. Department of Justice for funding the research reported in several chapters, we wish to thank the educators and school students who agreed to be interviewed, sharing with us so freely their hopes and frustrations. We thank also the colleagues and students at our various universities who have critiqued chapters for us and helped us to sharpen our arguments.

We have been energized by our research to redouble our efforts to counter violence in schools. We hope this book will encourage readers to redouble their efforts as well.

—Joan N. Burstyn

Acknowledgments

All the authors of this book would like to thank the administrators, students, support staff, and teachers who so generously shared their opinions and beliefs. We want, also, to thank our colleagues at the various universities where we teach for their support and insights.

Thanks are also due to the Syracuse University Violence Prevention Project (SUVPP), funded by the Hamilton Fish National Institute on School and Community Violence through a contract with the U. S. Office of Juvenile Justice and Delinquency Prevention.[1] SUVPP supported Joan Burstyn, Ronnie Casella, Domingo Guerra, Rebecca Stevens, and Kimberly Williams to conduct research in the schools of Northeast City. Chapters 2, 3, 6, 9, 10, 11, and 12 draw, primarily or entirely, on data collected during the first year of the project, 1997–1998. The group worked as a team during that year, so that each owes much to the discussions held at that time.

Joan Burstyn, as Director (1997–1998) and Principal Investigator (1998 on) of SUVPP, and Kimberly Williams, as Assistant Director

[1]The funding was from Grant no. 97-MU-FX-KO12 (S-1) from the Office of Juvenile Justice and Delinquency Prevention, Office of Justice Programs, U.S. Department of Justice. Points of view or opinions in these chapters are those of the authors and do not necessarily represent the U.S. Department of Justice.

(1997–1998) and Director (1998–1999) of SUVPP, benefited especially from discussions with colleagues at the other six institutions forming the Hamilton Fish National Institute. We thank them for their contributions to our thinking.

Syracuse University provided an Instructional Development Grant, from 1995 to 1997, to Joan Burstyn to develop and teach a graduate level course entitled "A Whole School Approach to Conflict Resolution." The framework for chapter 8, which originated while she developed the course with Rebecca Stevens, was refined as they co-taught the course several times.

Last, Joan Burstyn would like to thank: Dara Wexler for her skills in tracking down source materials and her careful reading of the whole manuscript; and Harold Burstyn, and R. Deborah Davis, Director of the Syracuse University Violence Prevention Project, for their comments on chapters 1 and 13, and for their forbearance with her while she prepared the final manuscript.

1

Violence and Its Prevention: A Challenge for Schools

Joan N. Burstyn

Syracuse University

People may view violence in schools as a discrete problem, to be addressed by school personnel without concern for broader social issues. The shootings at schools around the country during the last decade have led to a rush to rectify policies on student behavior—discipline more strictly enforced, zero tolerance for violence, and offenders banished to alternative schools. The buildings and grounds have been changed—bushes have been cut back, outside lighting increased, side doors kept locked at all times, and metal detectors installed at main entrances. We may be tempted to believe that we all agree on what school violence is—the use of guns to mow down classmates and teachers—and how to deal with it.

However, beyond wanting to end students' shooting at classmates and teachers, agreement evaporates on what school violence is and how to deal with it. Agreement depends on shared cultural assumptions about the causes of school violence, which institutions or people need to change, which behaviors are unacceptable, and which ways are best to handle conflict, express anger, and deal with fear. As a society, we are not united in our assumptions about these issues. Thus, the nitty-gritty of school regulations, the day-to-day procedures to prevent fighting and harassment, become more controversial than the initial decision to end violence.

1

The authors of this book acknowledge the complexity of the issues facing schools and society in trying to prevent the spread of violence in schools. Robert C. Pianta and Daniel J. Walsh, in *High Risk Children in Schools: Constructing Sustaining Relationships* (1996), provide a useful theoretical framework for considering this complexity. Pianta and Walsh develop a contextual systems model to explain the relationship among children, their families, and their schooling. This model suggests that the child–family system and the schooling system are each subordinate within a larger system that links them together. The authors argue that each relationship within any system, and between systems, is founded on interactions that take place over time. Hence, the history of those interactions is an important part of any relationship. According to Pianta and Walsh, "relationship systems exist between the child-family and schooling systems *regardless* of their quality (good or bad), the nature of the contact between the units (positive vs. negative, engaged vs. disengaged), or the even [*sic*] lack of contact. It is not the case that no relationship exists" (p. 67 italics in original).

Children, like adults, participate in other systems than child–family and schooling: these include systems of gender and race relations, the economy, the media, and the law. The nature of their interaction with each of these systems affects children's acquisition of knowledge and their behavior both inside and outside school. These other systems and their impact upon students is not the focus of this book, but several of the contributors allude to them. We believe that stopping violence in schools depends, not only on changing schools, but also on changing these systems.

Pianta and Walsh's framework offers researchers who are concerned with preventing school violence a way to talk about, and link together, the variety of influences—societal, familial, educational, and individual—that affect students' behavior. The responsibility for a child becoming "at risk of violence" has to be shared by all the systems to which that child belongs.

However, there are challenges to using a contextual systems model to explain school violence and then expecting people to change a system based on what they learned from the model. Changing the behavior of a system is more difficult than changing the behavior of an individual. In our society, changing the behavior of an individual has become the purview of professionals, such as psychiatrists, school counselors, teachers, or probation officers. It is hard enough, even with professional assistance, to persuade one person to change his or her behavior. It is even more difficult when people want to change the behavior of a system, as they must engage in a complex political process that is costly in time and money. Moreover, the ideas held by the agents of change are bound to be challenged. They will have to be defended, not only among professionals, but also in the media and other public forums, because to change the behavior of a system entails changing the opinions and behaviors of the public at large, as well as those of the professionals who maintain that system.

When change is suggested for a system, the individuals who must bring about that change, and in the process change their own behavior, are usually adults. This offers a second challenge. Up to this time, most programs introduced to prevent school violence have expected the students to change, and not the teachers or administrators. A student, who does not have all the legal rights of an adult, may be obliged to accept changes that an adult could refuse. And being young, students may adapt to changes more readily than many adults do. Thus, asking the adults in schools to change presents greater challenges than asking students to do so.

Despite the challenges, Pianta and Walsh's contextual systems model helps those of us working to prevent violence realize the link between our work at the micro level, where we attempt to change the lives of individual students in a specific school, and the work of policy-makers at the macro level, who attempt to counter the effects on children of inner-city poverty, rural decay, lack of public transport, suburban anomie, or the constraints experienced by affluent, professionally employed parents.

In Part I of this book, several authors look beyond the initial decision to end violence in schools to examine both the various meanings given to violence and the ways it impacts teenage boys and girls as they live through each day at school. Ronnie Casella (chap. 2) suggests that violence in schools includes far more than the use of weapons. It also includes jostling in corridors; name-calling that leads to fights in the playground; bullying and extorting food or money from the victims; suicide, which may devastate not only the individual and his or her family but the whole school; forms of sexual harassment that some teachers and administrators previously have not noticed or have accepted as "natural" behavior among children and teens, and the systemic violence embodied in coercive school policies. These forms of violence are hard to document. However, both Casella and Kimberly Williams (chap. 3) show how ethnographic research, including participant observation and in-depth interviews, can throw light on the historical and socioeconomic context for violent confrontations in schools, as well as the immediate motives and actions of those involved in them.

The importance of such research as a means to illumine what it means to be an adolescent today cannot be overemphasized. Niobe Way's *Everyday Courage: The Lives and Stories of Urban Teenagers* (1998) draws on stories told by twenty-four urban teenagers over three years to describe how they view their world and negotiate their way through it. She also emphasizes the dangers facing researchers when they interpret qualitative, ethnographic data. She writes that the adolescents' stories "reminded me that when social scientists, including myself, place their thinking into categories such as 'self-blaming,' 'individually oriented,' or even holding a 'split consciousness,' they risk oversimplifying the teens' desires, thoughts, beliefs, and values. The difficulty of complicating a story—of making it more authentic and real—while also revealing patterns, drawing broad strokes, and 'having a point' is an ongoing difficulty" (p. 267).

The students from Northeast City who are described in several chapters of this volume came from homes similar to those of Way's students. Like them, our students developed ways of coping. Chapter 12 describes a pilot literacy project for teens attending a program set up as an alternative to expulsion for possessing a weapon on school property. The teachers in this alternative (public school) program believed that the profiles of their students were similar in all respects to those of students who remained in regular public school. They referred to the students at the alternative school as good kids who had made a mistake.

Should we conclude, from studies such as Way's and our own from Northeast City, that the issues faced by urban teens, especially those from ethnic or racial minority groups, differ in kind from the issues faced by suburban or rural students from predominantly White families? Way suggests that the differences she saw among her students may be artifacts of the differing research methodologies used for her study (interviews and qualitative analysis) and for most studies of White, middle-class, suburban students (surveys and quantitative analysis). Perhaps, she suggests, if we used the same research methods with suburban and rural students that she used, we might find that the students expressed similar views. This is an issue that researchers must now address.

In the last decade, several authors have written about the difficulties boys encounter as they grow to manhood in the United States (e.g., Canada, 1998; Miedzian, 1991; Pollack, 1998). Among those difficulties are the rigorous codes to which boys must adhere to be considered manly by their peers. In this volume, Geoff Bender (chap. 4) explores the implications of these codes for young men in a suburban school whose peers identify them (and who identify themselves) as "freaks." While Bender provides a snapshot of one moment in the history of a suburban school, chapter 5 takes the reader on a journey through time to examine changes in the socialization of African-American boys during the last thirty years. Beginning with a short story by Howard Gordon from the 1970s about a lethal fight among teenagers, the chapter continues with Gordon's reminiscences, a quarter of a century later, on what he intended to convey through the story and what he has observed since that time in his work with African-American adolescents and youth. This is followed, in chapter 6, by Williams's discussion of the importance of "frontin' it in the 'hood" for a group of boys with whom she worked.

As they grow up, young women, often become the victims of violence perpetrated by men. That does not mean, however, that they are never victimizers themselves or that they never engage in violent acts. They do indeed, and with growing frequency. Moreover, girls often form an audience as boys and young men fight. As Gordon's story illustrates, they may urge the men on. More than boys, girls seem to be the purveyors of rumors, serving as a "he said/she said" rumor mill that starts many fights, whether between boys over a girl or between girls over a boy. Nevertheless, it is clear that every day in school, girls have to face, if not violence, then insolence that borders on violence from boys who assume they have the right to speak or act toward a girl however they choose. In this context, violence is often associated with the awakening of sexual desire in both teenage girls and boys.

Schools are not a place where the emotions aroused by sexual attraction between a boy and a girl can be discussed openly and easily. For example, in a middle school classroom, a girl, who has just enrolled in the school, looks furtively from time to time at an attractive boy sitting close by her. Smiling, he looks back at her. They exchange a few words. She giggles as he throws a ball of paper at her. She tells him not to do that. But she continues to throw glances at him, to smile and murmur comments to him. He does the same to her. Their playful interaction continues intermittently over several minutes as the teacher presents ideas to the class. Suddenly, the boy stretches and yawns. As he does so, his right arm brushes across the girl's chest. At once, she raises her hand and calls out to the teacher that the boy has hit her on her chest. This is not the first time that a girl has complained about the behavior of this boy, so the teacher sends him to the principal's office for misbehavior, possibly sexual harassment.

After I observed this interaction, I spent some time considering who had initiated it (the girl), how it had developed over time (both students had continued it), who had overstepped the mark of acceptable behavior (the boy), who had drawn the attention of the teacher to what was going on (the girl), and who had received punishment (the boy). I had watched the interaction build up to the incident reported to the teacher. I was not sure that the boy had deliberately touched the girl as he stretched. Nor was I sure that the girl believed he had done so deliberately. Nevertheless, she felt his attention to her had gone too far—she felt violated. Once the boy had been sent to see the principal, however, the girl appeared chagrined. She was new in the school; now she had made an enemy where she had wanted a friend. Sitting beside her at the table, the boy had offered her excitement during the lesson. Now she sat next to an empty seat and had to listen to the teacher. After the class, I found out about the confusion she felt because she and I had a few moments to talk about the incident. But such debriefings are unusual for boys or girls following such provocative, if superficial, sexual encounters in the classroom.

As I write about this incident, I recall an experience early in my own teaching career many years ago, in an urban school in London. Two students, age twelve, sat side-by-side at an old-fashioned desk. The boy put his hand on the girl's leg. She let out a yell. "He's being filfy [*sic*], Ma'am!" Like the teacher at the middle school, I sent the boy to the principal, who returned with him a few minutes later. He made the boy stand, with hand outstretched, in front of the class. Then, grasping a thick cane, the principal slashed it across the boy's hand several times. Each time the cane came down, I flinched, along with the boy. Never in my life had I seen a child caned—nor have I seen it since. In reaction, I vowed that I would never again send any child out of my room for misbehavior. Instead, I would handle all such problems myself. My recollection of this incident now reminds me that I dealt with the issue in a similar manner to the teacher I observed recently. Teachers sometimes have difficulty dealing with even minor acts of violence because outbursts in the classroom threaten their control of the class. I am reminded, also, that the problems teenagers have in managing their emotions and their sexual desires are not specific to this country or the present time.

In chapter 7, which is about the ways girls and young women negotiate their sexuality, Kristen Luschen explores the intersection of sexual expression and violence and the ways violence against women is condoned by society. Her findings and those of other feminist scholars provide clues to prevent such violence by restructuring the ways we socialize both girls and boys.

While these chapters offer insight into the social system, especially into the workings of discrimination by race and gender, they don't emphasize the totality of influences upon young boys and girls. Only touched upon briefly in the chapters of this book are the economic system, which impacts the lives of children daily through their families, their homes, their neighborhoods, and their schools; the media, which teach children what to emulate, what to desire, and what the adults in our society value at the same time as they entertain; and the legal system, which determines how much alcohol, which drugs, and which weapons are illegal and what the penalties for possession or use of them shall be. Each system is linked to the others. And, just like adults, children participate in all these systems. Their experience of each system shapes their attitudes; their experience of each also expands or limits their aspirations. In her book entitled *Lanterns: A Memoir of Mentors* (1999), Marian Wright Edelman comments upon the ways society causes young people to limit their aspirations:

> In our nation and world, White children have been assigned more value as a group than Black and Brown and Asian and Native American children. Affluent children are accorded more respect and resources than children who are poor and need them more. Children in single-parent families or born to teen parents are assigned the stigma we often attach to the parents they did not choose. Children with special physical, mental, or emotional needs are sometimes shunned and made the butt of jokes and jeers. Girls as a group face many barriers that boys do not in a world still characterized more by male privilege than by gender equality and mutual respect. Some boys—especially Black boys—are accorded no respect and are expected to control their rage from unequal treatment without crying or protesting—legally or illegally. And most boys are imprisoned by "male values" that teach that strong men don't cry and that life is a contest between winners and losers rather than between winners and winners and a struggle between self and God. (p. 134)

In discussing ways to prevent violence in schools, we cannot overlook decisions adults have made, for economic and legal reasons, that have increased children's ability to purchase guns during the last two decades. In his book *Fist Stick Knife Gun* (1995), Geoffrey Canada shows how in the late 1970s and early 1980s, lawmakers in New York state, responded to public concern by cracking down on drug dealers and mandating long prison sentences if they were convicted. The dealers then circumvented the new laws by employing teenagers to deal for them. If the teenagers were caught, they would be tried as juveniles and receive lighter sentences than the adults. Once teenagers began to earn large sums in the drug business,

they became potential targets for robbery. Naturally, they turned to pur-
chasing handguns for their own protection (Canada, 1995, pp. 78–80). The
manufacturers of handguns were not slow to take advantage of a new mar-
ket. They made their guns more attractive to teens and targeted their mar-
keting to them and to women, according to a report quoted by Canada
(1995, p. 123) and written by Josh Sugarmann and Kristen Rand of the
Violence Policy Center in Washington, D.C. Canada spends some time discussing the impact of guns on teenagers:

> Even more dangerous than the fact that there are tens of thousands of adoles-
> cents shooting and playing with guns is the psychological impact that having a
> gun has on these kids. There were always some natural checks on violence
> among young people before handguns were so common. There were many times
> that I wished I could have fought back when I was growing up but I didn't
> because I knew I couldn't beat the other boy, or I was afraid of his bigger
> brother, or he had friends who would come after me. Even when a fight went
> ahead, the outcome wasn't guaranteed; you might lose, or win but get a black
> eye or a tooth knocked out. As we got older and more sensible we recognized
> that there was a system of checks and balances on violence, we learned to weigh
> acting violently with the consequences. Sometimes, no matter how hard it was to
> accept, we just had to take the indignity of being ridiculed or cursed at and go on
> with life.

> Kids with guns often see no limits on their power (Canada, 1995, p. 100)

Recent shootings in schools have demonstrated all too clearly the psychological impact of a gun on children. While the authors of this book
acknowledge this impact, they perceive gun violence as simply the most
destructive manifestation of the valorization of violence in American society.

The reader needs also to be aware that, during the last decades of the
twentieth century, policymakers and the media have both disparaged the
role of parent. In a penetrating analysis, Sylvia Ann Hewlett and Cornel
West (1998) write that parents are confused about what prevents them
from doing well by their children. "Pop psychology lulls us into thinking
that as long as our intimate relationships are in order, life will be fine"
(Hewlett & West, 1998, p. 142). Thus, parents tend to analyze any problems they have in terms of personal shortcomings.

> They are much less clear about what the external obstacles might be, such as a
> tax code that discriminates against families with children or a labor market that

puts immense downward pressures on wages. One thing is for sure: it is
extremely difficult for parents to overcome a set of problems they do not see, and
when mothers and fathers fail to identify external pressures and tensions, the
tendency is to blame each other, which often weakens the family from inside.
(Hewlitt & West, 1998, p. 142).

In this book we point to the complexity of these issues. We urge our
readers to study the authors whose work we cite to grasp the full range of
issues that must be addressed if the United States is to become a less violent nation.

Part II of this book focuses on the authors' research on interventions
that are already in place to prevent violence in schools. For several
decades, a patchwork of activities on conflict resolution has been offered
to schools, largely by not-for-profit organizations. Some activities have
been add-ons provided by outside consultants and taught to the staff during in-service days or to students in workshops once or twice during the
school year. Certain organizations have offered longer courses and developed impressive materials for various grade levels. However, many of
these materials deal only with prosocial skills between one individual and
another; few of them suggest ways for teachers to integrate these skills
with the subject matter they teach daily; few encourage discussion of the
meaning of social justice for communities at a local, national, or international level; few offer curricula to build on a student's knowledge from
grade to grade, and few include everyone working in the school, from the
janitor to the principal, in the process of creating a school without violence. Yet a whole school approach to preventing violence is needed, as
explained by myself and Rebecca Stevens in chapter 8.

In the following chapters, several authors examine peer mediation in
one urban school district. Within the last few years, articles have claimed
the benefits of peer mediation programs at both the elementary and secondary levels (Angaran & Beckwith, 1999; Dagnese-Pleasants & Yvetta,
1999; Humphries, 1999; Johnson & Johnson, 1996). Nevertheless, in-
depth qualitative studies of the effectiveness of mediation programs are
hard to find. The research conducted by Casella, Stevens, and Williams
and reported in chapters 9, 10, and 11 of this volume is, therefore, an
important addition to the literature.

Peer mediation in schools is an offshoot of mediation for adults,
which has grown in popularity as the cost of litigation has risen. At first,
most programs of mediation for adults were run by trained mediators who
were not lawyers. However, some lawyers have also hastened to embrace

mediation. They have more than economic incentives: some states have mandated mediation in certain lawsuits; some lawyers, especially younger ones, find destructive the head-to-head, winner-take-all approach of litigation. They prefer to help disputants reach a consensus, or at least an acceptable compromise. Thus, mediation, which used to depend upon the voluntary participation of both parties to a dispute and was supervised by a trained mediator who was not a lawyer, has now changed, in many jurisdictions, to being mandated by the courts and conducted by trained lawyers.

The potential effects of mandating mediation (instead of allowing it to be voluntary) on the process, the disputants, and the viability of any agreement are important for educational researchers to examine as more schools decide to require, rather than encourage, students to attend peer mediation sessions to resolve their conflicts. I heard a heated discussion (at an American Bar Association annual meeting in the late 1990s) about the effects of these changes. Mediators without law degrees argued that disputants are less likely to internalize an agreement and abide by it without rancor if mediation is mandated. Lawyers trained in mediation, argued that mandates ensure that meaningful discussions must take place, and that lawyers are better able to shape a legally binding agreement than mediators who lack a knowledge of the law.

The mediation skills taught in schools follow the same rules as those for adult mediation. As described in chapters 9 through 11, mediation is based upon a belief that an unbiased, well-trained mediator, following specified steps and maintaining an atmosphere of calm reasonableness between the disputants, can assist them in reaching an agreement over the issue in dispute. Mediation includes negotiation skills that are essential to maintaining a democratic society.

Those who advocate mediation include creative thinkers who abhor the growth of violence in the world. In the last two decades, mediation has been advocated, and used successfully, for the settlement of international disputes. In the United States, mediation is seen as a way to ensure that democratic processes are sustained in a litigious society.

Mediation is based upon values of maintaining self-control, concealing emotion, and engaging in rational discussion, activities that are often associated with White males rather than others in society. Two comments made to me, by a Hispanic scholar and an African-American youth worker, illustrate this point. The Hispanic scholar told me about her family's way of resolving conflicts: there would be a loud argument, shouting, and tears as each disputant laid forth his or her position and had it countered by the others. Emotions were not held in by either men or women. After all the arguing, the parties expected to reach some settlement. Nothing like the steps of mediation, and nothing like the calm atmosphere insisted upon by mediators, was practiced by her family or the families of her friends. So, she asked, why should anyone insist that she, her family, or her friends use mediation to settle their quarrels? On the other hand, the youth worker explained to me that he and other African-American men he knew were brought up to cope with problems on their own, without discussing them with family or friends. If one guy had a "beef" with another, then he had to work out how to settle the matter by himself. That was it. Families he knew as a child did not generally sit down to discuss issues together. Only when he married someone who worked in the field of mediation did this man learn to see the value of talking things out as a way to resolve conflicts.

The varying ways in which different groups in society customarily deal with conflicts are important for educators to understand because some students in school may come from families or have friends whose ways to solve problems run counter to what is taught in school. When those students are required or encouraged to resolve a dispute through mediation, they may feel that the ways they have been taught to resolve disputes are being disrespected by the school. As a result, they may not only question the purpose of mediation but ridicule the whole process.

When school personnel feel that mediation is important to the well-being of the school, their task—an ongoing one, which must be repeated over and over because new students are constantly entering a school—is to explain to students why they believe in mediation. At the same time, they may need to consider adapting the mediation process to meet their particular students' needs and expectations.

In chapter 12, Domingo Guerra and I describe a pilot program to draw alienated youth into the community through having them tutor children in first to third grade in literacy. We believe that by engaging in caring activities with younger students, who are often related to them or their friends, these teens may gain positive images of themselves and their value to the community.

The book ends with a chapter by myself that discusses research described here and being conducted elsewhere to expand our understanding of how influential intervention programs can be for students if carried out and evaluated over a span of years. It is our belief, however, that violence in schools has its roots in many systems of our society and that it cannot be eliminated merely by changing rules or introducing prevention programs into schools.

REFERENCES

Angaran S., & Beckwith, K. (1999, May). Peer mediation in elementary schools. *Principal, 78*(5), 27–29.

Canada, G. (1995). *Fist Stick Knife Gun: A Personal History of Violence in America.* Boston: Beacon Press.

Canada, G. (1998). *Reaching Up to Manhood.* Boston: Beacon Press.

Dagnese-Pleasants, D., & Yvetta, G. (1999, Winter). Peer mediation: An effective program for reducing violence in schools. *Delta Kappa Gamma Bulletin, 65*(2), 19–23.

Edelman, M. W. (1999). *Lanterns: A Memoir of Mentors.* Boston: Beacon Press.

Hewlett, S. A., & West, C. (1998). *The War against Parents: What We Can Do for America's Beleaguered Moms and Dads.* Boston: Houghton Mifflin.

Humphries, T. (1999, October). Improving peer mediation programs: Student experiences and suggestions. *Professional School Counseling, 3*(1), 13–20.

Johnson, D. W., & Johnson, R. T. (1996). Conflict resolution and peer mediation programs in elementary and secondary schools: A review of research. *Review of Educational Research, 66,* 459–507.

Miedzian, M. (1991). *Boys Will Be Boys: Breaking the Link between Masculinity and Violence.* New York: Doubleday, Anchor Books.

Pianta, R. C., & Walsh, D. J. (1996). *High Risk Children in Schools: Constructing Sustaining Relationships.* New York: Routledge.

Pollack, W. (1998). *Real Boys.* New York: Henry Holt.

Way, N. (1998). *Everyday Courage: The Lives and Stories of Urban Teenagers.* New York: New York University Press.

Part One

The Social Context of Violence in Schools

2

What Is Violent About "School Violence"? The Nature of Violence in a City High School

Ronnie Casella

Central Connecticut State University

INTRODUCTION

An unprecedented number of shootings and killings in schools in Arkansas, Mississippi, Kentucky, Washington, Tennessee, North Carolina, Pennsylvania, California, Colorado, and elsewhere have made it evident that violence in the United States does not stop at the school gates. But as shocking as recent tragedies have been, the extent of violence in schools is more complex and far-reaching than most news stories and research suggest. Though not as tragic as the fatalities caused by shootings, nonetheless, fights, assaults, bullying, and harassment are damaging—and sometimes daily—occurrences in schools (Lawrence, 1998; Petersen, Pietrzak, & Speaker, 1998). In recent years, the extent of violence and the disciplinary and judicial reactions to it have become more varied, and sometimes more extreme (Arnette, 1995; Hyman and Others, 1994).

Since the time of President George Bush's initiative, *America 2000* (1991), which included as one of its six goals, "Every school in America will be free of drugs and violence and will offer a disciplined environment conducive to learning," most national reports and initiatives regarding public schooling have incorporated a concern for preventing violence. Yet the single-minded focus on gun violence in schools is misguided, for it misses the complexity of the problems and the real fears schools face. In this chapter, I note how violence is enacted in many forms and at different cultural and structural levels, which allows one to understand it in a more complex way than is usually portrayed in our popular discourses about school violence.

THE SCHOOL

The high school discussed in this chapter was located on the south side of a mid-size city in New York State, in an area primarily poor and African-American but abutting a rather wealthy community, primarily White.[1] The city has undergone devastating de-industrialization and the loss of many blue collar and professional jobs. The high school, which I will call Brandon High, is one of four high schools in the city. There are 1,400 students in the school, about half of whom are African-American and half of whom are White. There is a small minority of Latino students as well. The school has one principal, four assistant principals, five counselors, a psychologist, a social worker, a police officer, security guards, a dropout prevention staff, and about ninety teachers. Since the early 1990s, the school has had programs and committees aimed at reducing violence in the school, including a Peer Mediation Program, a Crisis Intervention Team, a Student Support Team, and a Drug Abuse Resistance Education (DARE) program. The school is considered one of the better public schools in the city, though during the 1997–1998 school year there were a number of articles in the city's primary newspaper targeting Brandon High as a particularly violent school.

METHODOLOGICAL AND THEORETICAL CONSIDERATIONS

The research reported here is qualitative and was conducted from August 1997 to July 1998 under the auspices of a federally funded violence intervention research project. The research was initiated with anthropology-based participant observations in the school and the surrounding community (Fordham, 1996; McQuillan, 1998). It then spread to other

---

[1]The name of the school and the names of its faculty and students are pseudonyms.

schools in the city and to community events and organizations involving youth, schools, and violence. Actual research in Brandon High was conducted two to three times a week, for about 15 hours each week. This involved semistructured interviews with the school's students and staff (especially its administrators, police officer and security personnel, teachers, counselors, social worker, and dropout prevention workers) observations of the school's violence prevention programs and committees, observations of classes (especially its Health and DARE classes), interviews with parents and social service workers, and time spent "shadowing" school faculty, students, and police officers in the school and the community. All interviews were tape recorded and then transcribed. During observations, copious field notes were taken and also transcribed to a computer program. Field notes and interview transcriptions were coded, and then the codes were condensed according to themes. Hypotheses were inductively generated, in the fashion of grounded theory, and conclusions were made "from the bottom up" and "from many disparate pieces of collected evidence that are interconnected" (Bogdan & Biklen, 1998, p. 6; see also Erickson, 1973). Also included as data were the booklets, handouts, and articles distributed by the school regarding violence. Again, these texts were coded and hypotheses generated inductively. In the tradition of critical ethnography, the study reported on here focuses on the everyday events and rituals—the assumptions and taken for granted "facts" that undergirded activities associated with violence in the school, and are, therefore, in many ways invisible to school policymakers, administrators, teachers, students, and, at times, researchers (Denzin, 1992; Lincoln, 1988). Consequently, this research takes to heart the belief "that the symbolic creativity of the young is based in their everyday informal life and infuses with meaning the entirety of the world as they see it" (Willis, 1990, p. 98).

Undergirding this research is the belief that people make meaning of the world through a symbolic interpretation of what they see, hear, and feel. As a phenomenological and semiotic alternative to positivism, this research functions on the basis of three premises: that people act toward things on the basis of the meanings these things have for them; that the meanings of things are derived from, or arise out of, social interactions; and that these meanings are modified through an interpretative process (Barthes, 1994; Blumer, 1969). At the forefront of this research is a concern for the perspectives and active energy of the people who are a part of the study and a recognition for the extent to which these individuals are always in action, sustaining as well as challenging the structures around them, including structures of violence and violence prevention (Thompson, 1994, p. 201). Central to this research, then, is a belief in the constraints and structures on which social inequality is built, but also a belief in people's abilities to challenge those structures and enact change. In this way, students' "lived experience [is] seen as an interpretative rather than a causal story" (Feuerverger, 1998, p. 703). Essentially, (and challenging more deterministic theories of social reproduction), this research recognizes how culture—its structures and patterns—is both produced as well as reproduced; it also recognizes that all people take part in the construction of society and its institutions, discipline policies, and rules and therefore are capable of preserving, as well as challenging, these aspects of the world around us.

Foundational to this research, as well, is an effort to problematize public discourses of school violence. Discourses are "institutionalized ways of understanding relationships, activities, and meaning that emerge through language (talk, rules, thoughts, writing) and influence what people in specific institutions take to be true" (Biklen, 1995, p. 81). Discourse is not rhetoric but rather takes into account how language shapes social relations—what people take to be true—and hence, how people come to interact with one another and the world around them. In his study of torture and prisons, for example, Foucault (1978/1995) demonstrated how symbols of the spectacle and the body, both integral to the public torture of criminals, were replaced in the nineteenth century with what he called a "pedagogy" of rehabilitation and correction based on new psychological models of deviance. Essentially, painful punishment was replaced with an economy of suspended rights, a manner of control meant to change criminals, not destroy them. Accompanying these changes—and also helping to define them—came new ways of thinking about, and constructing, apparatuses of discipline, confinement, surveillance, and deviance, all of which sheds light on current notions about violence and punishment. Ultimately, constructions of "truth" were integral to Foucault's notions of discourse:

> Each society has its régime of truth, its "general politics" of truth: that is, the types of discourse which it accepts and makes function as true; the mechanisms and instances which enable one to distinguish true and false statements, the means by which each is sanctioned; the techniques and procedures accorded value in the acquisition of truth; the status of those who are charged with saying what counts as true. (Foucault, 1980, p. 131)

In spite of criticisms that have linked Michel Foucault's work to abstractions and pie-in-the-sky theory, he always intended to emphasize that discourses circulate in our world and have a significant effect in people's daily lives and struggles. Discourses have had real consequences on shaping, for example, our discipline policies in schools and our notions of violence.

In this research, strains of discourse analysis and critical anthropology meet in a discussion of four forms of violence of concern to secondary school educators and students: fighting, systemic violence, hidden violence, and suicide.

While the news stories of shootings in schools have raised awareness about school violence, they have also created an image of school violence that equates it solely with gun violence; but as this chapter notes, violence comes in many forms and operates in schools at cultural and structural levels, causing fear and bodily harm, undermining educational opportunity, and giving impetus to various kinds of "zero tolerance" policies. While some school violence has caused bodily harm and even death, violence too is often hidden and systemic in nature (Epp & Watkinson, 1997). Some policies that are meant to prevent violence in schools, such as some forms of zero tolerance policies, actually increase other forms of violence, specifically systemic violence; other policies drive violence underground, increasing the number of cases of hidden assaults. Violence, too, may be self-inflicted, leading at times to suicide.

Ultimately, violence in U.S. schools is an outgrowth of violence in U.S. society. But when it is committed in schools, it not only leads to the same consequences as in society—death, crime, and victimization—but, in addition, it undermines students' chances of becoming fully educated. This happens both to those who are directly involved in violence and to those who are not (Prothrow-Stith, 1991). At times, violence undermines students' opportunities to graduate from high school. In some of its forms, it causes bodily harm; in others, mental anguish and fear. Structurally, schools become oppressive when control and discipline are emphasized over education (Devine, 1996). Noting how all this occurs— how violence as fighting, as systemic, as hidden, as suicide, operates in different forms and at different cultural and structural levels—allows one to form a more complex and accurate picture of school violence than is routinely portrayed in our news stories and in our popular rhetoric about school violence.

FIGHTING

Nobody never knows what happens in your house so you come to school having
a bad day, coming from home, and at school somebody just start with you and
on a regular day you be all happy coming from home and somebody say some-
thing to you smart, you just blow it off—but if you having a bad day and some-
body say something smart or pick on you about how you dress or something,
that make you want to fight.

–Zakia, a senior at Brandon High School

In the hallway on the third floor of Brandon High there was a sudden commotion. James Maddy, the coordinator of the afternoon school program and a special education teacher, was on hall duty on the third floor at the time and was called to the scene on his walkie-talkie. Two girls, an African American and a Hispanic girl, were on the floor, fighting, scratching each other's faces, and ripping out each other's hair. Amid the shouts and the commotion, two teachers attempted to keep onlooking students in their classrooms. Another teacher was struggling to hold a leg of each of the fighting girls high in the air so that they wouldn't be able to stand up and do more damage to each other. The girls were swearing back and forth repeatedly, calling each other "fuckin' whores." The African-American girl yelled, "You fuckin' whore, I'll kill you," while the Hispanic girl yelled, "I'll fuckin' kick your fat ass!" James Maddy had the two girls nearly separated and calm when the African-American girl broke free from his grasp and began kicking as hard as she could at the other girl who was still on the floor, holding her hand to a deep fingernail scratch on her face. The Hispanic girl yelled and kicked back and a teacher pushed the two girls apart, slapping the Hispanic girl. The Hispanic girl yelled at the teacher, "I'll kick your White ass!" The teacher yelled back: "Shut-up! Shut-up!" Things were out of control. The teacher held one girl's leg up in the air again. James Maddy had the other girl calm now and was escorting her to the main office. As she passed, she was primarily ignored by White students, but other African-American students, mostly girls, asked her what had happened. Some chastised her for fighting, saying, "Now you're out of here" (meaning suspended from school). The girl kept telling the other students, "I kicked that fat-ass cheerleader's ass!" Two students cheered her for doing so, another told her it was a stupid thing to do.

Both girls were suspended for five days and were scheduled for a judicial hearing at the Board of Education Building. (Starting in November 1997, all students caught fighting in school were summoned to a formal judicial hearing.) In the main office, Brian Arena, one of the school's assistant principals, lectured the Hispanic girl for fighting again and told her about the judicial hearing. Last year the two girls had also gotten into a fight, though it was less violent. Brian Arena gave the student a form to sign. It specified why she was suspended ("fighting") and that, according to district policies, she must report to the Hove Family Center for the five days of her suspension, to be tutored for two hours each day. The girl said that she couldn't go. If she was suspended and the social services department found out, she'd lose her child care money. Brian Arena told her to bring her son. "After all, it's a family center," he said, missing the point that she would lose the money for being suspended. The form that he gave the student said that students would not lose any class time or fall behind in their school work while suspended at the Hove Family Center, though of course they did. I interviewed several students who had been in fights and been sent to the center who remarked that they fell far behind in their work and that sometimes their tutors did not show up for their instruction.

In spite of its intensity—the brutality, the vicious language, the swift disciplinary procedures, the striking of the student by the teacher—scenes like this are not uncommon at Brandon High or at other high schools. It is not uncommon in the cafeteria to hear the shout of "Fight!" followed by the sudden turning of chairs, the opening of doors, and the movement of students rushing away or toward the fight. One student spoke for many when she noted, "If you sit in enough lunches you're bound to see a fight." In 1997–1998, 53 Brandon High students were suspended for fighting during the first four months of school. Of the 53 students, 31 were girls and all but 8 students were African-American. While the numbers no doubt fluctuate, in other city high schools as well the number of African-American students suspended for fighting is significantly higher than that of White students. While it appears that most fights are between African-American students, it also appears that suspension is often meted out more rapidly to poorer and African-American students than to others (Soriano, Soriano, & Jimenez, 1994).

At Brandon High, as at many schools, there was concern, and even shock, regarding the number of girls who were caught fighting. The school principal, two guidance counselors, the school police officer, and several teachers and students expressed their concern about "girl fighting." While part of this concern reflects stereotypes indicating that girls should not fight, and therefore their fights are viewed more critically and noticed more readily, there is also evidence suggesting that today, girls more often fight physically and even brutally now than ever before

(Boothe, Bradley, & Flick, 1993). Amy Rogers, a guidance counselor, told me, "Girls are the worst." The school police officer said: "The girls can be the most vicious. One minute they are walking down the hall with their books, talking to their friend, they see somebody they don't like, and whammo, they go at it, pulling out hair by its roots." And the school principal confided: "It's the girls we worry about. They're the ones who are fighting." During one week at the school there were five fights, all of them between girls. One student not only described the chaos that accompanies school fights but referred naturally to girls when describing one:

> It's just like all of a sudden you hear somebody yell, "Fight!" and like everybody rushes around to see. People are really serious, like girls are pulling out the other girls' weaves and people are just—they don't even care about what's around them. This one time, this fight between two girls broke out right in front of me on the second floor. And everybody just bomb rushed it. And I was like, just let me out! Let me out! And it's not like they are going to just let you out. I mean they're not going to let you out of it unless I really push myself out. It's just like crazy. And like people get injured. People are cheering and stuff. I mean it's like, for some people it's fun watching two people beating each other up.

The severity of some fights and the fact that so many are between girls was spoken about often, sometimes with great dismay. Equally shocking for school staff and some students was the reactions of some students who would rather watch a fight than try to calm the situation. Of the 136 students who were referred to peer mediation because of disputes, 96 were girls. That most disputes between girls involved a boy or man was supported by the guidance counselors, the school social worker, and many of the students. In general, most fights, including fights between boys, were started because of name-calling ("he said/she said"), stealing, or conflicts over lovers (boyfriends and girlfriends).

On their part, the administrators had a way of seeing fights as seasonal. Janice Street, the principal of the school, noted that November was always a bad time for fights because of the coming of winter and the gloominess of the city at that time of the year. (November, as the principal predicted, was a particularly bad month for fights at Brandon High.) The school police officer mentioned later in the year that September was often a bad time as well: "Most of what happens during the first few weeks of school is that students bring whatever didn't get resolved during the summer to school and they meet in the cafeteria or the hallway, and they start resolving it their own ways." He said that on Mondays, there were always problems because of the weekend. The school psychologist felt that the warm months were bad as well, though many students who would fight did not come to school when the weather was nice, so incidents of fights decreased in June, during the last weeks of school. With September, November, the warm months, and Mondays as particularly bad times for school fights, there seemed little room in the school for peacefulness.

In reality, fights occur in schools for many reasons. While these may include weather conditions, fights are, foremost, cultural expressions of frustration, and sometimes hatred. What occur in schools are not random acts—fights do not simply erupt, as is commonly thought—they are physical expressions of structured and patterned phenomena (Giroux, 1996). Students know that they are very often rewarded for violent behavior: increased attention and sometimes respect from one's peers come with fighting. Girls and boys fight in school because this is where they most often meet their enemies. Fights that occur because of turf disputes occur in school because turf lines and borders are blurred in school hallways and cafeterias, where all students, regardless of race, gang affiliation, or sex, must meet.

Meanwhile, there are patterns to school fights that preclude the notion that school fights erupt randomly. First, not all students fight. At Brandon High, girls fought more than boys. Students of color fought more than White students, and when students of color fought, they were more likely to be suspended than Whites.

Why do girls fight in school more than boys? Why are students of color more often suspended for fighting than White students? These are questions that must be answered by taking into account how each student's background and culture are expressed within the structure of the school. On one level, students most often fought because of rumors, stealing, and lovers. But they also fought to get attention. Those who received the least amount of attention from school staff were more likely to fight. Many students fought because they had learned—through our own society and popular culture, through their families, and through adult examples—that to back down and walk away from a fight does not earn one respect but rather is "chicken" or "pussy," as students explained in interviews (see also Fry, 1993). Ultimately, fights are not the problems of individuals who cannot control their behaviors, as many adults working in schools and in psychology believe; rather, they are expressions that make evident aspects of the United States that are unjust. In general, children who are raised in poverty, who feel threatened, who experience violence in their homes, whose experiences are violent, who are punished corporally, and whose lives are racked with frustration and hatred for circumstances that are not their fault are the children who fight and whose fights in school are the most dreadful and severe.

SYSTEMIC VIOLENCE

Students caught fighting at Brandon High were usually suspended for three to five days and were summoned to a judicial hearing. Between September 1, 1997, and January 8, 1998, a total of 584 students had been suspended from Brandon High for a range of offenses, some minor, some not. Students who were suspended for fighting and disruptive behavior (and sometimes attendance) would sometimes be placed permanently in the afternoon school program, which ran from three to five o'clock each day in the basement of the school. In May 1998 there were 105 students in the afternoon school program, but generally about 400 students enter and exit the program throughout the year, most either dropping out or getting a general equivalency diploma (GED).

At Brandon High and other city high schools, the days of the reprimand, the call to the parents, the lecture about "bucking up" and "straightening out" are gone. Now, as the principal claimed, fighting is "dealt with swiftly."

Disciplinary action at Brandon High involving fighting in school was much influenced by a November 6, 1997, letter from Dr. Steven Kolman, superintendent of the city school district, to all parents with school-age children. The letter introduced a new "zero tolerance" policy that was meant to combat school fighting. The letter read, in part:

Dear Parents,

With the increase of reported gang violence in our city, we want to assure you the [city] School District will take all necessary precautions to prevent the violence from entering our schools. Lately, however, the number of student fights in the high schools has been escalating, resulting in a disruption of the learning process. We have tried talking to students, warning them, placing them in the In-School Suspension Program, and suspending them for up to three days out of school. Nothing seems to affect those few disruptive, aggressive, violent students.

To address this threat to student safety, as of October 30, 1997, I have instituted the following: High school students involved in fights or committing an assault

on student or staff member will be suspended from school and subject to a
Superintendent's Hearing. If found guilty, the students may be transferred to
another school or placed in one of our alternative high school programs. This
placement means a change of school and, most likely, will result in a change of
courses, teachers, hours of school and inability to participate in interscholastic
sports. If the student has a record of aggressive violent acts, there is a very good
chance the student will not be allowed to attend any regular program and will be
placed on homebound instruction.

Students caught fighting in school could receive one of a host of disciplinary actions. While most students were suspended for about three days, some were given five days of suspension. Some students' actions were deemed "behavioral problems"; these students were sent to Cross School, a school for students labeled "violent" or "aggressive." Students who were caught with a weapon in school were sent to Garfield, an alternative school which had about sixty students and was located, at that time, in an area of the city with the greatest incidence of gun violence. Both these alternative schools—Garfield and Cross—were staffed mainly with part-time and overworked teachers, who attempted to teach in very trying circumstances. A student deemed unfit for any type of public institution was placed on Homebound Instruction, which lasted for many weeks and sometimes for six months to a full year. Such students were required to stay at home and receive instruction from a tutor who visited the house or, usually, arranged to meet the student at a public library. Essentially, these students were expelled from school, not even being allowed to take part in the afternoon school program or the alternative schools for violent youth in the city.

In most instances, when students were suspended for fighting and disruptive behavior, after attending the Superintendent's Hearing, they went before the high school's Screening Committee. The Screening Committee at Brandon High determined what programs the expelled, suspended, and, sometimes, transferring students, received. Transferring students most often arrived from other high schools or from alternative schools and detention centers. Many students arriving from out of state were African Americans, migrating from the south of the United States. Ironically, as the disciplinary apparatus regarding violence was developed, the definition of "alternative school" changed such that in the city, alternative no longer referred to experimental schools, which were often progressive in nature, but to "detention centers," which were often guided by behavioral notions of discipline and control rather than by pedagogy.

Such disciplinary action may seem like a necessary response to escalating violence in schools, but it, too, is a form of violence (Epp & Watkinson, 1997). As Paulo Freire (1970) and Pierre Bourdieu (1991) both noted, violence can be systemic in nature. Systemic violence refers to structural forms of restrictions, oppression, and brutality which can be state and nationally mandated—such as executions—and that cause the enforcement of rules and actions that demean, hurt, or, sometimes, kill people who are less powerful and influential than those committing the violence. The ramifications of the superintendent's letter (like other forms of zero tolerance policy and rhetoric), combined with a growing crackdown on kids in general, cleared the way for drastic and sometimes unjust disciplinary policies in the city schools (Fuentes, 1998; Noguera, 1995). Essentially, individual students—often demonized these days in our popular culture and imaginations—were no longer thought of as unique cases. Their fights were not examined and assessed. Rather, the zero tolerance policy made way for a kind of slate-clearing approach to fights: hallways, cafeterias, and classrooms were promptly cleared of disruptive students through disciplinary actions that included suspension, expulsion, the use of alternative schools, the afternoon program, and school tracking. While the administration insisted that their afternoon school program helped students who could not attend day school (because of a job or child), which was true at times, and that they helped students who were interested only in obtaining a GED diploma or were more interested in manual labor than academics, the program was also a form of tracking. Many students felt trapped in the afternoon school program, and given that attendance was not strictly enforced, it became for some students a jumping-off point for dropping out of school (Fine, 1991). Most students in the afternoon school, even those who had chosen to be there, had poor attendance and students were rarely reprimanded for not coming. Some students had as many as 60 absences during the school year. Not urging these students to come to school (even to the afternoon school program) sent the message that their attendance did not matter—that they, in fact, did not matter.

One student, Latoya, expressed her situation and in many ways reflected the stories of other students who violated school fighting and weapon policies. Latoya was an African-American student, extremely quiet, who had transferred to Brandon High after failing out of a private Catholic school (she had failed theology several times). Her father, who was very religious, had been addicted to drugs and had gone to rehabilitation. There had been times of domestic violence in her home. Soon after the superintendent's letter was distributed and reported in the main city newspaper, Latoya was suspended and then put in the afternoon school program for bringing a knife into a school dance. She explained:

> I kind of regret getting kicked out because I miss it [school]. This year hasn't been a good year. I got into a little trouble in the beginning of the year. It wasn't my fault. It was my fault but it wasn't intentionally. It was the first dance here, it started at dark time and I live in a very bad neighborhood [on Durbin Street, which the local news station in 1997 dubbed the most dangerous street in the city]. And me not knowing that they would have checked my pockets and bag. I wasn't intentionally coming, "Oh I'm going to fight someone at the dance." It was just my protection because I have to walk and it was nighttime. They had a little metal detector. I had a little pen that was the size of that [shows her pinky], it had a little blade at the tip. It was like the size of an art knife. I had it in my pocket and they asked me what was it. I pulled it out and gave it to them, like I forgot I had it on me and so they let me in the dance. I thought I wasn't in trouble because I gave it to them and I wasn't going to fight nobody. When the dance was over, they came to me and said, "You know you are going to get in trouble." But they also made fun of it [the homemade knife], saying, "What are you going to do with this little thing?" laughing. I was just going to class that Monday when I came to school, they called me to the office and said I was going to get suspended for five days.

Latoya had brought the homemade blade to the dance for protection. She was working that night at the local supermarket, and when she got off from work she had to walk through a neighborhood she feared. She told the principal of the school that her father had given her the knife and her father, in court, stood by the story (though she admitted in private to a different version). Latoya had never been in trouble before in school, had never been suspended, had not been in a fight. In fact, almost nobody knew Latoya. She was, in many ways, an invisible student at Brandon High. She insisted:

> I never been in trouble, I never had a record, never been in a fight, suspended, nothing. They gonna suspend me for five days, they had no mercy or nothing. That's what really made me think of the difference between Bishop Brennan [the private school she attended] and Brandon, because Bishop Brennan you can do a lot of stuff in there and they had the heart to forgive, even if you never been in trouble, they talk to you, you know. She [the principal at Brandon] was like, well you're suspended, wrote the paper, there's nothing you can say about that. They put me in this program that started at eleven to one o'clock at the Hove Family

Center. I had to walk over there for a whole week. I really didn't have any work because the teacher didn't have me do nothing. They tried to put me in afternoon school—I mean for a little knife for protection for walking up here. They was gonna try and put me in afternoon school. [The principal] recommended that I went to afternoon school until November 1st. That really upset me. Because me being a senior, I had goals and everything. That side tracked me big time. They didn't give me a chance.

Latoya was back in regular school when I interviewed her. During the school year, her attendance became more sporadic. She told me that she didn't have many friends in the school and wasn't very happy. She had mentioned that she wanted to attend the local community college, but when I tried to give her an application, I could not find her in school. It seemed she had left school, but the records office could not be sure since there was no paperwork about her dropping out.

This kind of entrance and exit of students was hardly considered abnormal at the city high schools. Teachers and administrators at Brandon High expected that many of their students would drop out of school, and as many as 30 percent did. In addition, in 1998 nearly 25 percent of seniors did not graduate (for academic and attendance reasons). In short, then, barely half the students coming into the school actually graduated.

Systemic violence led to unquestioned policies and actions that were, at the very least, demeaning, and at times devastating for some students. It negatively affected, not only individuals, but the environment of the school and relationships between people. Early in the school year, for example, the administration, responding to increased fighting, instated a policy that restricted all students to their classrooms for the entire day whenever there was a fight in the school. In a form of doublespeak, these days were called "learning" or "focus" days. This policy not only rationalized a kind of prison mentality toward school discipline, it undermined educational opportunity for all students, who could not then go to the library, get extra help during their free periods, use the bathroom during class, or make an important phone call. Both students who were academically successful and those who were failing their classes criticized this policy for its inhumaneness. Several students referred to focus days as "lockdowns." Girls, especially, complained that they needed to use the bathrooms for reasons they preferred to keep to themselves. They would rather not have to beg and thus expose themselves to an entire class.

Systemic violence made people's actions ugly. The presence of armed police officers, surveillance cameras, metal detectors, guards, and monitors with walkie-talkies may adequately describe a prison, but it should not be the description of a school. Nor should school faculty feel so threatened and powerless that such forms of discipline and policing are necessary. That so many teachers and administrators are fearful and feel strong pressure from community members to keep control of the school—and to squash the possibility of any bad publicity about the school—gives impetus to behaviors that are oppressive and damaging. At Brandon High, throughout the school day, routinely, administrators and the school police officer barred the way of young people entering the school. Often those trying to enter were expelled or suspended students, sometimes they were recent graduates with friends still in the school. To see so many students suspended and expelled—or "dropped"—from school and then to see so many turned away from entering the building has to cause us to question: Just how public are our public schools?

Perhaps most disheartening about systemic violence is the means by which impossible scenes become everyday occurrences that, at least on the surface, seem to be uniformly accepted and participated in. An example of this could be drawn from school basketball games. Because of great sports rivalries and gang tensions between the different sides of the city, especially the south and north sides, city high school basketball games are heavily policed. During one city game (Brandon vs. London, a north side school) there were about twenty police officers in uniform, with guns and clubs, patrolling outside and inside the school. There were two hand-held metal detectors used on each student who came in the door as a spectator. Some students were frisked. There were six marked police cars, one parked sideways in the parking lot, cutting off traffic to the back of the school. The other police cars were parked up the hill just outside the school, in front of the school, and in various parts of the parking lot. There was a paddy wagon in front of the school, as well. Standing outside the paddy wagon were men in black SWAT-like uniforms, with shoulder pads and automatic weapons slung over their shoulders. There was a helicopter circling above the school with a spotlight that bounced back and forth in the parking lot, climbed the side of the school, and returned to the parking lot, over and over again. The night was very dark, but there was a lot of glare from the spotlights. The spectators were nearly all African-American, with only about a dozen or so White spectators. In school the next day, one White teacher remarked, in referring to the different skin colors of the spectators and the police: "Imagine what it would have been like to be Black coming into this school last night. Imagine if it was the other way around."

It is much too easy to blame schools for systemic violence, just as it is too easy to blame kids for the violence they do. Matters are much more complex, and some reasons for systemic violence can be found elsewhere: in families, in gangs, in prejudices and fears, and in political rhetoric that sanctions forms of discriminatory punishment and policing. One could see, for example, the evolution of systemic violence, especially in forms associated with discipline and punishment, partly as an outcome of congressional backing on the national level, starting in 1994, of "three strikes" and "zero tolerance" policies with reference to adult criminals, especially drug offenders, and the imposition of mandatory prison terms for them. The mass building of prisons, the cutting of social services for delinquent youth, the increase in zero tolerance policies, the prosecution as adults of children as young as seven and the mean-spirited call for orphanages and better (read "stricter") detention facilities has trickled down to state, city, and school policymakers and has emboldened them—and in some cases created pressure for them—to install their own forms of zero tolerance policies and policing. To consider this a "symbolic" form of violence, as some individuals do, understates the real consequences on students of policies and institutional practices that confine, demean, and misunderstand young people—that create in our society a general feeling that teenagers are no good, out of control, and immoral and that therefore bolster punishment in place of pedagogy and control in place of understanding.

HIDDEN VIOLENCE: SEXUAL HARASSMENT, BULLYING, AND JUMPINGS

Unlike shootings and fights, but in some ways similar to systemic violence, sexual harassment and attacks, bullying, and jumpings are hidden forms of violence that are not always noticed, and sometimes the least discussed in conversations about violence, yet remain prevalent problems in schools (Besag, 1989). These are forms of violence that occur nearly every day and sometimes are committed outside the view and hearing of school officials. Ironically, though, they are also often committed in public places such as libraries, hallways, and outside during lunch or recess (Stein, 1995). Sometimes they occur rather quickly, as when a boy discreetly grabbed a girl's buttocks in the hall or a group of girls pushed another girl against lockers in the hallway. During one incident, a boy student quietly teased a smaller boy relentlessly about his size while on lunch line. While there were numerous examples of hidden violence occurring in public places, at times such incidents took place in areas of the school

"ribbed" about. Manuel explained that he was only "buffing" her. Again, the adult mediator wanted to know what he meant. Both Manuel and Keisha smiled and chuckled, no longer enemies but now the main figures in a secret joke and private language. Manuel explained that buffing was like a "big wet one." The adult mediator still didn't understand, so Manuel asked Keisha if she wanted to explain. Keisha didn't respond, so Manuel turned to the mediator and asked, "Are you sure you won't be offended?" The adult mediator told him to go ahead, and Manuel said, "It's like oral sex, buffing, a big wet one." Essentially, Manuel had been taunting her about having oral sex with him. The adult mediator told Manuel that ribbing and buffing could be "crossing the line." She said, "It might be fun to you, but it can also be sexual harassment." Manuel, becoming defensive suddenly, insisted: "I know that. I know what you mean."

Making evident the way that young girls so often accept sexual harassment, Keisha began to defend Manuel. She insisted that she sometimes could not take a joke, and that perhaps Manuel was only joking with her.

The student mediator in the room asked Keisha: "What do you think will solve this problem? Is it possible to not see Manuel anymore—that you two stay away from each other and don't talk to each other?"

Keisha nodded, then said, "We can have a little ribbing now and then."

Manuel, agitated, said: "No way. As far as I am concerned, you do not exist. I will not even look in your direction."

The adult mediator asked Manuel, "Do you always rib girls?"

Manuel, more agitated, said, "I don't want to be listening to those coneheads in the office always saying that I have problems with women." He said: "I love women. I came from a woman. My mother is a woman. I love women. I even rib my mother." Then he repeated: "We have to solve our own problems. My father was here yesterday, now he's going to be here again today." Angrily he went on, "I won't rib her anymore, I won't even talk to her."

Keisha became visibly upset whenever Manuel mentioned that he would not talk to her or see her any more. Not only did she not want to pursue the issue of sexual harassment, she told him that it was okay for him to "rib" and "buff" provided he not go too far.

Meanwhile, Manuel made reference to other formal complaints that had been made about his sexual behavior. After the mediation, the adult mediator told me, "Kids just don't understand sexual harassment. Some of them don't even think it is wrong."

Based on my own observations, it seems that few people, adults as well as students, understand sexual harassment. At the very least, individuals are quite unsure how to proceed with addressing this form of violence. And since most fights between boys and girls (and, sometimes, students of the same sex) have a sexual element to them, the inability to deal with this form of hidden violence affects people's ability to deal with more overt violence, such as a fight. Even when participants in sexual harassment incidents, both victims and perpetrators, are vocal about what has occurred, the stories that parties tell are often quite contradictory. Students keep many secrets from administrators, especially if their secrets include incidents of sex and secret trysts. In these cases, it becomes quite obvious that students do not tell all the details of their stories: issues involving relationships, past disputes, vulgar gestures, and friends of the disputants are often kept quiet, therefore increasing the *hiddenness* of hidden violence.

While the violence involved may be less physical and perhaps less serious than in other forms of confrontation, harassment, bullying, and jumpings are insidious because they occur underground, in out-of-the-way places, in secret; or, if committed in public places, they are done discreetly. Like systemic violence, hidden violence is a long-lasting and ongoing form of aggression. A student's fear of gang reprisals and their associated jumpings, for example, may never cease until he or she leaves the school by either graduating or dropping out.

Hidden violence is not hidden to the people involved in it: the tormenting that individuals do and the anguish that their victims feel are quite real. But the detection is difficult (Kramer, 1997). As a means of detecting hidden violence, some schools have turned to surveillance cameras. However, though cameras may document incidents of hidden violence, they will not teach us how to talk more adequately to students about violence. Sexual harassment, for example, remains merely a whisper in schools in spite of its frequency, partly because talking about it means also talking about sex, relationships, and students' bodies.

Similarly, there is no open discussion about the bullying and jumpings that occur in schools, often between groups of students who are different: from different races, gangs, or different social classes or with different sizes and body weights. Bullying and jumpings, as well as sexual harassment, are the result of student planning, they are ongoing forms of violence and therefore occur for reasons that are not completely spontaneous; they are not the result of a sudden flare-up. They occur for reasons that are inherent in historical, social, and economic relations between people—between boys and girls, Whites and people of color, gangs, and so forth. To address hidden violence in schools is to open a can of worms. To do so, we need to examine tense social relations that have a long history and discuss issues that make people uneasy, such as racism, poverty, sex, and sexism.

SUICIDE

Suicide is another form of violence that begins as a hidden phenomenon but, in some cases, becomes public quite quickly. It is a form of self-violence that can be most devastating for a family, school, and community. During the 1996–1997 school year, two Brandon High students committed suicide: one boy shot himself and another hanged himself. The two were friends and they were part of a group of students who called themselves the Crazy Ass White Boys (CAWBs).

The first suicide was Mark Fisher. On September 21, 1996, he borrowed his mother's car without permission. His mother came home unexpectedly, discovered what he had done, and when Mark arrived home with a friend, she argued with Mark outside their house. His mother threatened to ground him. Quite suddenly, Mark went inside the house to the basement to get shells for a gun that was kept upstairs, went upstairs, loaded the gun, and shot himself in the mouth. Linda Evers, the school counselor who worked closely with Mark's friends and family after the suicide, could not say exactly what prompted Mark to commit suicide—to react so lethally to his mother's reprimands. But she felt sure that it had more to do with a surge of frustration and anger than any long-standing depression. She, and others, felt that if something had distracted Mark, he would not have shot himself. She remarked: "To this day I believe had the phone rung, had somebody knocked on their door, Mark would be here today. He was really impulsive."

That Mark was impulsive was noted by others, including his friends. According to the school social worker, if an adolescent is very troubled, upset, or depressed (and many adolescents are) and then becomes furious or extremely frustrated, the availability of a gun "ups the ante." It makes suicide much easier. To the general public and most researchers, suicide is the outcome of depression, frustration, family situations, drug and alcohol abuse, relationship problems, alienation, loneliness, and identity problems

(Hafen & Frandsen, 1986). A society that romanticizes suicide—that cre-ates frustration for adolescents and often misunderstands young people—may also contribute to their suicide (Noddings, 1996). But often overlooked are the anachronistic laws and frontier mentality that prevent handgun legislation. In cases such as Mark's, the impulsive person, who could otherwise do less damage or be calmed by another, acts hastily and sometimes fatally when guns are commonplace in homes and on the street. Even if it is true that an individual will find an alternative method of suicide if a gun is not available, it is also true that the alternative method will probably not be as lethal as a gun. To have slammed a door, punched a wall, or taken pills and been hospitalized would have been less fatal out-comes of Mark's situation.

And yet, the availability of guns is not the lone culprit here. The sec-ond student at Brandon High to commit suicide hanged himself, and did so deliberately and quite methodically. His suicide was quite different than Mark's. Though always very quiet, Ruben became especially quiet after Mark killed himself. He did not open up to anybody, unlike his sister, who would suddenly begin crying in class due to thinking about Mark. On St. Patrick's Day 1997, without any warning and apparently for no reason (there had been no fight or argument), Ruben hanged himself from his weight bench at home. The day before, he had cleaned out his locker at school, written a suicide note, eaten dinner with his family. A psychologist who read the suicide note suspected that Ruben might have been gay. St. Patrick's Day had been Mark's favorite holiday, and nobody saw Ruben's timing as mere coincidence. His purposeful approach to suicide was very unlike Mark's. It shattered people in the school. Even in 1998, Linda Evers felt the school was still reeling from the suicides. She noted:

> The first one was kind of contained to that group, that group of friends [of Mark]. When you have a second one, when the second one hit, the ripples were felt much further out. It brought up just that much more for kids. I mean we had kids just falling apart, from March to June, just devastated. It didn't really calm down until January of this year. I was afraid it would start all over again with the anniversary of Ruben's [death]. We came back to school and then boom right away it was the anniversary of Mark's death. It wasn't so much the kids who were really tight with those guys, it was more the fringe. It was all those kids who it had rippled to. I guess I don't worry as much about the kids in that core group because they were pissed at Ruben. And just last week—that's why I was so uptight—it was the anniversary of Ruben's [death] and I was afraid what that would bring up with students.

Students were saddened by the deaths of Mark and Ruben, but many students became angry with the second suicide. A guidance counselor explained the anger: "Because they all agreed, after Mark, that they would never do that to each other. They all knew what it did to everybody else and they swore they would never do that to each other again." After the second suicide the dead boy's group became very divided. The girls, for the most part, wanted to keep remembering and talking about Mark and Ruben. The boys, in many ways, wanted to move on. They wanted to try to forget, at least for the moment. Eventually, the group dissolved. There developed some bitter feelings among them—the boys were accused of being insensitive and the girls of harping on the suicides. Some, who didn't want to talk about the suicides anymore or were angry with Ruben, felt awkward around Mark's sister, who remained in the school. Some parents in the community vocally blamed the school for being inattentive to the two boys, not seeing the warning signs. In the end, the suicides ended the lives of two young men. They also destroyed families, friends, part of a community, and relationships among people in the school.

After the suicides, the school became especially attentive to distressed students and signs of potential suicide. While it is impossible to know the extent of suicidal behavior in schools, one school counselor who screens for suicidal tendencies concluded that she assessed about forty to fifty students a year. Many of these students were then referred to C-Pep, a psychiatric ward in the city, for further evaluation. In 1998, there were at least three serious incidents involving potential suicides. In one case, a student found what could have been interpreted as a suicide note in the locker of a friend. Meanwhile, the friend who had apparently written the note was not in school. Phone calls were made, and it was discovered that the student was at home. She was feeling depressed, having broken up with a boyfriend. The school notified her parents about the breakup and the note found in her locker.

In another incident, a tenth grade girl found out during math class that an ex-boyfriend had been shot and killed during the night. He had also been a student at Brandon High. The girl left the school very upset and saying she was going to "kill." The math teacher who reported the incident was not sure whether the student wanted to kill herself or somebody else (perhaps the person who had shot and killed her ex-boyfriend). An administrator called the student's house, but there was no answer. The principal left the school to look for the girl. Later, it was discovered that the girl had not left the school but was cutting her classes and hiding in the gym, not talking to anyone.

Another situation involved a student by the name of Monica. Monica was a small girl, White, who dressed in "goth" black and, on most days, wore black lipstick and white face powder. She was in ninth grade. She had lived at Whitman House, a shelter for homeless and runaway girls. She did not get along with her parents, who had, to some extent, disowned her. In time, Monica was kicked out of Whitman House for breaking curfew rules. Meanwhile, because her parents were very religious—Monica's mother was the daughter of missionaries—Monica was also very naive about sex. Her parents did not speak to her about sex and, for religious reasons, did not permit her to take the sex education classes offered by Brandon High. Until recently, Monica did not know how girls got pregnant. Moreover, her boyfriend had herpes yet she didn't know what the disease was or how people became infected. In time, other girls explained these things to her, but Monica continued to have unprotected sex with her boyfriend.

During the year, Monica had cut her wrists superficially. On another occasion, she used a red pen to draw severed veins on the underside of her forearm. She had also come to school one day with a deep burn on her wrist, which, she noted, she made with a cigarette. The school administration tried to have her admitted to C-Pep for evaluation, but the psychiatric ward refused to take her because she did not have insurance. An administrator at C-Pep assured the school that they had already evaluated Monica (the year before) and had prescribed medication for her, which she refused to take: there was nothing else they could do. One day, Monica came into school very withdrawn and perhaps high on marijuana or alcohol. She had not slept in two days and had only eaten candy bars. School administrators tried to take her home, but her family (who had, by this time, entirely "disowned" her) suggested that they take her to a relative's house. Once there, Monica refused to sleep. She was exhausted but complained that she would die if she fell asleep. Monica's relative emphasized to the school administrator who had brought her there that Monica could only stay a couple of days.

There exists a certain amount of inattentiveness and lack of caring that also, in some cases, contributes to suicide. In many ways, adults have given up on delinquent and poor children and on the social system aimed at helping them. Monica was supposed to call the school the following morning, but by noon she still had not called. An administrator noted that the principal was going to suspend Monica for coming into school high on marijuana, that she would have a Superintendent's Hearing (just like students caught fighting in school), and that she would most likely be expelled. She was, according to one administrator, "out of control." The administrator believed that Monica was probably going to drop out anyway, and probably would not even attend the judicial hearing. A school counselor worried that Monica would end up killing herself. Another administrator said that Monica would probably end up "squatting" with other runaways in an abandoned building. Given the fact that Monica was working sporadically (labeling envelopes) at night on the north side of the city, one administrator felt that she would be "victimized" while taking the bus late at night. It seemed that many administrators could foresee Monica's future yet none felt capable of doing anything to prevent it.

In these cases at Brandon High, causes of suicide and potential suicides ranged from sudden bursts of self-destructive emotions and grief to long-standing relationship, identity, and family problems. Because suicides are sometimes not reported as such (in order to avoid the stigma that accompanies suicide), it is difficult to say exactly how many young people kill themselves each year. Some estimates suggest that about 5,000 youths commit suicide each year and that for every successful suicide, there may be as many as 50 to 150 additional, unsuccessful attempts (Guetzloe, 1989; Hafen & Frandsen, 1986; Marcus, 1996). That boys tend to kill themselves whereas girls tend to "threaten" suicide, as in these cases at Brandon High, is typical, as well.

According to the National Center for Education Statistics (1995), among individuals between the ages of fifteen and twenty-four, between 1988 and 1992, the suicide rate (number of suicides per 100,000 individuals) for White boys jumped from 8.6 to 22.7. There was a similar increase among African-American boys where the rate rose from 4.1 to 18.0 per 100,000 individuals. However, the overall rate of suicide among African-American boys remained lower than for White boys. The number of suicides per 100,000 among White girls was lower but also increased form 2.3 to 3.8. Among African-American girls, who had the lowest rate of the four groups, there was, also, an increase in suicides from .05 to 2.2 per 100,000. That the students at Brandon High (Mark, Ruben, and the girls who threatened suicide), with the exception of one, were White is quite typical. White students in general commit suicide more frequently than students of color. In interviews, African-American students sometimes criticized White students for suicide, the way that White students criticized Black students for shootings. Viewed from a different perspective, shootings of African Americans by African Americans can be seen as an outcome of self-hatred and not so unlike suicide; perhaps they are a form of "indirect suicide" (Marcus, 1996). But whether talking about Black students or White, girls or boys, the increase in suicides is startling. Suicide, as well as what could be interpreted as indirect suicide, are unnerving forms of self-violence: they are unnerving due to the apparent inability of adults to comprehend or to stop them.

THE FOCUS ON GUN VIOLENCE

In spite of the range of violence that exists in schools, as I noted so far in this chapter, the administrators and staff at Brandon High channeled most of their energy into various activities meant to prepare the school for prospective gun violence. Again, school violence was reduced to that which involves a weapon, most specifically, a gun. For example, toward the end of the year, Brandon High staged a planned "surprise" drill meant to prepare the school for a crisis involving a shooter in the school. The drill was called the "Mr. Lion Drill"—the lion is the school mascot—and was conducted in the following manner. At 1:30 on the chosen day, an announcement was made on the school intercom: "Mr. Lion, please report to the auditorium foyer." "Mr. Lion" was code to let all staff know that there was a shooter in the school. The instruction to "report to the auditorium foyer" really indicated that the shooter was in that location. This was meant to be standard code in the case of a real emergency.

Once this announcement was made, teachers were required to usher all students into their classrooms and to lock their doors, which most did. The rest of the communication between administrators and the school police officer was conducted through walkie-talkies: first, the school police officer was called to the scene, then the school nurse was called because there "was a student down," then an emergency unit was called, and finally, all staff who knew cardiopulmonary resuscitation (CPR) were asked to report to the foyer. The drill lasted about thirty minutes and was met with confusion and mistakes: many students continued to roam the halls during the drill; other students thought that the drill was related to the bomb threats that the school had been receiving; some teachers did not participate; it was noted that the nurse might have been shot had she reported to the foyer without any form of "backup;" and when teachers who knew CPR were called to the scene, over twenty arrived.

Rather than this spectacle having the effect of preparing the school for a crisis, it made evident the misguided nature of notions of violence in schools. Essentially, the school prepared for a form of violence that was unlikely to happen while shifting its focus away from violence that already existed. I do not want to downplay the seriousness of gun violence in schools. But fears of gun violence plus the misconception that school violence equals gun violence cause the spectacle of a "Mr. Lion Drill." It also undermines the time given to other violence prevention activities that are well intended and effective. For example, at Brandon High there is a Crisis Intervention Team, made up of administrators, teachers and counselors, that was developed in response to the two student suicides. Originally, the focus of the team was to help students through periods of "grief and loss." The Crisis Intervention Team counseled the friends of the two suicide victims, helped other students who were suffering because of a death in the family, and talked to any students who seemed depressed or were victims of any form of emotional pain. With 1,400 students in the school, incidents involving grief and loss were common, and it was admirable that the school had developed a responsive committee.

Unfortunately, though, in 1998, the focus of the Crisis Intervention Team shifted from "grief and loss" to "crisis management." In the last meeting of the year, the school psychologist led the group with a plan for how the team would respond to a shooting in the school. Late in the 1997–1998 school year, the team invited an intake counselor from the C-Pep psychiatric center to discuss how to evaluate students with emotional traumas. The meeting with the counselor focused abstractly on how teachers and administrators should respond to the aftermaths of deaths caused by gun violence while virtually ignoring any discussion regarding the already existing student problems in the school.

When I asked students if they felt safe at Brandon High, most said they did, though some noted occurrences of violence and times when they did not feel safe. Overall, none considered gun violence the immediate problem in the school. Rather, they noted the high number of fistfights in the hallways and cafeteria and discussed explosive tensions between races, gangs, and social classes of students. Some felt unsafe during the bomb threats; during the last three months of the school year in 1998, over fifteen such threats were called into the school. Some students said that they did not feel safe when a fight broke out, mostly because students gathering around the fight were themselves dangerous. Students sometimes felt afraid to go to particular places in the school—usually the bathrooms or locker rooms—because of bullying. One student was afraid to come to school because he owed money to somebody who had threatened to beat him up if he failed to pay it back. Those who did worry about gun violence expressed greater fear of their neighborhoods than their school. Teachers and staff had similar reactions. Though their discussions of gun violence at times ended in a kind of tongue-in-cheek, "Well you never know," most considered the school safe and worried more about the forms of violence examined in this chapter than gun violence. And yet, again, outside the schools—in political rhetoric and in much of the literature on "school violence"—the focus is on guns. This has the effect of channeling important resources and attention away from very real forms of violence that already occur in schools.

CONCLUSION

Ultimately, when people talk about violence in schools, most often they are referring to conflicts that entail weapons, from box cutters to guns. Meanwhile, in most schools in the United States, violence is a persistent but less dramatic problem. In fact, most schools are safer than their surrounding communities (Apter & Goldstein, 1986; Goldstein, Harootunian, & Conoley, 1994). School violence, then, is an ongoing and somewhat underground problem that entails forms of verbal and physical harassment, bullying and jumpings, self-destructive behavior, systemic and structural oppression, and fistfights. There are other forms of violence that stretch the boundaries of these categories, but in general, these are the kinds of violence that most affect school environments and cause school staff and students to fear for themselves and for others.

Meanwhile, in spite of everything that accompanies school violence (fears, drills, new Crisis Intervention teams, and grief and loss), oddly enough, violence in schools, along with its consequences and security apparatuses, has become a natural part of the day (Bushweller, 1993). This is exemplified by students' offhand remarks about "another fight in the lunchroom," by the zero tolerance policies that have become institutionalized, by the everyday personnel in the school—including hall monitors, assistant principals, and the school police officer—who are charged with the task of school control, and by the walkie-talkies, metal detectors, guns (carried by the school police officer and the visiting police officer who taught the DARE program), and other security devices in the school. Many students today, unlike students of the recent past, accept violence and policing as an everyday component of schooling. The presence of military metaphors in the language of teachers and administrators, the apparent need to "fight" violence with policing by declaring a "war on school violence," the strict regulations and rules all create a school environment that is oppressive and, in some ways, violent in the forms expressed by Bourdieu (1991) and Freire (1970). Essentially, school becomes oppressive when control and discipline are emphasized over education. Greater security apparatuses, including school police officers, metal detectors, video cameras, and zero tolerance policies, have been incorporated into many schools, sometimes at great expense. And while these forms of precaution and policing may, in some ways, curb violence, they also produce an alternative form of violence that becomes a natural part of our political and popular discourse and security mechanisms (Foucault, 1978/1995).

The outcomes of school violence, including teachers' fears, student unrest, and bodily harm, not only undermine the education of those involved in violence, but create obstacles for all students in their attainment of an education. Violence is a serious problem, not only because of the immediate damage that it does, but also because it undermines each student's chances of being educated in a safe environment. It also thwarts any possibility of introducing young people to a public institution and, in many ways, adult society in a joyful manner (Craig, 1992). A person's first attendance at a public institution is often at school, and today that introduction is met with fear, a firm discipline policy, police, and other devices that demonstrate each day that we, as a society, continue to focus on the policing of people rather than the elimination of weapons and the foundational reasons for violence. We prefer a one-size-fits-all policy of discipline rather than an understanding of how issues of poverty, race, gender, social status, sexual identity, prejudice, and fear are central to varying forms of school violence. While gun violence remains a serious problem in incidents of homicide and suicide, our focus on gun violence causes many to forget how violence in schools operates at many levels, involves many forms, is particularly devastating to certain groups of students, and can mean widespread anguish and loss for families, individuals, and schools. School violence is part of a broader problem of violence in U.S. society and, therefore, can only be eradicated by addressing the social injustices, poverty, availability of weapons, rewards that often accompany violence, and the misunderstandings and prejudices of individuals, all of which fuel most forms of violence.

REFERENCES

Apter, S., & Goldstein, A. (1986). *Youth violence: Program and prospects*. New York: Pergamon.

Arnette, J. L. (1995). Weapons: A deadly role in the drama of school violence. *Update on Law Related Education, 19*(2), 30–32.

Barthes, R. (1994). *Mythologies.* New York: Farrar, Straus & Giroux.

Besag, V. E. (1989). *Bullies and victims in schools: A guide to understanding and management.* Milton Keynes, England: Open University Press.

Biklen, S. K. (1995). *School work: Gender and the cultural construction of teaching.* New York: Teachers College Press.

Blumer, H. (1969). *Symbolic interactionism: Perspective and method.* Englewood Cliffs, NJ: Prentice-Hall.

Bogdan, R., & Biklen, S. K. (1998). *Qualitative research in education: An introduction to theory and practice.* Boston: Allyn & Bacon.

Boothe, J. W., Bradley, L. M., & Flick, T. M. (1993). The violence at your door. *Executive Educator, 15*(1): 16–22.

Bourdieu, P. (1991). *Language and symbolic power.* Cambridge, MA: Harvard University Press.

Bushweller, K. (1993, January), Guards with guns. *The American School Board Journal,* pp. 34–37.

Craig, S. (1992, September). The educational needs of children living with violence. *Phi Delta Kappan,* pp. 67–71.

Denzin, N. (1992). *Symbolic interactionism and cultural studies: The politics of interpretation.* Oxford, England: Blackwell.

Devine, J. (1996). *Maximum security: The culture of violence in inner-city schools.* Chicago: University of Chicago Press.

Epp, J. R., & Watkinson, A. M. (1997). *Systemic violence in education: Promise broken.* Albany: State University of New York Press.

Erickson, F. (1973). What makes school ethnography "ethnographic"? *Anthropology and Education Quarterly, 4*(2), 10–19.

Feuerverger, G. (1998, Summer), Neve Shalom/Wahat Al-Salam: A Jewish-Arab school for peace. *Teachers College Record, 99,* 692–730.

Fine, M. (1991). Framing dropouts: Notes on the politics of an urban high school. Albany: State University of New York Press.

Fordham, S. (1996). *Blacked out: Dilemmas of race, identity, and success at Capital High.* Chicago: University of Chicago Press.

Foucault, M. (1980). *Power/knowledge: Selected interviews and other writings, 1972–1977.* New York: Pantheon Books.

Foucault, M. (1995). *Discipline and punish: The birth of the prison.* New York: Vintage Books. (Original work published in 1978)

Freire, P. (1970). *Pedagogy of the oppressed.* New York: Continuum Publishing.

Fry, D. (1993). The intergenerational transmission of disciplinary practices and approaches to conflict. *Human Organization, 52,* 176–185.

Fuentes, A. (1998, June 15/22), The crackdown on kids. *The Nation,* pp. 200–22.

Giroux, H. (1996). *Fugitive cultures: Race, violence, and youth.* New York: Routledge.

Goldstein, A., Harootunian, B., & Conoley, J. C. (1994). *Student aggression: Prevention, management, and replacement training.* New York: Guilford Press.

Guetzloe, E. C. (1989). *Youth suicide: What the educator should know.* Reston, VA: The Council for Exceptional Children.

Hafen, B. Q., & Frandsen, K. J. (1986). *Youth suicide: Depression and loneliness.* Evergreen, CO: Cordillera Press.

Hyman, I., et al. (1994, October 28–29), Policy and practice in school discipline: Past, present and future. Paper presented at the conference, "Safe Schools, Safe Students: A Collaborative Approach to Achieving Safe, Disciplined and Drug-Free Schools Conducive to Learning." Washington, DC.

Kramer, L. (1997). *After the lovedeath: Sexual violence and the making of culture.* Berkeley, CA: University of California Press.

Lawrence, R. (1998). *School crime and juvenile justice.* New York: Oxford University Press.

Lincoln, Y. (1988). Do inquiry paradigms imply inquiry methodologies? In D. Fetterman (Ed.), *Qualitative approaches to evaluation in education.* New York: Praeger.

MacDonald, I. M. (1997), Violence in schools: Multiple realities. *The Alberta Journal of Educational Research, 43,* 142–156.

Marcus, E. (1996). *Why suicide?* New York: HarperCollins.

McQuillan, P. J. (1998). *Educational opportunity in an urban American high school: A cultural analysis.* Albany: State University of New York Press.

National Center for Education Statistics. (1995). *Gangs and victimization at school.* Washington, DC: Author.

National Governors' Association and President's Education Summit. (1991). *America 2000: An Educational Strategy.* Washington, DC: Author.

Noddings, N. (1996). Learning to care and be cared for. In A. M. Hoffman (Ed.), *Schools, violence, and society.* Westport, CT: Praeger.

Noguera, P. A. (1995). Preventing and producing violence: A critical analysis of responses to school violence. *Harvard Educational Review, 65,* 189–212.

Petersen, G. J., Pietrzak, D. R., & Speaker, K. M. (1998). The enemy within: A national study on school violence and prevention. *Urban Education, 33,* 331–359.

Prothrow-Stith, D. (1991). *Deadly consequences: How violence is destroying our teenage population and a plan to begin solving the problem.* New York: HarperCollins.

Smith, P., & Sharp, S. (1994). The problem of school bullying. In P. Smith & S. Sharp, (Eds.), *School bullying: Insights and perspectives.* New York: Routledge.

Soriano, M., Soriano, F. I., & Jimenez, E. (1994). School violence among culturally diverse populations: Sociocultural and institutional considerations. *School Psychology Review, 23,* 216–235.

Stein, N. (1995). Sexual harassment in school: The public performance of gendered violence. *Harvard Educational Review, 65,* 145–188.

Thompson, E. P. (1994). *Making history: Writings on history and culture.* New York: New Press.

Waldner-Haugrud, L. (1995). Sexual coercion on dates: It's not just rape. *Update on Law Related Education, 19,* 15–18.

Willis, P. (1990). *Common culture: Symbolic work at play in the everyday cultures of the young.* Boulder, CO: Westview Press.

3

The Importance of Ethnography in Understanding Violence in Schools

Kimberly M. Williams

State University of New York at Cortland

Those of us who are researchers, educators, and instructional designers struggle to define "conflict" and "violence" as we design research projects and interventions around these issues. All too often, we impose our social construction of reality onto those we are studying or educating instead of trying to find out, first, how these individuals interpret their own reality. I submit that our definitions of conflict and violence will vary dramatically based on our social location (i.e., gender, race, social class, geographic location, age, and religious affiliation). As Delpit (1995, p. xiv) argued: "We all carry worlds in our heads, and those worlds are decidedly different. We educators set out to teach, but how can we reach the worlds of others when we don't even know they exist? Indeed, many of us don't even realize that our own worlds exist only in our heads and in the cultural institutions we have built to support them." We must begin the process of research and design by looking inward to examine our own standpoints or "worlds." Then we must engage in qualitative inquiry to better understand the worlds of others from varied social locations; this is essential if we want to improve our understanding of violence and our attempts to reduce it.

As researchers, educators, and instructional designers, we need to ask individuals from various backgrounds and social locations how they make sense of violence in their lives before we can design effective prevention and intervention efforts. We need to know what individuals in certain geographic locations are already doing successfully to prevent such violence. Finally, we need to examine how new efforts might conflict with, dismantle, or render such existing systems ineffective. We need to know what the motivation is for buying into a new system. We cannot simply identify "promising practices" and assume these will work in all environments. We must examine qualitatively the following. First, what are individuals currently in the location doing to prevent or reduce violence? Second, how might a selected "promising practice" interfere with existing structures or strategies already being used? Third, what can realistically be accomplished and internalized into this system? And fourth, what is the motivation for adopting a new strategy?

In violence prevention and intervention work in schools, we have had a history of identifying so-called promising practices (usually practices educators and administrators feel good about) and imposing them on the culture of the school. Typically, students are never asked what they already do to keep themselves safe. They are never asked what they think would work better to prevent violence. However, before we can create any lasting change, we need to examine the students' perspectives. In addition, teachers are rarely asked what they do to keep their classrooms safe and peaceful or they are rarely asked what successful strategies they see students using. How can we find out what various groups of people within a school or community think about violence? How can we find out what these groups are already doing to keep themselves safe? Qualitative research strategies provide the ideal starting point.

Qualitative methods such as ethnography, participant observation, journal analysis, and interviews have a necessary place in the examination of a community's (including the school community's) perception of violence and its attempts to address and reduce it. A better understanding of the community's perception is essential in conducting a needs assessment for any program charged with developing educational interventions designed to reduce and, ultimately, eradicate violence. Qualitative research allows us to examine some of the inequalities and oppression that groups from various social locations experience and the ways these inequalities influence violence and perceptions thereof. This chapter examines the usefulness of such qualitative strategies as in-depth interviews, journal writing, and participant observation in conducting a needs assessment of an urban school district.

INTERVIEWS

Interviewing is particularly useful in examining how individuals make sense of violence in their lives. Feminist methodologists such as DeVault (1990, 1996), Oakley (1981), Reinharz (1983, 1992), and others have written extensively on the importance of interviewing as a way to gather information from the perspective of the individual—particularly individuals whose voices have been underrepresented in the literature. Interviewee-guided interviews tend to yield rich information. However, in the case of certain topics, such as violence, people sometimes have difficulty speaking. Sometimes the words are not available. In conducting interviews with young people, I have found that it is sometimes difficult to have a purely interviewee-guided interview and recommend that the interviewer start with some basic questions. Trust, also, is an essential element in a productive interview with youth—particularly concerning issues that involve illegal behavior such as involvement in, or knowledge of, violent crime.

To conduct interviews on violence that yield information, the researcher first needs to become someone the informant knows and trusts. In my experience, building trust with young people who have had considerable trouble within educational structures has been difficult. Also, as a White female, I found it a challenge to build trust with students of color, particularly males. When I changed my role of researcher to a more active role in the lives of the youth whose voices I wanted to hear, I found that students were more open with me about the role of violence in their lives. Creating ways to build relationships with young people before conducting in-depth interviews is a helpful strategy that allows access to the words of young people who have traditionally been silenced.

Second, the researcher should ask open-ended questions that are grounded in the everyday reality of the informant—this requires some understanding of the informant's life which can be gained through observation and relationship building prior to the interview—to allow for an interviewee-guided discussion about violence. The researcher needs also to view him- or herself, *not* as an unbiased, objective data collector of the life researched, but rather as a reflective interviewer helping another person create a personal narrative. Researchers need to take into account their personal social location, their interests, their thoughts about what brought them to the research, and so on. As Taylor, Gilligan, and Sullivan (1995) observed in their study interviewing teenage girls about race:

> A narrative account is produced interactively, depending not only on the questions of the interviewer and the experiences of the narrator, but also on the "social location" of both. Hence, any telling of a "story" may be affected by race, ethnicity, gender, class, age, sexual orientation, religious background, personal history, character—an infinite list of possible factors that form the scaffolding of relationships between people. (p. 14)

Being aware of issues of race and class (and other aspects of one's social location) and questioning one's own social location and biases are critical in this type of work.

I found that interviews with individuals whose social location was similar to mine (i.e., White, female, middle class, and professional) were fruitful and easy. The similarity that seemed most important was that of being a professional. For instance, I had very informative interviews with teachers, the youth violence task force coordinator, community members, administrators and counselors at community agencies dealing with young people, and curriculum developers. Many of these people were from different social locations than mine, but what we all had in common was the role of being a professional who was working with youth in the community. This common ground served as a starting point for our interviews.

One in-depth interview, with the administrator of an alternative school for students who had been found on school property with a weapon, yielded rich data about the struggles faced when educating students whom society has labeled as "at-risk," "violent," or "behavior problems:"

> A lot of kids I deal with here are kids who come from parents who didn't have positive school experiences themselves. Many of them did not complete school for whatever reason. Many of them were young mothers or young fathers. So they have a really bitter taste in their mouth about school settings and stuff and a sense of what's just and not just. And so sometimes when you try to discipline children in school you don't get cooperation from the parents. And the parent will say to you, "I told him to do that." Now, I'm trying to say to the child there are other ways to solve a problem than punching someone in the face. And the parent is telling him, "I told you if someone gets in your face that you hit him." So, you've got that dual message here. And as much as I can say, I can't control

what goes on in their immediate home and on the street, but I can say in the confines of this building it will not happen, because it is not acceptable. In society as
a whole, it's not acceptable. But in certain communities, handling problems that
way is acceptable.

In this example, we get a picture of this particular administrator's perspective on violence and how it is perceived differently in the home versus in the school. We also hear that the administrator finds it difficult to
discipline students who come from families and communities where violence is not defined in the same way as the school personnel define it.
From her social location as a middle-class, middle-aged, professional
woman, this administrator found any form of violence unacceptable. For
some of her students, violence was, not only acceptable and supported by
family and friends, but seen as a necessary part of their culture.

The interviews I found more challenging were with youth whose
social locations were quite different from mine. These were young people
who experienced various forms of violence in their daily lives, either as
observers or participants. Their reality was quite different from mine, and
I struggled to gain entrée and acceptance in their worlds in order to hear
their words. Once I had established honest, caring relationships with these
students, I was allowed access to their emotions. These young boys and
girls were not as angry as I had thought at first glance. I later watched
them interact in violent ways with their peers. From the interviews I had
conducted with them, I gathered that my first assumptions about their attitudes toward violence and their concern about the effects on their own
lives of engaging in violence were not always accurate. I noticed that the
interviews I had conducted with them gave me a deeper level of understanding about how adult perceptions of violence and subsequent violence
prevention efforts were socially constructed. For example, consider a
statement by one student that is similar to many others I heard in interviews and focus groups:

Now you're going to think about getting that person down on the ground and
beating the hell out of that person. That's all. . . . You're not going to be thinking
about, "Oh am I gonna be kicked out of school?" By that point you're not even
thinking. . . . Later, afterwards, you're thinking about, "Oh! Am I going to be
suspended?" Right? You don't care about getting suspended. What's suspension? All you got to do is get put into another school. As long as you still getting
put into another school, people's not going to care. That's why I'm here. I was at
Brandon School before.

The perceptions of many students were that violence and fighting were part of life. At least, this was the image that many students portrayed. This image of toughness—of being willing to fight at the slightest provocation—was seen as necessary for survival. Students referred to this image as "thuggin' it." Privately, in interviews, students told narratives that were different. There was more talk of the violence they experienced. For example, a student named Paul told me about being chased and beaten by the police. Other students told me about their struggles in school from the time they were very young—about feeling "stupid" and having nobody take the time to read to them. Donise told me about her mother hitting her and her retaliating, and why, at age fifteen, she needed to run away from home and go into hiding with her unborn child to avoid being put in foster care or in juvenile detention for violating probation.

Administrators, teachers, and other adults who would tell these students that fighting was wrong seemed not to understand life from the perspective of youth. Students and teachers were often frustrated. They did not listen to each other. Teachers explained to me that they had classes to teach and that disruptive students needed to be removed. They would send students to the office. Sometimes, the administrators would send the students home.

Thus, the students' needs clashed regularly with those of teachers and administrators. To maintain their standing with their friends, students needed to "front" it—to act tough, as though school did not matter. Teachers needed to teach their courses and cover material mandated by the state in math, science, English, and social studies. Many students told me that they would figure out ways to fight because fighting was an important way to protect oneself and to demonstrate toughness in order to avoid future fights. Fighting was an important means to prove oneself in one's relationships. Most students brought their "beef," as they called the issues they fought about, to the streets once the school adopted a zero tolerance policy, for fighting in school. Students admitted that school was a safer place to fight than the street because fights at school would quickly be broken up. They saw street fights as more dangerous because, there adults were not around to break them up.

Intervention strategies have typically been designed by individuals who share the same view as the administrator quoted earlier—violence is unacceptable and students should be punished if they are disruptive or violent in the classroom or school building. However, if we are trying to change the violent behaviors of those who view violence as necessary, we need to address their perceptions as well and to inquire why violence is so perceived. We need to listen to, and analyze, the perspectives of youth who feel that violence works as a way of interacting within relationships, and we must take these perspectives into account when developing interventions.

NARRATIVE ANALYSIS

Journals allow people time to think and write about a difficult issue such as violence. In a previous research project that I conducted on college women's drug use (Williams, 1998), I analyzed journals that college women kept about their drug use. Because openly talking about an illegal behavior, such as the use of illicit drugs, requires that informants feel safe sharing this information with the researcher, I collected these data within the context of a course I taught about drugs. Women students felt safe opening up to me about their illicit behaviors, and some were willing to be interviewed. Journal writing provided useful data as well as a starting point for later interviews with more regular users.

An important part of journal reading is examining the subtle nuances in individuals' writing about their social location, particularly about issues of gender, race, and class. Bannerji (1995) argued that race, ethnicity, gender, and nationality are part of any social act and that any feminist research must take these differences into account. It is also necessary to read journals for less obvious examples of how aspects of social location are taken up in discussions and in writing. As Bell and Yalom (1990) wrote in the Introduction to their edited book, *Revealing Lives: Autobiography, Biography, and Gender:* "Individuals writing about themselves have traditionally been prone to take their gender as a given, usually conflating it with sex, and to reflect upon it less than they do their race, class, religious and political affiliation, which have appeared to them as more idiosyncratic" (p. 7). They argued, further, that "men rarely make an issue of their gender because the generic masculine has been the norm in Western society for at least three millennia, with woman conceptualized as derivative from and secondary to man" (p. 7). Similar to "maleness," "Whiteness" is often taken for granted in autobiographical material. However, the researcher should reflect on his or her own social location and on how this position may be affecting the reading of others' journals.

Asking people to write about their experiences with violence and conflict can be a useful way to have individuals share information that they might otherwise find difficult to discuss. For example, I asked a group of seventh and eighth grade students living in subsidized housing to write about a recent conflict they had experienced. In response, they provided painfully honest and revealing answers about the violence that some of them experienced at the hands of their parents, their peers, and law enforcement officers. One young woman wrote:

> One time my brother and my father was fighting and my mother side [*sic*] to my brother don't be hitting him so my mother jumped in. Then I said well you is not going to jump my brother so I jumped in and my sister and then my brother['s] girlfriend jumped in so we were all fight[ing] the next door people called the police and they came my mom opened the door and closed it the police kicked our door down then we started fighting the police my brother['s] girlfriend was throwing plates at them then I hit a police man in the head with the arin [*sic*] then they took all of us to jail. We all had to stay there over night.

A lot of fighting happened to protect younger siblings or cousins. One boy described that he fought a kid who was "talkin' shit" to his little brother, who was "really little" so he "snuffed him" (i.e., fought him). Also, if a cousin or sibling was in a fight that you witnessed, you had to get involved, too. One girl described this in her writing (spelling as in the original): "Once when I was in school and my friends were fighting and than my friend had pulled out some mase and tryed to mase my sister cousin than my sister cousin had polled out a knife and stabbed her in the thigh. Than they both went downtown and went to [juvenile detention home] for 2 days."

We get a picture from these young people's written narratives that violence is a part of the daily round—at home, on the street, and at home again. We must understand the culture in which violence is occurring before we can develop strategies to reduce it. How better than by collecting written information (through journals and writing assignments) or spoken information (through in-depth interviews) from young people in response to open-ended questions?

I would like to add a word of caution here. Many youth who have been labeled "at-risk" for violence also tend to have low levels of literacy. I have had such students refuse to conduct a writing assignment about violence and suspected that for some, this refusal was due to their poor writing skills. As researchers, we need to be sensitive to students' fears concerning, for example, a problem with writing. When people have difficulty communicating verbally or through writing, we, as researchers, can still gain a picture of their culture by becoming a participant observer—not just any participant observer, but one who challenges his or her own social location, biases, and beliefs.

PARTICIPANT OBSERVATION
AND ETHNOGRAPHY

Ethnographic fieldwork involves observation, participation, archival analysis, and interviewing. Within this methodology, researchers search, not only to better understand the perspectives of others, but to better understand themselves, their social locations, and their standpoints. Ethnographers have developed a continuum of involvement, from "complete observer" to "complete participant" roles. I have found in my research that adopting the "complete observer" role is not effective if I am to obtain a depth of information about a setting, because the informants are less likely to trust the aloof researcher or to share information, especially about illegal behavior. Some believe that being a "complete participant," or engaging in total immersion, is the best way to get at the kind of information the researcher is trying to obtain and understand. Teachers writing about violence they experience in the classroom, community workers writing about their experience in the streets, clergy writing about their work with gangs—there are a variety of individuals who are complete participants in the culture of violence and could write about it. Hearing the voices of the most marginalized individuals from within the most violent subcultures would be helpful to those people developing programs for them. However, gaining entrée to these worlds and words can be challenging.

Participant observation is useful as a means by which to examine a variety of sites without being immersed in any one of them. For example, I have been a participant observer in peer mediation training programs at several schools, including an alternative school for youth caught in school with a weapon. I have also served on a community task force on youth violence and on a community management team dealing with juvenile gun violence. These varied experiences have allowed me access to the perspectives of various individuals, all of whom are invested in reducing violence in the school and community.

LESSONS FROM THE FIELD:
THOUGHTS ON THE ALTERNATIVE SCHOOL

Researchers cannot study the causes of violence and ways to prevent it merely by observation without interacting with those at the site; and they cannot simply analyze data without analyzing their own thoughts and perspectives about the site. The following paragraphs are taken from my memos to myself in the field, which were intended to examine my thoughts and concerns about my position as researcher:

> Recognizing that people tend to use the term "culture" to gloss over race, socio-economic class, ethnicity, geographic location, educational background, religion, family structure, and a whole host of other aspects of one's social location, in my most recent qualitative project . . . I have begun to revisit some of my own assumptions about the culture of those groups in our society who have been socially constructed as "violent." I know that there are images that are conjured up when we think about the word "violence." Think of the picture that the word conjures up in your own mind. Are there images of physical fighting, gangs, guns? Is there a particular location that you think of, *a bad part of town*? Is there a particular age group? Color? Gender? Do the images ever include sexual violence?

> I have begun to examine my own definitions of violence—something I think is critical for researchers as well as those conducting needs assessments in this area. I have been forced to think about it relative to my own social location and the social location of my informants. As a White woman going into sites where I am obviously the minority as far as my gender, race, social class, educational background, geographical location are concerned, I am "other." I am "different." I am the "outsider." So what does this mean for me? Truly, it means that I am frequently uncomfortable in these sites. I am silent. I am ignored. I look for others who look like me. I sit beside those who look like me—not always consciously. Does this affect the way I treat those who are different from me? Does my social location affect my feelings for these students and how they are treated? Does it make it easier for me to go home at night because I think that these are "other people's children?" Would it be easier for me, if I were a teacher, to send students to an alternative school if they were from different social locations than mine? It is so difficult to know. But the questions need to be asked: Are teachers intolerant of cultural differences? What are cultural differences? If a child behaves in a classroom counter to the way we have been taught that a student should behave in a classroom—what do we do as a teacher? I have only had the experience of playing teacher at a university, a two-year college, and during

summer programs for seventh and eighth graders—one group from public housing and one from a local Native American reservation. In each of these circumstances, I did not have a principal's office or an alternative school placement as a place to send disruptive students. I could not send them home. I was forced to change my dominant paradigm to fit what the students in the class needed—a very tough thing for a teacher to do.

I had images burned into my brain from the time I was very young about what appropriate classroom behavior involved. Yelling out, getting up, talking when others were talking, refusing to do what the teacher asked, cursing the teacher, and refusing to call the teacher by his or her name were not part of my paradigm of appropriate classroom behavior. Such actions were disrespectful. They made me physically sick. If I had had the option to send the most "obnoxious troublemakers" out of the room, I might have done it, reluctantly, for the "good" of the others. If I had had a student who consistently failed to meet my expectations of the role of student (i.e., sitting quietly and respectfully in class and working hard on projects I assigned, eager to please me as teacher), I would not have felt very upset about removing this student from my classroom permanently, because, I would have told myself: "It's for the good of the others."

This permanent removal from the classroom is what happened to the students sent to the alternative school. Because there is a "zero tolerance" policy in the school district, students with paring knives, nail files, and other items that can be construed as a weapon (regardless of whether or not they have been or are intended by the student for use as a weapon) can be sent to the alternative school for as long as a year. From what I have gathered from discussions with teachers, administrators, counselors, and students, some students are scapegoats or "troublemakers" and the alternative school is a convenient place to send them to keep them from disrupting the educational experiences of the "good" students. Troubling to me is the fact that nearly all of these "troublemakers" are poor and Black.

By analyzing my own reactions to my informants and to the ethnographic research in the alternative school, I have begun to "unpack" the notion of institutionalized racism. I have struggled to think about the ways race, social class, gender, and so on influence the ways students make sense of the classroom experience. The way that we, as a society, have defined appropriate classroom behavior has resulted in students who do not learn this way of behaving at home or who do not accept it at school being put into an alternative school setting. Students who do not successfully navigate the classroom environment may withdraw and become chronically truant—frequently resulting in their placement in alternative educational sites such as juvenile detention facilities, group homes, or alternative schools for students with "behavior problems." Students who misbehave in classroom settings on a regular basis may be suspended from school (placed in either in-school or out-of-school suspension). Students placed in out-of-school suspension for long periods must rely on individual tutorials for their learning. These students may also be placed in alternative learning sites. Frequently, after being placed in an alternative learning site, students find it difficult to get back on track academically and their chances for pursuing higher education become slim.

I understand the ideas behind the alternative educational setting. If there are students who consistently make the learning environment unsafe and unproductive, it seems easier to remove them from a situation where they can have a negative impact on other students. So, instead of following the mainstreaming movement, we take certain students out—we remove them from the stream entirely. They are placed on the banks, where they watch others in the mainstream continue their educational pursuits—taking classes that will help them graduate from high school and maybe get into college. They sit by and watch others in the mainstream learn teamwork through participation in cocurricular activities, including athletics. They sit on the banks as those in the mainstream are taught about sexually transmitted diseases and drug abuse and learn mediation skills, French, Spanish, art, music, and creative writing—and the subjects the state has determined are the most important subjects to learn—social studies, English, science, and mathematics.

After a year on the banks, some students may elect to jump back into the mainstream. During their wait, however, some have run off into the woods, some have been killed, and some have been caught doing something the dominant culture did not approve of as they tried to survive. These students were captured and imprisoned. Some of those who ran off to survive found a group of others who had been through similar experiences and who solemnly vowed to keep them safe from harm, a group that adults have labeled "a gang" and have called for strategies to eliminate.

Qualitative ethnography allows researchers to explore the complexities of an issue such as the efficacy of the alternative school. The lessons I have been forced to learn in my own research should allow the reader the opportunity to realize the complex and challenging nature of qualitative research as well as the incredible amount of rich information the researcher can gather in this manner.

CONCLUSION

Although quantitative measures allow us access to causal relationships and some ideas about the effectiveness of programs, qualitative measures are better able to give us a depth of understanding about perceptions of violence and violence prevention efforts, which is also important to understanding the ways that a community (including a school community) defines, understands, and reacts to violence. By examining ways that community programs influence schools, and vice versa, from their inception to their implementation and beyond, we become better able to understand the subtle nuances that accompany these kinds of relationships.

How does a community define violence? Each defines it differently, and for most, a definition is not clearly established before community groups begin to conduct "violence prevention and/or intervention activities." There seems to be some implied understanding about what kinds of violence are most destructive and thus are worthy of programming to prevent. For example, in the urban community where this research was undertaken, with the advent of a seperate Office of Juvenile Justice and Delinquency Prevention grant designed to reduce juvenile gun violence, much emphasis was placed on this effort while other forms of violence (e.g., verbal attacks, including racial slurs, physical abuse, and sexual violence) seemed to be overlooked. Programs are generally based on past programs that have "demonstrated success," yet the definition of success is often based on a somewhat simplistic outcome—fewer shootings, fewer drug arrests, fewer truant students, and so on. Qualitative methods begin from the question of how individuals define violence and then proceed to questions such as, "What does it mean for a violence prevention project to be successful?" The answers to these questions are highly variable, but they yield a richness of information not attainable through survey data, meta-analyses, and other quantitative approaches. Through qualitative strategies such as in-depth interviews, narrative or journal analysis, participant observation, and ethnography, we can examine the similarities and variations in the ways people make meaning of violence in their lives. Then we can develop interventions and measure their success from the perspective of those living in the targeted community.

After reflecting on my own experiences, reading and listening to the words of other community members (including youth with a history of being involved in, or witness to, violence), and analyzing the literature, I have become convinced of the clear need for projects using qualitative methodologies. Only in this way can we take into account the complex, multiple, and shifting social locations of people to help explain violence and violence prevention from the perspective of those who are, directly and indirectly, involved.

The literature on violence and violence prevention has failed to include the subjective experiences of young people as active and experiencing subjects in their social worlds. As a result, the role of violence from young people's perspectives has yet to be depicted. We need projects that fill this void in the literature by describing how individual students make meaning of violence in their lives. These projects should include a more diverse array of voices, including those who have previously been marginalized in the literature. In addition, we need to consider how groups address issues of gender, race, geographic location, social class, age, and privilege when expressing their experiences involving violence.

REFERENCES

Bannerji, H. (1995). *Thinking through: Essays on feminism, Marxism, and anti-racism.* Toronto, Canada: Women's Press.

Bell, S. G., & Yalom, M. (1990). *Revealing lives: Autobiography, biography, and gender.* Albany: State University of New York Press.

Delpit, L. (1995). *Other people's children: Cultural conflict in the classroom.* New York: New Press.

DeVault, M. (1990). Talking and listening from women's standpoint: Feminist strategies for interviewing and analysis. *Social Problems, 37*(1): 96–116.

DeVault, M. (1996). Talking back to sociology: Distinctive contributions of feminist methodology. *Annual Review of Sociology, 22,* 29–50.

Oakley, A. (1981). Interviewing women. In H. Roberts (Ed.), *Doing feminist research.* New York: Routledge & Kegan Paul.

Reinharz, S. (1983). Phenomenology as a dynamic process. *Phenomenology and Pedagogy, 1*(1), 77–79.

Reinharz, S. (1992). *Feminist methods in social research.* New York: Oxford University Press.

Taylor, J. M., Gilligan, C., & Sullivan, A. M. (1995). *Between voice and silence: Women and girls, race and relationship.* Cambridge, MA: Harvard University Press.

Williams, K. M. (1998). *Learning limits: College women, drugs, and relationships.* Westport, CT: Bergin & Garvey.

4

Resisting Dominance? The Study of a Marginalized Masculinity and Its Construction Within High School Walls

Geoff Bender

Syracuse University

This chapter presents a short ethnographic study of a marginalized population of high school males in a moderately large high school in a suburban community in the northeastern United States. The study points to the significance of a male student's use of violence as a means of constructing his identity as "masculine." As marginalized members of this school community, the boys in this study occupy a conflicted social space vis-à-vis traditional male uses of violence: at times, they are victims of aggression by more socially powerful peers; and, at other times, they take up the tactics of the dominant group to secure the social status they would otherwise lack. Over the course of the chapter, I will seek (1) to review the literature on masculinity and schooling as it is relevant to my study, (2) to define the significance of violence in the context of a boy's construction of his masculine identity, (3) to present an analysis of the most salient features of my findings, and (4) to offer some reflections on this work and how it may be used to further our understanding of the needs of boys in public schools.

HEGEMONIC MASCULINITY:
AN ETHOS OF THE BODY

In his work with men and boys in school contexts, Blye W. Frank (1996) identified three areas of traditional masculinity that he considers "central to the maintenance of (monolithic) masculinity" (p. 117). These are the body, sports, and sexuality. These areas, considered together, form a hegemony, which becomes the culturally dominant way of enacting gender in the school setting (Connell, 1996). Hegemonic masculinity in schools centers around a male's use of his body. Belonging is determined by demonstrated physical prowess ("Didn't he make a great play?" "Did you see how much he drank last night?"), assumed physical prowess ("Don't mess with him," "The girls love him"), or endorsement of hegemonic norms ("I'd like to knock her up," "he's such a queer"). Excellence—or the perception of excellence—in these areas gives a male privilege among his peers. Failure results in consignment to the margins of masculinity; or, worse yet, relegation to the realms of the feminine. Boys who do not endorse this "holy trinity"—or who cannot excel in these areas of traditional male "accomplishment"—often become the victims of male-on-male aggression (Boulton, 1995; Shakeshaft et al., 1997). In fact, boys are more likely recipients of peer aggression than are girls (Siann, Callaghan, Glissov, Lockhart, & Rawson, 1994), sometimes dramatically so (Nolin, 1995).

Victims of this aggression are subjected to what Casella, in chapter 2 of this volume, calls "hidden violence," particularly bullying and sexual harassment. The term "hidden" is a bit misleading, though, as bullying and sexual harassment are seldom entirely hidden. Hegemonic masculinity is a publicly constructed and maintained masculinity. It is never stable and secure; it must be proven over and over before an audience of the male's peers (Kimmel, 1994). In schools, the corridor, the classroom, the playing field, and the cafeteria become proving grounds where a boy—through verbal ridicule or physical intimidation—can establish or reestablish his membership in the club of masculine hegemony. The social value of bullying and sexual harassment lies, to a large degree, in the recognition that male peers will confer on the perpetrator in the form of increased status within the group. Entirely private enactments of these forms of violence, while undoubtedly occurring, do not carry the same social merit and so—in terms of the peer social order—are worth less.

If these forms of violence are in any sense hidden, they are hidden because they are so common and accepted that they have become invisible to any adults who may be supervising student interaction. In her article,

"Sexual Harassment in School: The Public Performance of Gendered Violence," Stein (1995) reported on numerous incidents of male-perpetrated violence—in the forms of bullying and sexual harassment—that went completely unacknowledged by adults with the authority to stop these incidents. The following example should serve as case in point concerning the degree to which some kinds of male-on-male crime can assume invisibility:

> After a football game, [a] young man . . . was restrained by four of his teammates and painfully taped naked to a towel rack after he left the shower area. He was humiliated further when a girl was involuntarily dragged in to view him. [The young man] claimed that this team ritual was well-known to the coach and school officials. (Stein, 1995, p. 155)

The school's officials reacted to this incident, when it went public, by writing it off as "gender appropriate" (Stein, 1995, p. 156). When the case went to court, the suit was filed on the basis of sexual harassment statutes. The judge dismissed it "because plaintiffs have not alleged that defendants' conduct was sexual in any way. . . . [The] allegations are not sufficient to base a claim of sexual harassment" (*Seamons v. Snow,* 1994, p. 1118, cited in Stein, 1995, p. 156). But, contrary to popular opinion, it *is* indeed the case that male-on-male harassment, illustrated here by an extreme example, is often, in some way, sexual. In fact, the line between bullying and sexual harassment is often blurred. When a young man is called a "faggot"—a common taunt from one seeking to establish himself in masculine hegemony—is he being bullied or sexually harassed? The distinction, in my mind, becomes semantic rather than substantive.

Perhaps the truly hidden violence among schoolboys is what I will call "tacit violence": it is violence that is understood rather than expressed. Tacit violence warns students not to cross certain social boundaries for fear of more overt repercussions. Tacit violence ensures that the girlfriend of a boy in the hegemony will remain untouched by a boy in the margins; it also ensures that boys in the margins will not frequent parties given by those in power; it ensures that boys in the margins will not have too much voice in student government or in shared decision making. Tacit violence is the expectation that violence will occur, based on prior experience or inference gained through the gritty clashing of interests and abilities among boys. Tacit violence as a form of violence has remained largely, if not wholly, unexplored in the literature I have encountered, but I will touch upon it later in this chapter.

THE SOCIAL
LANDSCAPE OF MY RESEARCH SITE

As explained, the institution where I conducted my research is a moderately large high school (population = 1,500) in a suburb to the west of a small, industrial city in the northeastern United States. For reporting purposes, I shall refer to this school as Welton High.[1] Racially, the school is almost entirely White (96.86%).[2] There are small proportions of African American (.95%) and Asian (1.53%) students. There are even smaller proportions of Native American (.29%) and Hispanic (.37%) students. Although the first language of most students in this school is English, there is a small but visible population of immigrants, mostly hailing from Ukraine.

The socioeconomic status of most students' families ranges from lower-middle to upper-middle class. White collar and semiprofessional jobs are held by 64.9 percent of fathers with children at this high school and by 70.6 percent of mothers. A large segment of parents also hold blue-collar jobs, fathers (22.6%) significantly more than mothers (9.6%). Parents involved in agricultural work remain proportionally marginal (fathers = 1.3%; mothers = 0.5%). A small percentage of mothers are homemakers (12.5%), with just a few fathers occupying a similar position (0.7%). Fathers and mothers who are unemployed comprise 3.1 percent and 5.3 percent, respectively. The remaining parents (fathers = 7.4%; mothers = 1.7%) describe their work as other than the categories listed here.

The students' social landscape is populated by numerous cliques. In my informal discussions with students, they identified the following cliques in operation: jocks, preps, nerds, burnouts, and freaks. Jocks, I am told, can be recognized by their tendency to wear athletic attire (team jerseys, etc.), usually preceding a game. Preps dress more conservatively, often wearing khaki pants and dressy shirts or sweaters. These two groups are most closely aligned with the educational agenda of the institution and inhabit most of the student government positions.

---

[1]This and all other names have been changed to protect the identities of the people and places connected to my research.

[2]This and other numerical demographic information come from a synthesis of three school-produced documents: (1) "Information for College Admissions Counselors," (2) an informal, administration-generated spreadsheet providing enrollment statistics for the entire district (dated April 1996), and (3) a document prepared for the Middle States Accreditation Board prepared from statistics available for the 1992–1993 school year.

Burnouts, nerds, and freaks populate the margins of power in this high school's peer order. According to students, the single most defining characteristic of a burnout is his or her publicly advertised drug use (though drug use is by no means confined to this group). A burnout makes him- or herself known by wearing tie-dye t-shirts and Birkenstock sandals and sporting long, often unkempt hair. In contrast to the burnouts, the nerd population tends to dress conservatively and espouse conservative political views. The appearance of nerds in this high school is in striking contrast to their depiction in the literature. For example, Eicher, Baizerman, and Michelman's (1991) interviews with high school students yielded descriptions of nerds as wearing "flood pants" and "ugly sweaters" and having "unkempt hair" (p. 683), an appearance that is supported by a nerd's image in popular culture. In contrast, in both appearance and attitude, Welton nerds seem to be more closely aligned with Welton preps than with the nerd sterotype.

FREAKS: A CLOSER LOOK

Freaks at Welton High belong to what Penelope Eckert (1989) called the "progressive" category in the adolescent peer order. Eckert maintained that this progressive category—whose various instantiations have included beatniks, freaks, and punks—challenges the hegemony of the conservative, stable categories of jock and burnout, which reproduce local class structures within the schools. Because the progressive category poses a threat to the stable "class system" of the school, Eckert (1989) believes that "this accounts for the intensity of their hostile reception" (p. 18) within the school walls. The animosity felt between jocks and burnouts in Eckert's study of a suburban Michigan high school was exceeded only by the animosity both groups felt toward the progressive category of the punk. This pattern of social dichotomy between jock and burnout, as well as their united animosity toward the progressive category (in this case, the "freak"), was reproduced in my own study through my participants' stories.

Before choosing participants for this study, I observed several school literary magazine meetings and interacted with magazine staff members. Welton's literary magazine is known as the school's haven for its "freak" population; staff meetings appear to create a safe space in which these creative young people can interact without much inhibition. My informal interaction with them helped me to identify prominent members of the group whom I could interview.[3] After choosing four willing participants, we met for three participant-guided interviews. Field notes were taken during the interview process, transcribed to a computer soon thereafter, and then coded thematically.

My four participants included Filbert, Word Painter, Bobby Joe, and Super Flamer.[4] Filbert is an eleventh grade White male, who comes from a working-class family. Because he repeated a grade in elementary school, he is one year older than many of his junior peers, a fact that he admitted with some degree of self-consciousness. Word Painter is a twelfth grade White male; he, too, is from a working class home. At Welton, Word Painter is a prominent poet and serves as the literary editor of the school's creative writing magazine. Bobby Joe is an eleventh grade White male. His family is solidly middle class. Bobby Joe is good friends with Filbert and a recent addition to the literary magazine staff. Lastly is Super Flamer, who is, to my knowledge, the only "uncloseted" gay male at Welton. He chose his name for this study, he informed me, to reflect his awareness that others define him solely by his sexuality. Super Flamer makes no effort to hide his sexual preference, which has resulted in his being targeted for many acts of aggression by homophobic members of the student body. He, as well, comes from a solidly middle-class, White family.

Our first task, as a group, was to explore the meaning of the social category into which these boys placed themselves (or were placed) and then elaborate their connections to this category. Filbert put forth this definition of the word "freak": it means "basically trying to be yourself." "Being yourself," however, denotes very specific attributes of personal style, most notably in tastes in clothing and music. And male freaks often *link* clothing style to the kind of music they like. One who listens to "punk" or "ska" music is therefore likely to wear a wallet chain, a large-bead "choke" necklace, and pants that balloon out at the shoes—concealing them—and drag on the ground. He may also boast a goatee, if his facial hair is sufficient, and exhibit many earrings. Those who profess themselves as "punk" often voice a notably leftist political agenda, though their understanding of the political concepts that comprise it may not exceed a listing of names and basic tenets. Those who listen to ska alone are con-

---

[3]Though several of the young men I chose were outspoken and so gained attention and prominence that way, some were not. My assessment of "prominence" was gauged more by peer recognition—either nonverbal or verbal—of these staff members in their contributions to group decisions than by any one member's verbosity (a sometimes unreliable trait to indicate clique affiliation).

[4]All participants selected their own pseudonyms.

sidered more "laid back." Filbert identified himself as "punk"; Bobby Joe called himself "ska-punk."[5]

Word Painter described himself as "very industrial." Industrial music is characterized by a driving rhythm, little melody, and a metallic sound—rather like the collision of thick metal objects. Word Painter wears his hair long and tied in a ponytail, and he sports long, tapering sideburns. As he was describing his musical tastes, he showed me a t-shirt with the logo of an industrial band embossed across the front—a band I had not heard of. He, like many other freaks, display band logos as tokens of affiliation. Indeed, Freaks often wear their identities on their shirts.

In terms of personal style, Super Flamer is perhaps the most complex. Rather than defining himself *as* his musical genre of preference, his contribution to a discussion on the connections between music and style was phrased differently: "I *like* Ludwig Van as much as Taco." His response didn't indicate a preference for a particular kind of genre at all. In his attire, Super Flamer rarely, if ever, sports band t-shirts. He often wears plain, black, loose-fitting outfits that balloon at the bottom. His hair is usually elaborately gelled and often highlighted. Sometimes he has been known to wear eye makeup. The ensemble produces a very androgynous image. Super Flamer makes his otherness quite clear through the effects of his apparel.

Although Filbert and Bobby Joe dress in a similar fashion, there are, overall, notable differences in the tastes of these young men that produce very different visual appearances when they stand side-by-side. Difference is, in fact, the keynote to these young men: they mark themselves as "different" from the mainstream through distinctly visual accouterments. The issue of difference as a uniting factor is central to understanding how an eclectic group of teenage males can find solidarity amidst their varying tastes. Freaks define themselves in contrast to conservative, dominant styles, which they describe as "cookie-cutter" like.[6] One of the most prominent among the elements of style is clothing. In fact, Word Painter elevated clothing to perhaps the single most important marker of belonging and difference when he stated, "Clothing constitutes class in high school." As mentioned earlier, preps—particularly male preps—who

---

[5]I noted while conducting my interviews with these young men that they did not express their musical tastes as things that they liked; rather, what they listened to was who they were. So Bobby Joe did not say, "I like ska-punk." He said, "*I'm* ska-punk." This illustrates the degree to which these young men identify with the music they listen to.

[6]In a poem titled, "Bless the Freaks," Word Painter wrote: "You promote our chaotic behaviors / With your cookie cutter life / You bring about our rebellion / With your conformity and strife."

occupy the center of power in the peer social order at Welton, usually sport khakis or jeans, college sweatshirts, button-down plaids, or sweaters. Male jocks, who share the center of power with preps, dress similarly, unless a game is at hand, in which case they don their athletic jerseys or sport a dress shirt and tie.[7] A male freak's attire sharply contrasts with the casual and conservative prep/jock appearance. In a sense, a male freak defines himself as "not prep/not jock." Prep/jock styles are viewed by the freaks as conformist, and they are repudiated for that reason. A freak views the prep/jock jeans–sweatshirt combination as a signifier that represents "buying into the system" through style.

These young men, in adopting such an antistyle, are rebelling against the perceived authoritarian prescriptions of hegemonic masculinity, which dictate, among other things, how the body must be packaged for commerce in the heterosexual marketplace (for a discussion of the heterosexual marketplace, see Eckert, 1996). The reasons for such a rebellion are, no doubt, complex.[8] One obvious outcome of the adoption of an antistyle (which, of course, is a style in and of itself, with its own concomitant norms and expectations for conformity) is the resistance to bodily definition that more conservative styles of clothing often produce. Freak styles are notably more androgynous. In contrast to many of their male preppy cohorts—who often wear "athletic cut" shirts to enhance the contours of their shoulders and chest—male freaks wear loose-fitting clothing that enhances no contours. In fact, much of the male freak's attire could be exchanged with that of a female freak without producing a striking difference in appearance. In addition, male freaks may exhibit other symbols that violate conservative masculine norms: multiple earrings, elaborately sculpted hair, rings with demons or dragons on them. Such markers of difference set them up as "othered" commodities in the heterosexual marketplace. In contrast to their "hypernormal" peers (Eicher et al., 1991, p. 685), who may spend hours in the weight room (or present themselves as if they do), body sculpting appears unimportant to the freak. Rather, in general, physical style is dependent on decorative elements—like jewelry,

---

[7]In fact, when asked what differentiates a jock from a prep, Super Flamer replied, "There is no difference between preps and jocks." Word Painter added to this by noting that members of a particularly prominent male sports team—who occupied the most prestigious position in the peer order—consisted solely of preps and jocks.

[8]Interestingly, by defining himself in opposition to those in power, a freak's rebellion preserves, rather than dismantles, the binary logic that underlies the exclusionary practices of hegemonic masculinity.

wallet chains, and hairstyles—and a clothing ensemble aligned with a certain musical genre. In these stylistic ways, freak males offer resistance to hegemonic notions of the body; they "write" their bodies differently, and they face the consequences for their transgression, which often come in the form of violence.

The difference in physical style between freaks and their more conservative counterparts sets up oppositions with more socially powerful males that clarify the marginalized positions of these young men. This is particularly true in the heterosexual marketplace:

> *Word Painter*: Bottom line about girls: If it looks good, we'll look. But other
> guys try to prop themselves up by putting you down. . . . You risk bodily harm
> if you look at a jock's girlfriend. Lisa [Word Painter's current girlfriend] hugs
> everyone. What can I do?

Here, Word Painter indicates powerlessness on two fronts. First, he is unable to "look at" (and, presumably, flirt with) girls courted by males in more prestigious social positions without risking retaliation by these males in the form of bodily harm. It is Word Painter's perception here that physical violence is the means by which a male jock will "protect" his "property"—a girlfriend acquired in the marketplace—and that this physical violence will be something against which he will be unable to defend himself. For this male freak, violence stands as an invisible, yet ubiquitous, threat that is broadcast from those at the center of power. The strength of those in power lies in the strength of this threat; it need not be acted upon to be felt. It is, rather, tacit. Such is the power of hegemony.

Second, at a level more embedded than the first, Word Painter indicates frustration at his inability to perform as a jock; he cannot "own" his girlfriend as a jock would. Thus, while Lisa's act of hugging "everyone" appears to be acceptable by the rules of freak heterosexual conduct—since he feels he cannot "legally" stop her—Word Painter indicates a longing that things would be otherwise ("What can I do?"). His desire to participate in a practice typical to hegemonic masculinity, subjugating females and transforming them into property whose use can be controlled, seems to belie both the professed (sometimes anarchic) equality that is central to the freak creed and the ever-present distaste for conservative gender roles. Rather, in this example, Word Painter seems to be covertly embracing, not rebelling from, hegemonic masculinity.

This subtle embracing of hegemonic sexual attitudes is borne out in another example, again offered by Word Painter:

> We [male freaks] pick on ourselves rather than picking on each other. We joke
> about sharing each other's girlfriend [*sic*]—not joking to injure. It shows we're
> comfortable with each other in our sexual orientation, friendship, and mutual
> respect for each other.

In the beginning of this example, Word Painter distinguishes freak
expressions of camaraderie from those typical of jocks. Jocks will often
mock each other to signify bonds of friendship and establish intra-group
hierarchy. According to Word Painter, freaks do not engage in such a
practice. "Picking on oneself," or self-deprecation, if done throughout
the group, serves the function of establishing a common ground on
which these friends can operate. In effect, it promotes a sort of lowly
egalitarianism.

This common ground, evidently, does not include their girlfriends,
who appear to be subterranean in status. As with the previous example,
here females are cast as objects that can be owned, and can therefore be
shared. A male freak's respect for his comrades apparently does not
extend to his mate. Instead, this degradation of females serves the interests
of hegemonic masculinity well. It satisfies one of the primary requirements of "being a man": the visible endorsement of heterosexual practice,
which, in this case, as in many others, means the objectification of
women. Thus, while male freaks may visibly endorse an antistyle that
resists masculine hegemonic practice through participation in androgynous dress, a repudiation of athletics, and an endorsement of countercul-
tural music, their links to the hegemony through attitudes toward the
opposite sex remain somewhat intact, as does the tacit violence that goes
with such attitudes.

If these heterosexual freak males negotiate the boundaries between
rebellious and hegemonic practice with some degree of complexity (and
hypocrisy), the negotiation processes become significantly more complex
when a homosexual male tries to navigate the same heterosexual marketplace:

> *Super Flamer*: I can get away with anything when it comes to girls.

Rather than viewing young women as objects of desire, Super Flamer
instead uses them as important elements of a support structure aimed at
protecting him from the violent censure of his homophobic male peers.
Faced with an onslaught of physical aggression daily from his menacing
male cohort, Super Flamer has developed ways of defending himself

without the use of force. Instead, he uses people, particularly young women, to negotiate the boundaries for him. For example, he told me that when one of his "enemies"—likely a virulent perpetrator of violence against him—began going out with one of his female friends, the violence he experienced from that person significantly decreased. Super Flamer revealed that, should this young man pick on him, the young man's girl-friend would quickly break up with him. Close friendships with young women can thus serve as a partial buffer between Super Flamer and his potentially hostile male peers. The effectiveness of this buffer is, of course, dependent on the relationships Super Flamer's "enemies" have with his female friends. If a relationship turns sour, Super Flamer's buffer will begin to erode.

In addition, Super Flamer appropriates the bodies of other male freaks for his defense. For example, in the boys' locker room, a haven of hegemonic masculinity and perhaps one of the most threatening sites for a young, openly gay male, Super Flamer utilizes the protection of Bill, a towering young man with a Mohawk haircut and the body of a line-backer, who is scheduled for the same gym class. Prior to Bill's appear-ance as body guard, Super Flamer talked of the many times he pulled gum out of his hair during his gym period—the results of a tactic employed by young men seeking to gain in social power at another's expense without the use of overtly physical violence and the concomitant threat of suspension.

Super Flamer's experiences in the boys' locker room bring to light the significance of locker space as a site of confrontation between males on the margins and those espousing the hegemonic practice. By locker space I mean the terrain both in and around the locker, in addition to the actual locker surfaces. Locker space is institutionally sanctioned as semiprivate space. Students often personalize the interiors of their lock-ers with images that symbolize social affiliations and individual inter-ests. In a sense, many students make their lockers "like home"—with the inside door not significantly different from a wall in their room. Stu-dents know, though, that this space is violable. The administration can open any locker with a claim of "reasonable suspicion." Students, too, can open each other's lockers. Combinations are seldom kept a secret. It is fairly common for a student to share two or three lockers with other students through an informal combination exchange. The wide disper-sion of an individual's locker combination can result in break-ins by unwanted parties who have obtained the combination through a particu-lar social network.

Exterior locker space is popular congregating territory for students before school and between classes. Friendship groups often huddle around a particular student's locker, frequently choking hallway traffic. When inter-group confrontation occurs between males at these sites, members of the group and, perhaps, other passers-by become an audience for the unfolding performance. The audience makes the confrontation public, which by hegemonic standards is preferable, as these young men go through the moves of constructing their masculinity. Males who are perceived as weaker, either psychologically or physically, become easy targets for male predators trying to accrue masculine status in this public arena (cf. Boulton, 1995). Freak males, who pride themselves on resisting the norms of hegemonic masculinity and often shy away from such confrontation, become easy targets of such violent confrontation. Word Painter became one such target:

Word Painter: R.G. used to pick on me with all his little cronies. I used to hang art I drew (on the inside of my locker)—just shapes—a horse running through a clock.

Interviewer: Why did R.G. pick on you?

Word Painter: He needed to elevate himself by putting me down. I told him off: "I never see you in any of my classes. You don't know anything about me." He pushed me. I slammed his fingers in my locker. He said he wanted to punch the hell out of me. We were to meet at the mall. There was a big rumor: I was going to get pounded into the dirt. I showed.

Interviewer: Did R.G. show?

Word Painter: The big men always show. He pushed me, knocked me to the ground. I took him by surprise and punched three of his teeth out.

Interviewer: How was your status affected by this?

Word Painter: It pumped me up. I was the guy who took G. out.

In this example, Word Painter was able to use physical violence in his favor. He accepted the invitation to the proving ground initiated by R.G.'s threat: "I'm going to punch the hell out of you." Contrary to popular expectation—that Word Painter was going to be "pounded into the dirt" due to R.G.'s size advantage—Word Painter "won" the match by taking R.G. off-guard and bloodying him with a blow to the mouth. His "win" was rewarded by enhanced social status. Word Painter here fulfilled two social obligations of hegemonic masculinity: his showing up at the fight demonstrated that he was made of "no sissy stuff"; and, once there, he "gave 'em hell."[9] Word Painter, then, aligned his social practice with hegemonic practice. His competent use of his body for defensive purposes earned him respect from his peers and reduced the threat of future violence. That is, in this case the threat was reduced, although fighting, as a rule, gives no assurance of future peace, as the promise of revenge is often predicated on the last blow of a current conflict.

Those young men who are unwilling or unable to use their bodies to match violence with violence often become the targets of relentless verbal, and sometimes physical attacks, at the hands of bullies like R.G. Many of these young men belong to the freak group; Filbert is one of them. As an example of the kind of violent confrontation that he must undergo, Filbert recalled a conflict he endured during his ninth grade year. At the time, he was going out with Lisa (currently Word Painter's girlfriend). She laced his shoes in the reverse direction, so the bow ended where the laces usually begin. A group of boys responded to this unobtrusive bit of unconventionality with this provocation: "Oh, look at that fairy. He must be gay." This taunt was followed by an attempt to trip Filbert, after which he was kicked in the back of his shoes. When I asked Filbert how he dealt with it, Filbert responded that he was always taught to turn the other cheek, having been brought up to be a pacifist, so he ignored the taunts and moved on.

This incident is striking for a number of reasons. First, it seems clear that the verbal taunt, "fairy," is used to address more than sexual preference. A "fairy" may or may not be homosexual, but a "fairy" certainly (in the eyes of the taunter) is "unmale" in that he has failed to uphold the standards of hegemonic masculinity. In this case, Filbert's reverse-tied shoe laces seemed enough of a deviation to warrant rebuke. Anyone who does not visibly subscribe to the prescriptions of the dominant form of masculinity—and that, evidently, includes its dress code down to one's

---

[9]"No sissy stuff" and "Give 'em hell" are two of four themes that David & Brannon (1976) claim "underlie the male sex role in our culture" (p. 12). The other two are: a man must be "the big wheel": he must achieve wealth, status, and admiration from others (David and Brannon, 1976, p. 19); and he must be "the sturdy oak": he must exude "a manly air of toughness, confidence, and self-reliance" (David & Brannon, 1976, p. 23).

shoelaces—risks being stripped of his manhood entirely. The insult hurled in Filbert's direction was an attempt to do just that (cf. Kimmel, 1994). Being called "fairy" or "faggot" can be the initiating move in a physical confrontation, as it seems to strike at the core of a young man's identity, his entire sense of himself as "masculine." However, the insult is often issued in the direction of those who, it is thought, will not pose a physical challenge. Filbert fulfilled this hope by his pacifist response. Even after the physical violation of his person, through tripping and kicking, Filbert maintained a determined aloofness.

Filbert's aloof response is, to me, the second noteworthy event in this exchange. It opens up a series of difficult questions. For one, is such a tactic a viable alternative to fighting? Filbert, evidently, displayed no cowering, which no doubt diminished the intended effects of the intimidation; Filbert's response was, rather, visibly neutral. This position apparently neutralized his attacker, which saved Filbert from continued struggle, but at what cost? Filbert remains a target, unlike Word Painter, who, by his willingness to meet a bully at his own violent level, likely eliminated future conflicts with him. In contrast, there is no indication that Filbert will get such a reprieve through his pacifist approach. His reputation was likely little enhanced, and he admitted that he finds such exchanges personally embarrassing. In a sense, his refusal to respond in terms acceptable to the hegemony confirmed the implications of the taunt: he was a "fairy." And yet, if violence only begets violence, where does that leave a gentle young man who, perhaps out of fear or perhaps out of compassion, seeks another way?

LOCKER SPACE:
VIOLENCE IN THE ABSENCE OF A VICTIM

Conflict between marginalized and hegemonic masculinity is not limited to face-to-face confrontation. Hegemonic masculinity can challenge members of marginalized groups, like freaks, in their absence as well. One prominent example of this is locker vandalism. As mentioned, the locker is an institutionally sanctioned, semiprivate space allocated to a student within the institution. In some respects, the locker represents the student him- or herself: the exterior must conform to institutional standards of appearance, while the student has some freedom to construct the interior along the lines of individual tastes (though it never remains inviolable, nor is the interior design at the entire discretion of the student). In this sense, then, the locker, through some sort of metonymic shift, "stands in" for the student, and violence can be inflicted on it just as violence can be inflicted on the student.

Such was the case for Super Flamer's locker. He reported that his entire locker frame was bent and the word "faggot" and a swastika were scrawled across it. According to Super Flamer, the perpetrator of this vandalism was known but never punished (an allegation I could not confirm). What seems clear, though, is that the branding of Super Flamer's locker simultaneously branded his person, and rendered him a victim of peer-order heterosexism with facist overtones.

Word Painter's locker was similarly violated this year, except this vandalism reached into its interior. Word Painter reported that "they" (he suspects a group of burnouts who gather near his locker in the morning) ripped pictures out of his locker: a picture of his family; a picture of "T," a local freak icon; a picture of the Crow, a popular culture icon; and a sticker reading, "Demon to Some, Angel to Others." In black, permanent marker, the word "Freak" was written in his locker. This assortment of images—destroyed by one or more vandals—represents the complexity of one freak's psychological and social self. The images identify his freak affiliations locally (the picture of "T") and also reference a larger freak network (the Crow). The sticker's relativist message underscores the relativism that many freaks tout: We all have a right to our own opinion; mine is just as good as yours. Relativism is often a stance freaks assume to gain argumentative power. Word Painter's family is also referenced as important to his makeup. The ripping away of these images from the interior locker space, images that in many ways represent Word Painter's psychic interiority, and the superimposing of the monolithic label "Freak" in many ways signify the operations of hegemonic masculinity *in toto*. To one in the "club" of hegemony, psychological complexity, a lack of straightforward definition, is intolerable. You are either "in" or you're "out." The principle of belonging is binary and reductionist. It must obliterate complexity to work, much the way a totalitarian regime maintains its power.

CONCLUSION

I would be remiss if I did not point out some of the limitations of this study. For one, the time and scope of my work were both narrow. Studying a greater number of participants—and from different cliques in the school—over a longer period of time would have generated a richer cache of data, which no doubt would have informed a more complicated analysis. In addition, my participants were fairly homogeneous in terms of socioeconomic background and entirely homogeneous in terms of ethnicity. The degree to which race and class restricted both the data and the analytical framework remains, in this study, entirely unexplored. Future work in this area would need to take this into account in a more self-conscious way and, hopefully, remedy the problem by the inclusion of a broader range of participants and theoretical texts.

In spite of these limitations, I feel confident in concluding that hegemonic masculinity is alive and well, at least at Welton and probably far beyond Welton's walls. I believe it is also safe to conclude, based on these data, that hegemonic masculinity—an ethos rooted in bodily attitude and performance—is dependent for its perpetuation on violence of speech, action, and attitude. A societal and institutional climate that supports such an ethos is not good for the men and boys, who must negotiate their stance toward this ethos, often at their own expense—nor is it good for the women and girls, who face subjugation as a likely consequence.

Yet, there is hope. The work of Connell (1996), Frank (1996), and others has done much to dismantle the myths of a monolithic, hegemonic masculinity. Such master narratives of gender are being replaced by models with more promise. For example, Connell and Frank both suggest that masculinity is not singular and simple but rather multiple and complex: an individual may inhabit layers of "contradictory desires and logics" (Connell, 1996, p. 210) beneath an apparently unified persona. This is heartening, because it gives men and boys room to move. Models of multiple masculinities give voice to the margins: both the margins that define the territory of a man's psyche and those that define the broader social territory, including school settings. If the rash of school shootings by disenfranchised white boys teaches us anything, it should be that those voices on the margins need to be listened to, for they are often sources of some of the most creative, intellectually vibrant energy; and, when excluded, they can often cry silently with a pain that sometimes turns terrible.

REFERENCES

Boulton, M. (1995). Playground behaviour and peer interaction patterns of primary school boys classified as bullies, victims and not involved. *British Journal of Educational Psychology, 65*, 165–177.

Connell, R. W. (1996). Teaching the boys: new research on masculinity, and gender strategies for school. *Teachers College Record, 98,* 206–235.

David, D. & Brannon, R. (1976). *The forty-nine percent majority: The male sex role.* Reading, MA: Addison-Wesley.

Eckert, P. (1989). *Jocks and burnouts: Social categories and identity in the high school.* New York: Teachers College Press.

Eckert, P. (1996). Vowels and nail polish: The emergence of linguistic style in the preadolescent heterosexual marketplace. In N. Warner, J. Ahlers, L. Bilmes, M. Oliver, S. Wertheim, & M. Chen (Eds.), *Gender and Belief systems: Proceedings of the Fourth Berkeley Women and Language Conference.* Berkeley, CA: Berkeley Women and Language Group.

Eicher, J. B., Baizerman, S., & Michelman, J. (1991). Adolescent dress, part II: A qualitative study of suburban high school students. *Adolescence, 26,* 679–686.

Frank, B. W. (1996). Masculinities and schooling: The making of men. In J. R. Epp & A. M. Watkinson (Eds.), *Systemic violence: How schools hurt children.* London: Falmer Press.

Kimmel, M. S. (1994). Masculinity as homophobia. In H. Brod & M. Kaufman (Eds.), *Theorizing masculinities.* Thousand Oaks, CA: Sage Publications.

Nolin, M. J. (1995). Student victimization at school. Statistics in brief. Rockville, MD: Westat.

Shakeshaft, C., Mandel, L., Johnson, Y. M., Sawyer, J., Hergenrother, M. A., & Barber, E. (1997, October). Boys call me cow. *Educational Leadership, 55,* 22–25.

Siann, G., Callaghan, M., Glissov, P., Lockhart, R., & Rawson, L. (1994). Who gets bullied? The effect of school, gender and ethnic group. *Educational Research, 36*(2), 123–134.

Stein, N. (1995). Sexual harassment in school: The public performance of gendered violence. *Harvard Educational Review, 65,* 163–173.

5

Someone Is Screaming

Short story by Howard W. Gordon
State University of New York at Oswego

Followed by Joan N. Burstyn's account of an interview with the author
Syracuse University

Artie Graham had probably thought all day long about how he would kick Sterne's ass. I hate Sterne. Artie kept watching the clock, anticipating the bell for the beginning and ending of each class. I also hate bells. They remind me of being forced to go to church each Sunday when I was a little boy. I hated church then, as much as I hate Sterne now. Several times during study hall Artie flicked out a left jab at the imaginary Sterne's face the same way he had seen Muhammad Ali do to an opponent time and again. Artie looked around the room to make certain that no one had seen him. No one else had, and I pretended to read from my World History book as he followed his jab with a perfect right cross.

Now I don't know or really care a damn about World History, but I do know and care a lot about Artie. He's my best friend, my cut-buddy, and we've known each other since we were only six. I've seen him fight

---

This story, from the late 1970s, is published here as it was written. Later in this chapter, the author explains his intentions in writing the story and comments on changes since the 1970s in the lives of African Americans, especially boys and men.

many times before—I've even fought with and against him—and I respect him more than any one else in the world. But I know that there is just no way Artie can kick Sterne's ass.

"Sterne" is Ivan Sterne's last name, though everyone calls him Sterne as if it were a nickname. I guess it makes him all the more tougher, which is the way he enjoys being thought of. Everyone knows that Sterne is a bad motherfucker, but he insists on proving it to his doubters. I know. I was one of those doubters, and then he proved it to me. But I would fight Sterne all over again just to protect Artie, and I know that this time I'd win. I'd kill him. Yeah, I'd fight Sterne without a second thought—and head up too—just so he couldn't hurt Artie. But I also know that Artie wouldn't let me do that; he has too much pride to let anyone else fight his battles. He'd fight Sterne even though he probably doesn't remember what started their argument. It won't matter to Artie that they argued over the usual trivial bullshit which niggers always seem to find time to argue over. He'll fight Sterne because you just don't back down from a test this important and expect to live in this neighborhood past the age of eighteen. It's all a part of growing up, even a part of dying—and no one can back down from those things forever. Everyone has to grow up or die some day.

I hope this isn't Artie's day, but I feel as if I'm waiting to go to a funeral. He's probably outlined the entire fight in his mind—how he will jab and hook, then move away and jab and hook again, the same way we've done to each other while just fucking around—yet, I know he's really scared. He didn't even fall asleep during Mrs. Minarcheck's class the way he usually does. She preached all period long about the history of civilization; how history repeats itself in cycles, over and over again, no matter what the culture, and she went on endlessly—I almost fell asleep myself, but I listened to her carefully and rubbed the lump inside my pants' pocket.

When the bell rang, Artie sat stiffly in his chair, a blank expression on his face. I guess some of the other students understood, as I did, that he was scared to death. A few of them stood over his desk with sad looks on their faces and shook their heads in pity as they filed by. Most of them probably wish that Artie would not go, that he wouldn't leave the building to fight Sterne.

"Maybe if he rapped to the brother—" someone suggested.

But not Artie. He wouldn't take back what he had said. Sterne was a dirty motherfucker for doing what he did, and Artie Graham would never be the one to do the apologizing. I can easily understand Artie's reasoning. Apologizing would be like repenting a sin that you had never committed, and Artie would rather die than do that. It would be like giving up swearing.

At the end of study hall, we walked slowly down the school's winding staircase, and Artie appeared to be composed. His hands were stuffed into his front pockets as usual, and he was silent. There was even a slight pimp in his walk; and yet, when I asked him was everything going to be all right, Artie would not look me directly in the eye. He merely nodded and gave me a sort of a half-smile as we continued the long walk down the stairs.

When students who were leaving other classes heard that there was going to be a fight, they followed us in swarms; many of them were jumping, laughing, and yelling as if delighted over the potential shedding of blood. From time to time Artie looked around nervously, but I knew that Sterne had skipped his class and was already waiting outside. That's Sterne's style: to wait for you after school, cussing and bragging about the way he was going to kick him some ass. Those of us who are in awe of him—and many of us are—would wait with him, listening in admiration to his details of the way he was "gonna break that nigga's face," or "stomp that chump's ass into the ground."

"He ain't tit-shit," Sterne would say of his next opponent. And usually he wasn't.

My best friend Artie is different. He won't stop fighting no matter how badly he's being beaten. He'll just keep picking himself up and going back for more. And Sterne, of course, will gladly give it to him. He'll give much more until Artie just won't be able to pick himself up any longer. No, Artie is different from people like you and me; he'd never surrender. And just yesterday Mr. James, our Social Studies and Black History teacher—who seems to enjoy bragging about being a recent prisoner in Vietnam—said that young black people didn't know a thing about trying to survive in this world. I nearly fell asleep in his class too, but he insists that we take notes. As I nodded out, I missed something he was saying about black-on-black crime but I copied down the good part, the part that made me mad.

"Young blacks," to quote Mr. James, "give up too easily and much too soon. You'll always find them screaming for help in the face of a crisis or death. When young black people are able to stop screaming, the help will find them, and only then will they be able to understand what survival is all about."

Well, I just wish that Mr. James could see this fight.

When we emerge from the building, Sterne is waiting outside, just as I expected him to be, the way I remember him the last time. As soon as Sterne sees Artie, he boguards his way through the crowd of twelve, maybe fifteen, boys who have gathered like flies around his muscular presence.

"Here comes the mothafucka now," Sterne shouts, and he takes a long drag on the expiring cigarette butt in the corner of his mouth then spits contemptuously as we approach. Sterne looks a lot bigger than his seventeen years would seem to indicate. He is taller and built stouter than Artie though they are both the same age. The shirt sleeves of his shirt are rolled to the shoulders in their usual manner so that his sinewy biceps, which have been over-developed through weight training, are proudly exposed. I size Sterne up, and he stares Artie straight in the eyes as they confront each other. Artie is still looking around nervously at the sidewalk and the crowd and at passing cars, as if he's expecting a hundred Sternes to appear.

"I hope you ready faggot," Sterne says, re-rolling one of his sleeves. "'Cause you gonna take this ass-whipping."

"Ready as your momma was when she farted you out," my best friend replies. And I recognize a note of feigned indifference in his tone.

"Then let's go to the alley an' get it on."

The crowd roars its approval at this brief exchange, and the two fighters begin walking toward Bronson Avenue.

"Kick his ass Sterne," someone yells, and he follows behind his idol's heels like a trained dog.

Sterne walks up front, pushing and bullying people from his path, and the crowd eagerly follows. I walk at Artie's side, feeling like a bodyguard, and several yards behind us another portion of the crowd follows.

"Bus' him upside his fat head Artie," one of the older boys encourages, although Sterne could probably give him the fight of his life also.

We walk, some of us yelling and laughing, others running to keep pace, and a few even engaging in mock battles. People stick their heads out of the windows of houses and cars, and some motorists blow their horns at us. Seeing us approach, an old woman in a tattered green dress and a mustard-yellow hat grips the large leather pocketbook which hangs from her shoulder. Clutching her treasured possession in a decrepit brown hand, she quickly crosses to the other side of the street, glancing back several times to make sure that she isn't being followed. Behind me, a short, fat girl boldly shouts:

"Y'all niggas need to be 'shamed of yallselves, always fightin' 'n' cuttin' up each other." Then she lets out a startled squeal when someone sticks his hand under her thigh-high dress and feels her plump behind.

The crowd quickly grows as we march across Bronson with half the people walking in the middle of the street as if to dare frustrated drivers to zoom their cars through.

"Fight," someone yells, and more excited people, friends and strangers, join the frenzied procession. Up ahead, Sterne still leads, and Artie continues to look around nervously as we walk, now farther behind than before. Artie's hands are sweating noticeably. He tries to wipe them on the sides of his pants legs, then stuffs them back into his pockets.

"Hey. Get the hell out of the street," a man screams from the doorway of his store.

"Fuck you," a voice yells back, and a stone is hurled by a nondescript somebody which just misses the store's huge display window.

A city bus screeches to a halt as it has to make a sharp turn at the corner of Bronson and Jefferson. The startled bus driver shakes his fist out the window and curses as more people running from that direction join the crowd. Attacking several hurrying feet, a barking dog follows the crowd for more than a block until its bare-chested master hurls an empty beer can, and a small T-shirted boy, running so that he will not miss the fight, stumbles against the curb and scrapes his knee. Finally, the crowd pushes itself through the alleyway near Number Four school to await the coming battle.

In the alley, a circle forms around Artie and Sterne. Older people and small children push and shoulder each other in order to get a better view, while most of the students begin to urge the two boys into war.

"Come on y'all; get the shit on."

"Break his back Sterne."

"Aw, they don't wanna fight."

"Kill 'im Art."

"Hey, what they fightin' ovah?"

"Somethin' 'bout Sterne takin' the dude's comic book and flushin' it down a toilet."

"Nigga, you bedda get your hands offa my ass."

"You mean they fightin' ovah a mothafuckin' comic book?"

"Now ain't that a bitch."

"Hold this." Sterne jerks a ring from his finger and throws it to a friend.

Artie, forever nervous, looks over the crowd and then the alley as he unzips his windbreaker. The alley smells of stench. It is filled with toppled and unlidded garbage cans, and nearby are two recently made urine pools. Pieces of broken glass and empty wine bottles lie half-embedded in the dirt. There are two wide, crumbling buildings on each side of the alley. Both are covered with a variety of Black this and Black that slogans. At the alley's far end, a brick wall closes the place off from the next street. Artie looks at the wall. On it someone has written in red paint: THE GHETTO IS THE ONLY DEAD END.

I wonder how many years those words have been there and how many times before us people have come to this alley for the same reason that we are here. A number of children manage to climb and sit on top of the wall. Next to me, a young boy deeply inhales the smoke from a tiny reefer joint, then hands it to an eager friend.

"This place good enough for you?" Sterne demands. With a nod of his head he indicates the alley to Artie's wandering eyes.

The ring of people pushes back and forth, and short necks begin to stretch around longer necks and crops of hair as everyone seeks a clearer view. The reefer joint is passed to another hand, relit and sucked on with a final desperation, then ground into the dirt by a sleek, black platform shoe.

"Hell, is y'all gonna talk or fight?" Someone shouts. And Artie looks around the alley again.

"I guess it looks okay to me—"

"Sucka."

No sooner had Artie gotten his words out when Sterne slaps him hard across the face. His right eye waters, and the crowd "ooes." Instinctively, Artie's hands go up and close into small fists. Sterne begins to circle him.

My heart thumps loudly against my chest, then leaps to a terrific-pound when Sterne suddenly charges. He sends two wild hooks at my best friend's head. Both swings miss as Artie easily backsteps out of danger. Sterne's guard is bodaciously low, the way I remember it, and the same killer gaze that once challenged me follows Artie's every move.

"Stan' still nigga," Sterne shouts after missing with another wild hook.

I hear a voluminous roar in my ears. Is it the crowd? Too occupied to find out, must dance. "Yeah, dance away," I hear myself cry out. "Jab and dance away like Ali."

But Artie isn't like Ali. He flicks out a half-hearted jab that bounces harmlessly off Sterne's forehead when he charges again. This time, Sterne catches Artie with his own jab, a solid left to the jaw. My teeth lock and Artie tries to dance away, but his legs just will not move the way he wants them to. Two more lefts catch Artie on the jaw. A hard right snaps his head back. I feel dizzy. Artie staggers, almost falling to his knees. I feel my pants, and the lump is still there. Suddenly, Artie fights back. He catches Sterne twice with surprising combinations. My hands tighten into fists. Artie can fight. Goddamnit, he can fight. But he cannot fight Sterne and live.

"That's it Artayyy," a voice I do not recognize screams. And Artie sends a straight right into Sterne's mouth.

"Stick 'im," another voice encourages.

But Sterne is just too big and too strong. He muscles Artie into a clinch, then shakes him with a wicked uppercut which lands flush on the chin. Artie and I grunt at the same time, and somehow he manages to squirm free. Artie tries backing away, again and again, but Sterne is on him each time, catching him with hooks and crosses to the stomach and the head. Blood flows freely from Artie's nose and I am nauseous although he continues to fight. And the crowd continues to yell and scream, and we push and shove and we elbow as the fighters stagger within our human circle.

Artie hits Sterne with a left, then a right; then he throws another right and left, but Sterne just keeps coming. Suddenly, he dives at Artie's legs and they wrestle. I plant my feet in the dirt, trying to dig in though I don't know how long I can hold on.

"Slam the nigga Sterne."

"Punch him in his head Artie."

Finally, Sterne lifts Artie's struggling body above his head, and I am dizzy again. He whirls Artie around twice, then slams him to the ground. Sitting across Artie's chest and pinning his arms with his knees, Sterne pounds away savagely at my best friend's face.

"Dirty bastard."

I moan, and several people without faces grab Sterne and pull him off. Artie leaps up, and my fists tighten again. There is a new fierceness in his bloodshot eyes, and he courageously charges Sterne. A crushing right connects, and the crowd's roar bursts in my ears. Artie charges again, but this time there is no strength in his effort. My mouth is dry. Sterne lifts Artie again and flings him into the crowd. I elbow back as the crowd pushes, and Artie is shoved to his feet. He is met by a hard kick to the stomach, and I am nauseous again. But despite the pain, Mr. James' haunting words are fresh in my mind. And I want to scream, but I won't.

"Come on mothafucka. Fight," Sterne or somebody urges. But my eyes are getting blurry. Something creamy and sour trickles down the side of my mouth.

Artie fights. He charges again and again, but the punches he throws have no power, and I am angry because it is hard for me to close my hands into fists any longer. Every mad rush by Artie is met by at least one solid blow from Sterne's bloodied knuckles. Artie swings wildly, and Sterne catches him with a hook or a left, or maybe they were rights or kicks. But every time a blow lands, the crowd "ooes" and "oh shits." Artie's face is covered with blood and his swollen features are almost unrecognizable, but he staggers gamely into Sterne. Not this time, goddamnit. I'm not giving up this time. Sterne is also tired, but he will fight to the death if that's what Artie wants.

"Stop it. Stop it, somebody," a girl's voice screams.

The crowd pushes me down, and I feel shoes on my back and legs. But I do get up, and I just wish that Mr. James could see me now.

"Damn, he's tryin' to kill the nigga." And I am up watching several people pull Sterne away.

"Come on Sterne, man. The nigga's had enough." But Sterne shakes himself free, and I tremble.

Artie is lying in the dirt. He sees Sterne coming again, and I reach for the lump in my pocket. Artie closes his eyes and covers his face with his shaking arms as Sterne kicks and stomps. Somehow I close my eyes too. But it doesn't matter; my arms do not shake.

"Get the fuck out the way. The nigga's crazy." And other voices scream when I fire the gun.

Quickly, the crowd scatters, leaving Artie and me alone. People still scream as I step over Sterne's body, and Artie is still covering his face with his arms. He jerks away from me after I help him up.

"If you laugh at me mothafucka," he cries, "I'll kick your ass too." But I understand, and I pull him to me again. He is my best friend, and he has survived.

Someone is still screaming loudly as I walk Artie home.

DISCUSSION

Howard Gordon wrote "Someone Is Screaming" in the late 1970s when the fist fights among boys of his generation, fights that might end in a bloodied nose or broken tooth, were giving way to fights with guns that ended in injury or death to one of the parties. What follows is the distillation of a discussion between myself (Joan Burstyn) and Howard Gordon in 1999, about the story and the changes he has seen among African-American youths in the last thirty years.

I began the discussion by asking Gordon what he had in mind when he was writing the story. He replied:

> The ritual that kids the age of the character of this story go through, and that is conflict that turns to violence and the kind of tension and peer pressure and maybe the inner forces that compel you into those conflicts. . . . If you are the kind of child that I was, growing up as [an] African American in Rochester, New York, you saw this a lot. I think the thing that intrigued me was that I saw sort of an era passing . . . maybe once in a while somebody would use a knife or, you know, something like that but really it was mainly people using fists and that era moved into people coming up with other violent means to hurt other folks. I wondered what did that say about young people and what they were. What was impacting their lives to cause them to make that sort of transition? So I think a number of things went through my head.

Indirectly, Gordon said, he was also exploring Black on Black crime:

> My point is that I didn't necessarily go into the story thinking that we often as Black males hear about quote "Black on Black crime," but that became one of the issues. . . . As an issue sort of that other people frame about African-American communities and what I was interested in is: What do people who are in those communities think about that particular kind of issue? And maybe it's not Black on Black crime that's the issue in the minds of people, maybe it is simply that this is a form of violence and it's not thought of as crime. But what if someone were trying to make that point? I think that that's what Mr. James [the teacher in the story] attempts to do. He attempts to get students to understand what he means by survival. Of course, what he means by survival is taken incorrectly by the narrator who thinks that he simply means stand up for what you believe in and go out there and don't stop, don't give up. So I think that is how that piece got there regarding crime and violence against one's own group or community.

In the United States, said Gordon, we get caught up with violence as spectators. That is not a new phenomenon: lynchings had spectators.

Some may try to stop violence when it erupts, but others egg it on. In a fist fight, Gordon said, the crowd and the fighters become one. The crowd, for instance, will push a fighter up if he falls. The crowd encircles the fighters, making it hard for one or the other to walk away. With the crowd in place, there is bound to be a winner and a loser, and the crowd ensures that everyone comes away with more or less the same story. Without it, each fighter could make up his own version of the outcome. Death was a likely outcome, said Gordon, if a fighter used a gun.

When Gordon was growing up, there were fights each week, but anyone fighting with even as much as a knife was thought to be psychotic. Gordon interpreted young people's resort to weapons as a sign that they no longer felt safe without them, that fists were not enough to get them through the dangers in life. For such dangers, they needed a weapon. That transition, he commented, meant "the coming of the wild, wild West" to urban America. The Vietnam War, indirectly, may have influenced the transition. According to the narrator in "Someone Is Screaming," Mr. James (the teacher and Vietnam veteran) "said that young black people didn't know a thing about trying to survive in this world. . . . 'Young blacks,' to quote Mr. James, 'give up too easily and much too soon. You'll always find them screaming for help in the face of a crisis or death. When young black people are able to stop screaming, the help will find them, and only then will they be able to understand what survival is all about.'"

"When you are thinking now about Mr. James, what did he have in mind when he said young Blacks give up too easily and much too soon?" I asked.

> Well, I think he was trying to make one of those critical assessments of his own people and if I remember . . . Mr. James says that young Black people have to stop screaming, and until they recognize, sort of look within yourselves and understand that no one else is going to help you. The issue is not out there. The issue is right here. If we are killing ourselves, then obviously it is impossible to survive. So, if you simply scream and shout that it's, you know, these other forces out there, which are very real. Racism is very real, violence against community by people who brutalize. I am sure that in many stories I have tried to make those kinds of points about, for example, police brutality and there are those outside forces. But, he is saying: What about the things that we are perpetuating within the community that are senseless acts of violence against ourselves, and in the end cause us to not be able to survive the way we want to? That was, without him saying it, that was it.

Gordon commented that the narrator, misunderstanding what Mr. James meant by survival, "thinks that he simply means stand up for what you believe in and go out there and don't stop, don't give up. So, I think that is how that piece got there regarding crime and violence against one's own group or community."

I asked Gordon whether he could describe the issues that led to the fight in "Someone Is Screaming" and compare them to issues that caused fights among the youths he grew up with and issues causing the fights that young African-American men speak about to him today. In reply, Gordon talked of issues of loyalty, kinship, and friendship. Two guys who are best friends come to know each other's strengths and weaknesses. They fear for each other. In the story, the narrator tells of his own fears even while he describes Artie and what is in Artie's head. Gordon said: "We are never really in Artie's head." Friends sometimes "know" something erroneous about the other. What they "know" may be merely a projection of their own fears or longings.

The fight in the story, like fistfights at Gordon's school, was also over issues of pride and respect. The narrator knows Artie won't end the fight because of his pride and the fact that he looks for respect. Though the issue causing the fight might seem trivial and might be forgotten by the participants shortly after the fight, it was considered an issue of respect by Artie, his opponent, and the narrator at the time. "In this case," said Gordon, "Artie and Sterne are fighting over a comic book, which is the only piece that is actually true about that story. I can remember being in a fight over a comic book and that is another thing that sort of got me started on that story." Respect is always an important issue to African-American men, said Gordon. "If I walk down the street you just can't make assumptions about me and show me some sort of lack of respect, because that is disrespect. I mean, that is what 'dissing' is all about. You can't 'diss' me. You don't know me, and even if you did know me, you've got to maintain some level of respect because I am another human being. So, that is one of the struggles that I think people grapple with as they are growing up."

Groups or gangs provide some people with the respect they seek. Despite that, Gordon claimed that some people found alternatives to joining one by asking what it was about themselves, as individuals, that separated them from people who felt the need to belong to a group. Sometimes, he suggested, the search for self is curtailed by our quickly seeking something to lean on, some group to join. "There have always been gangs; there have always been groups, but what has happened is that evolution of the kind of violence that I think I talk about in this story has certainly changed." One of the changes he identified was that gangs now try to intimidate individuals, as when he saw people in a car recently try to run down someone on a bicycle. He considered fights today over boy/girl issues as similar to ones in his day and basically being about questions of respect.

Racism makes the issue of respect especially salient for African-American men. Gordon claims that "African Americans have never believed . . . [they have] achieved the respect of people outside of their communities. So it is very important to have respect within your community."

Emphasizing the impact of racism on young African Americans, Gordon said:

> You do grow up with the sense that, well, those folks out there don't care about me. They have this particular kind of opinion about me. They have constructed me as, you know, every kind of stereotype you can think of and that is reinforced by what we see on television and the movies, and I think it changed a little bit in certain media but really the images are the same. The ones that bombard children as they are growing up are reasons why people have to wrestle with issues of lack of respect, self-esteem, identity. I mean, people are still being told that they are savages, that they are beasts, that they are hyper-sexual, that crime is committed by them only, that everybody that is on welfare is African American or brown, that they are the root of the problem.

Gordon commented about a racist ad he had seen shortly before our interview: "It's that kind of thing that you see every few weeks that just alarms you that you haven't gotten anywhere." That realization is especially painful for Gordon, who was a high school student in the 1960s.

"When I grew up," he said, "the [American Dream] really was a dream that, despite all the problems, all the racism, and all the difficulties, the obstacles in front of us, there was this hope that the civil rights movement was going to make . . . the dream accessible. So that you could dream of really getting a job, having a nice family, and having . . . that kind of 'normal' stuff that everybody just wants." During the Vietnam War, when Gordon graduated from high school, New York State had opened its state higher education system to students coming under the Educational Opportunity Programs, and so Gordon went to study at Oswego. "Hundreds, probably thousands of students went to school— Brockport, Geneseo, Oswego, etc. and they were coming from all these urban places like Rochester, New York City, and we would descend upon these predominantly White schools." There was excitement among the African-American students. "I mean, it was like this is *our* time. This idea that there really was this sort of revolution coming. . . . Going to college then became an extension of that."

Even though there was excitement among the African-American students Gordon met at college, he felt pressure from some of his peers not to do too well. Success had its price. As he expressed it, to be successful: "It means that you can't go home again. We would talk about those things. . . . There'll be people out on the corner saying: 'So, you up at school, Oswego. You must think you are White or something.' You know, you have to deal with those issues. Those were the issues." Not all his peers were successful, not all made it through college. Gordon described the importance he felt, as an African-American man, of developing his own *identity*. "You fail—or you will fail and that is sort of it. So why go through the effort? But someone has got to be there saying that people still succeed after they fail. I mean, failure doesn't mean that it is permanent, that there is going to be this kind of chronic condition that you're in. As a matter of fact, you know, people have written literature about how some people fail in order to succeed."

Gordon emphasized the need for students to learn to think for themselves. Today, they learn regulations, rules, and discipline, but "there is a real complex world out there that requires people to be able to think on their own and sometimes we simply hit them with this sort of 'Here is the structure that we need to put you through in order to make sure there is not chaos.'" He emphasized the need to teach young people to make decisions for themselves and not allow their peers to decide for them.

I raised the issue of interactions between men and women in the story. A young woman in the story was groped by a man in the crowd. Attitudes have changed since the 1970s, but I wanted to know: "Would it be something that would be discussed in any way? Or is it something that is accepted generally? Is there any difference in terms of different groups in society and what they perceive to be sexist issues and other groups in society that don't perceive [them]?"

Gordon replied that "on the street, so to speak," issues aren't necessarily addressed intellectually as they are in other venues. Intellectuals will sit and talk about issues; others will not do that. There was sexism, he said, among the people in his story that was not addressed by anyone, just as drinking and smoking were accepted social activities that were not addressed. Does sexist behavior still happen? "People disrespecting women? Sure, certainly, . . . [and] that leads to conflicts. We were talking about some of [the issues] earlier which may cause violence. Someone got touched the wrong way or, at least, someone said she was touched incorrectly and again this issue of disrespect becomes the focal point of some violence and potential violence."

These thoughts led him to ponder the ways that people deal with alcohol and drugs nowadays compared to the 1970s. When he was in high school and college, he said, most alcohol and drug use was hidden; now, it takes place in the open, in public spaces.

He spoke about the bitterness felt by African Americans when societal problems, such as alcohol and drug abuse, were tied in people's minds to one or two particular groups in society. For instance, "America is a homophobic society and we certainly have communities that have wrestled with those same issues. You know, Hispanic communities, or Latino communities, African-American communities, Italian communities. . . . Is there any real different, special, strange, or whatever way that homophobia plays out in the African-American community as opposed to others? . . . I guess I refuse to believe that."

Gordon sees a widening gap between the wealthy and the poor:

A lot of [achieving the American Dream] was possible for only certain people and because of the racial politics of this country, [others]—I mean they have always seen this dream as a nightmare and it really can't happen and it won't ever happen. It's just a lie. . . . And then there are other people who believe that it is just one great social program that hasn't done anything except take money out of my pocket for these people who don't deserve it and don't do anything for themselves. I keep saying racial politics because I really believe that we played this game in this country of blame. . . . We like to place blame, or if we want to get rid of—if we want to address—an issue like crime, we have to design a way of framing crime around groups, and that kind of racial politics has caused this deep bitterness and disenchantment among a lot of people who really see integration as a failure.

Other changes Gordon mentioned were that some people reading his story today might be bothered by the swearing in it, or they might find words in it that are not acceptable today, like "nigger," and "faggot." He'd thought about changing them, but he'd decided to leave the story as it was written because that was the way people spoke at the time.

Did Gordon see any way, I asked, to prevent Black students from being shunned by their peers for performing well academically and thereby being accused of "acting White"? He replied that he and his wife had showed their sons that they would have to discount their own parents, who are both college educated, if they attached themselves to that view. Students have to learn that there can be multiple perspectives on issues. Gordon felt strongly that too few African-American students today understand the historical context of their lives. He described his first Black history course at Madison High School in Rochester with Mrs. Brown, an African-American biology teacher:

> We were caught up in that stuff. I mean King was killed in 1968 and my biology teacher said to us, when we were talking about "We want to tear this place up!" . . . she said: "I'm no longer going to teach biology in class. We are going to shut this class down right now and it is going to become a Black history lesson because you don't understand why this man died and how he died for you." And she wanted us to do conferencing. These were tutorials where we would study on our own and do biology and she would get us through the exam at the end of the year. From now on, every day she was going to have a Black history lesson for the rest of the semester, so into June we started talking about Black history. That was my first Black history course. . . . After that I was just filled with it. I just couldn't get enough of wanting to learn about who I was.

Many Black students today know too little about Black history and the civil rights struggle. "We certainly never deal with race, and we certainly never deal with homophobia," commented Gordon. "I mean you do in certain educational arenas . . . in certain classrooms . . . in a course on multiculturalism, or in a leadership class . . . you may talk about some of these issues, but it is not the curriculum. It is not the canon. That is what we give them, we give them the canon. And even though the canon may have been modified to include people like them, that is really a stretch. Do you know what I mean? We are giving them what we have always given them."

"Just added a little bit of something else," I said, and Gordon replied,

"Yeah, it's a way of bringing them into, those that are successful, bringing them into the work world so that they can become consumers, not thinkers."

6

"Frontin' It": Schooling, Violence, and Relationships in the 'Hood

Kimberly M. Williams

State University of New York at Cortland

I selected the title of this chapter based on the term used by students at an alternative school in an urban area to describe how they survived within their relationships, school, and neighborhood. The students had been sent to the school because they had been caught on school property with a weapon. The descriptions in this chapter are based on the results of a year's observations of, and interviews with, students at this alternative school, as well as on research I conducted working with a subgroup of these students who were involved with a pilot literacy project. In that project, which is described in greater detail in chapter 12, students at the alternative school served as literacy tutors for elementary school students. This chapter focuses on how students socially constructed violence and on the roles of violence and drug use in relationships within this school.

Violence is socially constructed. What is violent to me may not be considered violent to others—particularly many of the young people with whom I worked for a year at the alternative school. Within the classroom and hallways and on street corners, I frequently observed mock fights between friends and fellow gang members—actions that I labeled as violent. Fighting, hitting, slapping, and verbal threats were a part of daily life at the school and at the community center where the literacy project was conducted. The young children in the literacy project also used verbal threats, cursing, and slapping when interacting with the older students— but in a joking or friendly way. Violence, as I defined it from my social location as a middle-class, White educator, was a part of daily life for these young people, who were predominantly lower class and Black. Relationship behaviors for young people in the school and in the community center, although gendered, were fundamentally based on the need for safety and self-protection. Even relationship decisions concerning one's own sexuality, which appeared to be of primary importance to many young people, took into consideration personal safety. The teachers in the school, who tended to come from backgrounds similar to my own, struggled to teach within what they, too, considered to be a culture of violence. Students were frequently reprimanded and punished for "violent" acts— acts that the students considered simply a standard part of their relationships with their friends and intimate partners.

Students described to me in a variety of ways how it was critical for their survival that they never show *any* vulnerability. *Frontin' it* was an overall term for acting, walking, and talking as if willing and ready to fight at the slightest provocation and demonstrating no weaknesses. Publicly demonstrating that one deeply cared about another person, such as a romantic partner, family member, or close friend, was sometimes viewed as a weakness or vulnerability. Walking, talking, dressing, acting, and having gender-appropriate relationships were all very important when *frontin' it* in the 'hood. The young people who were bullied in this culture were those unable to *front it*. They were quiet, shy, and did not carry themselves as though on the way to a fight. They were the ones who, according to one administrator at the school, "have victim written across their forehead."

Students at the alternative school would decide that there were others whom most students "didn't like." These students sometimes became outcasts whose lives eventually were made so miserable that some stopped coming to school. It was important to "fit in" and follow the norm. The norm was to act tough, to act as though school were unimportant, to claim to be in a romantic, heterosexual relationship (for girls) or to have multiple sexual partners (for boys), and to hang (around) on the block. Because fitting in was important to survival and *frontin' it* was part of the norm, students had to learn to act tough to avoid becoming an outcast.

WHAT STUDENTS TOLD ME VERSUS WHAT
THEY TOLD EACH OTHER

I noticed in my participant observations in the field, both at the alternative school and during the literacy project with students from the school, that the students each had a story about how they ended up at the school. Since what they all had in common was that they had been caught with a weapon on school property, every time someone new came to the school, they had to "tell their story" of how they got there. In every case I overheard, these stories were very dramatic. They all involved a big fight and a big weapon. Paul, for example, said that he was caught with a "sword" when he was in a huge fight. James said he had a gun (even though students found with guns were usually sent elsewhere than the alternative school). Tone said he brought in a big knife and held it to the throat of a kid who had "jumped" him and threatened to cut *his* throat. When someone (a young male trainer) asked him what would have happened if he had actually cut the kid's throat, Tone said, "I'd probably end up in jail."

For Tone, part of frontin' it was saying that he would have gone through with slitting his enemy's throat, even if it meant prison time for him. In some settings, frontin' it meant that Tone would have had actually to go through with it to prove his toughness, as Howard Gordon's story in chapter 5 of this volume demonstrates.

In their interviews with me, Paul, James, and Tone each downplayed the weapon and gave me the "adult" version. This occurred after they knew I had overheard their stories to one another. Paul told me a story of having a fishing knife in his pocket that he had put there the day before to keep his little brother from playing with it and hurting himself. In his words, "It wasn't very big . . . it wasn't a very big knife." His "sword" had been reduced to a small knife when talking to me. What had happened was that when his brother got into a fight in school, Paul jumped in and the knife fell out of his pocket. His brother was suspended and sent to "afternoon school," an alternative education program located in their high school. Paul was suspended and sent to the alternative school because he had the knife.

James said he had found a bee-bee gun and was showing it to his friends when the principal caught him. That was not the kind of gun he had depicted when talking to his friends.

Tone told me that he just had brought in a knife, not that he was about to cut a person's throat with it. These stories indicate the importance of acting tough within this setting. Stories for peers needed to demonstrate one's willingness to fight and use weapons if necessary. Stories for educators did not seem to need to demonstrate toughness. I watched students downplay their stories for adults in an effort to show why it was unfair that they had been sent to the alternative school. Nevertheless, students seemed to know that they needed to be careful to avoid being accused by peers of *frontin'*, which meant that they were just pretending to be "hard" or "thugs" but were not actually that tough. Boys, like Jared, were thought to be *fronters*, and their toughness was often challenged by threats to fight. Those suspected of *frontin'* were often targets of violence, so it was important never to let one's guard down around peers.

In the protected setting of the literacy project and one-on-one discussions of their private worlds with me there, the students did not need to act tough. After they got to know me, they did not seem to act as tough in front of me as they did in front of their peers. The five students in the literacy project described to me the pain and difficult times in their lives, and their relationships with their family and friends, and also their goals and aspirations. But they were careful that nobody saw them talking to me about personal issues for fear that they would be challenged. Outside this private and protected interview setting, these young men were forced to pretend to *thug it out in the 'hood*. Tone and Paul knew they did this. One day, on the way home from tutoring as they got out of my car in their neighborhood, they said to each other: "Let's go! We're thuggin' it out, thuggin' it out," almost as a chant. Leaving the security of my car seemed to mean that they had to act tough for their own safety.

FIGHTING FOR PASSION:
LOVE AND FRIENDSHIP AS UNDERLYING
MOST CONFLICTS

Despite the need to act tough and show no weakness, students carefully negotiated the delicate interpersonal relationships with friends and sexual partners. Having friends and partners was important, but the nature of these relationships varied greatly between boys and girls. I noticed that although boys and girls appeared to have different expectations involving intimate relationships (both friendship and sexual), at the most fundamental level, young people were looking for relationships that kept them safe.

Joining a group or gang, as these groups are frequently called, and making certain that one was not considered homosexual were two of the ways boys used relationships to stay safe. Girls also joined groups or gangs, and they coupled with strong, popular boys to keep themselves safe. Despite these strategies, violence did occur, and for a variety of reasons; usually, however, the root cause was within the context of an intimate or sexual relationship.

I quickly began to realize that the underlying cause of nearly every fight (and there were several daily during my observations) was conflict involving a sexual or romantic, boyfriend–girlfriend relationship. I realize that this statement is focused on heterosexuality, but in the high schools I observed this was the only kind of sexuality that was acceptable. Any time homosexuality came up in a conversation or a talk it was viewed with outward disgust and name-calling. Homosexuality in these environments was simply not tolerated, and, in fact, suspicion of someone's homosexuality might result in violence against that person.

Boys attempted to keep themselves safe by making it clear to others that they were heterosexual, usually by boasting of multiple (actual or fictional) sexual conquests and by remaining distant from other boys. At the alternative school, boys described their relationship with other boys and the ways that they would demonstrate that their friendship was not *too intimate*. They would not spend too much time together. They would not walk too close to each other. They described leaving a seat between themselves and other boys at the movies or in the cafeteria. They would not share anything too personal. I saw this at the literacy project. The boys would not sit too close to each other, and even the two boys who were the closest friends often denied knowing anything personal about each other.

I saw this behavior magnified in the setting of the human sexuality workshops, where boys and girls were separated. Within the male groups, the most popular boys were those who could boast about multiple sexual experiences (whether true or not). Those who were thought to be virgins (even in the seventh grade) were at high risk of being considered homosexual and being publicly humiliated until they could somehow prove their heterosexuality. I watched as adolescent boys called each other "faggot" and as the boys suspected of truly being gay, because they did not boast of their sexual exploits, got teased, ignored, ostracized, and hit with books and backpacks. These boys were unpopular and unprotected from victimization, and therefore girls did not consider them worthy romantic partners. As a result, they had difficulty getting the sexual experience they needed to become popular. Thus began a vicious cycle that meant a boy needed to start his heterosexual experiences young in order to avoid being victimized. The norm of masculinity that centered around demonstrating one's heterosexuality was seen as so critical that those perceived as outside this norm were treated cruelly and sometimes violently.

Within the groups of girls, there did not seem to be the same fear of being considered homosexual, although girls were very harsh when the topic of homosexuality arose. Girls would scream hurtful things such as "Eeew gross!" and, "Git away, faggot! Queer!" to someone (usually a boy) who was considered gay. In a group discussion among the girls where students were asked what or who made them most angry, a group yelled, "Faggots!" and the whole room erupted into a series of words meant to demean homosexuals. However, despite their talk about lesbians as "disgusting," the girls did not seem to fear being considered lesbian in the same way that boys feared being considered gay. Close girlfriends did not hide their relationship from others. They spent time together and sat next to each other. I heard a group of boys and girls talking about the fact that boys do not have close male friends because they do not want to be considered gay; the girls thought this was "sad."

However, there were very few obviously close friends at the alternative school. Perhaps this was because the population was so transient; students both entered and left the school throughout the year. Perhaps it was because they did not know whom they could trust. Or perhaps it was because of the importance of acting tough and the fact that having a close friend made one vulnerable. One girl said at her intake interview for the alternative school: "I ain't gonna git in no trouble here, 'cause I ain't gonna talk to nobody." Instead of having a few close, intimate friends, both boys and girls seemed to feel safer having many acquaintances to protect them. These groups of acquaintances, often called *gangs* or *street crews* by the adults in the community, were considered by the young people to be essential to their own protection, whereas having only one or two close friends could put one at risk of attack without adequate defenses.

For girls and boys, sexuality was extremely important. Being sexually attractive to the opposite sex was necessary for one's popularity. Having a boyfriend seemed to be more important to a girl than having a girlfriend was to a boy, and girls were much more likely to talk about having boyfriends than vice versa. Boys seemed more concerned with boasting of multiple sexual conquests in an effort to prove their masculinity, although there were a few boys, like Paul, who talked about having a regular girlfriend.

A relationship I watched develop and end within the course of two months occurred between Donise and James. They were both in the literacy project, and Donise considered the two of them to be a couple. Donise called James her boyfriend, but James did not consider her his girlfriend. This different understanding among girls and boys of what it meant to be a boyfriend–girlfriend couple led to much conflict between other boys and girls, as it did for Donise and James. Having sex, talking regularly on the phone and at school, and "going out" often led a girl to assume that she and her partner were in a relationship and that the boy was her boyfriend. This did not seem to be the case for boys. James, for instance, did not consider himself Donise's boyfriend. Therefore, he felt eligible to be with other girls sexually. When boys were with two or more girls at a time sexually, conflict would most often erupt between the girls because each would feel that the other girl had moved in on her man. This was the reason why several fights erupted between girls.

Heterosexual coupling (having a boyfriend, for girls, or having sexual experiences, for boys) was viewed as perhaps the most important goal in these adolescents' lives. Because being in a heterosexual romantic, or at least sexual relationship, was viewed as so important, many students became involved in conflicts because of jealousy, fear of losing a romantic partner to another, flirting, he said/she said rumors (about a love interest or romantic partner), or standing up for a romantic partner.

Some girls in the school, including Donise (who was fifteen at the time), became pregnant. (Although she considered James her boyfriend for a time, he was not, apparently, the father of her expected child.) During intimate, girl-only conversations in human sexuality workshops I attended, I discovered that using any form of birth control was viewed as a sign that one did not trust or love one's partner. A sign of true love was to refrain from using a condom during sex. In fact, among the middle school students at the alternative school, despite knowing how HIV and other sexually transmitted diseases were spread, the use of a condom was not seen as an option. The students role-played how to persuade their partner to get tested for HIV before they had sex. This role-play quickly became silly because students knew they wouldn't ask a romantic partner whom they loved to get tested. Such a request would throw their love into question and the signs of their trust, and they would risk losing their partner.

My work within the environment of the alternative school forced me to examine the ways that I, the staff, and the students constructed violence. There were many examples in which what I viewed as violent acts played a significant part in interpersonal relationships. In romantic relationships, I observed that flirting frequently involved threats of violence, hitting, slapping, and teasing (more often overtly displayed by the young women than the young men). In addition, young men and women described that the best way to demonstrate one's loyalty to a girl/boyfriend was to physically fight for them. In a time of life when romantic relationships were tenuous at best, young men were not supposed to let on (at least, not to their male friends) that their romantic relationships were important to them. However, they were expected to fight if the honor of their girlfriend was at stake (e.g., if another person was talking about her in an insulting way). Paul demonstrated this when he described "beating the shit" out of a friend who had told Paul's girlfriend's parents that she was pregnant after Paul had confided in him.

Young women were expected to fight other young women to demonstrate their love to their man. For example, I was told that, as a young woman, if someone was talking to your man, you had to fight to show the depth of your feelings. Donise described this when she told me about a fight between two girls in the school. She said that the girls were "actin' all stupid because of a guy." She told me that a girl would fight if another girl looked at her man a certain way.

The reasons for violence when defending close friends (including relationships with fellow gang members) were similar. Fighting was a way to demonstrate one's loyalty and caring without appearing weak. In friendships, as in romantic relationships, the expectation was that the person for whom you were fighting would do the same for you. For example, Jared got suspended from school for getting into a fight. Tone said Jared was just a "flunkie" who was fighting for his "boys" (in this case, a fellow gang member) because this is how you show that you are one of them. Jared later admitted to me that he was fighting to help out one of his friends who was fighting over a young woman. Most fights I observed were at least on some level because of a romantic interest or partner.

DRUG USE, VIOLENCE, AND ROMANCE

Drug use (mostly smoking marijuana and drinking alcohol) also played an important role in relationships among friends and between boyfriends and girlfriends. The young men and women hung out on the street corners together after going somewhere to get high. Although Paul said he did not "smoke weed" because his father would "kill him," most of these young people drank alcohol and smoked marijuana when they were "hanging out." I asked James in an interview what folks did when they "hung out." He said that they "pretty much smoke weed and drink." He said that he wasn't smoking as much any more because it was almost football season and he was lifting weights and running for preseason training and smoking made it hard to exercise. In most groups I observed in the school, however, some students were high in school and proud of it. I watched as students would walk into classrooms and announce that they were high and would laugh out loud. One time a young woman came in who was irritated because her dealer had stood her up that morning and she had not gotten her "weed." She said to another student: "Shut up! Timmy stood me up this morning and now I gotta sit through this and I ain't even high!" Some groups of enterprising young people had even begun making their own "moonshine."

In my book *Learning Limits* (Williams, 1998), I described the role of drugs in interpersonal relationships among college women. I found the role of drugs among the young people at the alternative school to be similar to what I found among the college women. Both groups would go to parties where they would drink alcohol and smoke marijuana so they could become less inhibited and more open about their feelings. The more popular and social students at the alternative school would get together with other teenagers from the same neighborhood, sometimes within the same gang, and rent out hotel rooms. They would have older siblings and friends buy alcohol for them, and they would gather to drink and smoke weed. It was in this setting that James and Donise first "started talkin,'" as Donise said. This meant they were becoming an exclusive couple to Donise, but not to James.

Pregnant young women seemed to know the effects of drinking and smoking on their unborn children, and they would try not to drink or smoke "too much," Donise told me. However, Tonia, who was also pregnant, told me that smoking weed was essential to helping her remain calm enough to stay out of fights. Students frequently mentioned self-medicating and using primarily alcohol and marijuana to ease the stress of becoming sexually intimate, to deal with school, and to handle frustrating family situations.

VIOLENCE IN THE HOME

Nearly all of these young people witnessed and experienced violence first-hand in their home. According to the school counselor, who knew the family situations of most students in the alternative school, many students, and particularly the girls, were victims of sexual violence, often at the hands of the mother's live-in boyfriend or a stepfather. Violence in the home affected relationships with friends and romantic partners. This was certainly the case with Donise and James. The violence in Donise's home was one of the factors that caused them to break up. Donise went into hiding because she feared being locked up after she violated her probation by hitting her mother. This brought an end to her romantic relationship with James.

Paul also described the abuse he took from his father. He described in detail the time when his father beat him (he described his father as a "big guy—like six two and almost three hundred") because he heard that Paul had gotten his girlfriend pregnant. It was after his father beat him that Paul went to school and beat up his best friend for betraying Paul's confidence in a way that led to his father finding out. Tone described an instance when his older brother came home drunk and threatened to beat up his mother. These instances were described by students involved in the literacy project. I suspected, based on conversations I heard in the corridors at the alternative school and my discussions with the school counselor, that many students at the school came from homes where violence was modeled for them.

DRAMA, SURVIVAL, AND ACTING TOUGH ON THE STREETS

Violence experienced in the home was carried out into the street. Both boys and girls described their lives on the streets as being filled with drama. Part of the drama of "hanging on the block with your boys or girls" after drinking and getting high was to threaten or make plans to get even with a rival gang. These threats could be over a girl- or boyfriend, turf, money, or drugs. Sometimes, fights or threats could be over a bump or stare or what the young people referred to as "he said/she said" rumors. And some deeply entrenched rivalries involved revenge for a shooting or killing that had happened months or years ago. Mostly, James admitted, gangs had rivalries because of "people tryin' to show off for the girls— you know what I'm sayin'?—like tryin' to make a scene. People just tryin' to make a scene . . . some blocks you just gotta jump out of your car and act all tough—if you chase somebody, if you jump somebody—you know what I'm sayin'?—they'll look up to you on most blocks . . . they'll think you're all hard."

Girls also tried to be "hard" in their gangs. Girls talked about initiation rituals that involved having sex with multiple partners, who were most often older men. As Terika said, "All the girls who are pregnant have basically the same fathers [for their babies]—they're the older guys who have sex with them to get into [the gang names]." Both boys and girls could join a gang by being "jumped in" (beaten by the gang members). James said it "wasn't too bad—it usually only lasts like fifteen minutes." These acts seemed like small prices to pay for protection from what could happen if you were alone on the street or not "down" (allied) with a gang.

THE STUDENTS AT
THE ALTERNATIVE SCHOOL:
VIOLENCE AND TEEN CULTURE

Teen culture, for many of the students whom I observed and spoke with, seemed to be centered around violence. There was a great deal of talk about it. Some, but not all, of this talk translated into violent action.

The perception among most of the young people I spoke with was that most adults don't understand or care about what teens need to do to protect themselves. If young people's perception is that one needs to carry a weapon or belong to a gang to survive, then they will indeed carry weapons and belong to gangs. This was certainly the case among many of the students at the alternative school—gangs and weapons were very important to them.

At the time the observations reported here took place (1997–98), the alternative school was located in a center of gang violence. Three of the high school young men told me that they could not be seen outside the school because if they were seen by members of a rival gang, whose turf included the school, they could be jumped or shot. Was this dramatic? No. I saw the groups congregate on the corner, waiting for these youths to leave the school. Family members would escort these young men out the back entrance before and after school so the groups on the corner could not get at them.

Whether a young person engaged in violent behavior seemed to depend on two major issues: the prospects for one's future and for one's love interests. However, sometimes violence happened out of passion; in such cases, the teens failed to consider the consequences because they were overcome with emotion.

"WHAT'S AT STAKE?"
AS A PREDICTOR OF VIOLENT BEHAVIOR

The students in the alternative school were asked, in a variety of settings and by various adults, "What are your goals for the future?" Or they were asked some variation of the question, "What do you want to be when you grow up?" The answers remained consistent for students, almost as though they had to have a pat answer for a question they were asked so often, without any thought given to what they would need to do to accomplish their goal. Shaun was probably the best example. Although standing only about four feet tall, he wanted to be a professional basketball or football player. Did he even play these sports in school? Not usually, but this was his goal. The boys often said that playing sports was their goal; the girls would say things like "Singer, dancer, have kids." Some responded, "Go to college," "Get a good job," or "Own a business."

I had a conversation with a group of middle school boys, some of whom said that they wanted to go to college. I told them about some programs and how they could go to college, but that they needed to do well in school. They got a dazed look in their eyes when I talked about the reality of actually getting into college: filling out an application, the importance of getting good grades, and so on. So, I asked them what they thought college was like. The response was nearly unanimous—it was all about partying—drinking, smoking weed, and hanging out. Never did it come up that they would attend classes or do homework. College meant partying, and that was why they wanted to go. They thought, also, that college would help them get a job at which they could make a lot of money. This explained to me why students who say they hate school still wish to attend college.

James was the only student who saw the connection between doing well in school and getting into college. However, he wanted to go to college to play Division I football. I heard that he was a very talented player and might make it, but that academically he was far behind. He spoke about his academics more than the others—what courses he would take, when he would take them, and the fact that he was worried about most of them because he was a weak student. Even so, in James's mind, college was still not about more school. It was about playing football.

DETERMINING WHAT'S AT STAKE

Through my observations at another high school in the district and at the alternative school, I began to realize that students who engaged in violent behavior felt that they had nothing to lose and a great deal to gain by fighting (with or without a weapon). Those students who did not fight or engage in violent behavior abstained because, as nearly all of them said, they were "good students" and "wanted to graduate." Some "wanted to go to college." For nearly all the students who refused to view fighting as an option, there was a lot at stake if they did engage in a fight. They would be sent to another school. They would miss school because they'd be suspended and would fall behind in their studies. They might not graduate or be able to go to college. These students were on a path that they believed was leading them forward. They felt that being a "good student" was an essential part of staying on that path.

Students who *did* engage in violent behavior felt that they had a lot at stake if they refused to fight. They would be "punked"—jumped, hurt, or shot in the back—if they walked away. Walking away from a fight was not seen as an option for these students. Because these young people saw school as offering them little, and were generally not very interested in school, as demonstrated by their grades, they did not have as much to lose by fighting as by refusing to fight.

It seems important for educators to understand what each young person views as important—what is at stake for each. Those who foresee a successful future in which they play a dynamic role are perhaps less likely to behave violently. Those who do not see themselves as having opportunities for a successful future or, indeed, believe that they will end up in jail or prison (as some students at the alternative school claimed they would) are more likely to behave violently.

CONCLUSIONS

Most young people, like most adults, want to be safe, protected, cared about, and accepted. The young people I observed and interviewed were no exception. Many of the students were searching for intimate relationships within a context where showing no vulnerability and acting tough were the norm. Acting tough was a way to protect yourself from getting too close to others and to project an image such that others would not "mess with you" or hurt you. These young people attempted to create relationships that would keep them from being victimized. For boys, this most typically meant showing heterosexuality by maintaining a safe distance from other boys, logging multiple sexual conquests, and belonging to a gang. For girls, this usually meant having a strong and popular boyfriend and joining a gang.

An important factor in whether students tended to behave violently in school was whether they perceived that they could be successful by staying in school. Most of the youths at the alternative school did not see themselves as successful students. They did not see school as playing an important role in their futures. As I observed in class discussions held between students and the assistant district attorney for the city, many students stated that jail was where they would end up spending at least some of their adult life. They believed this because so many of their relatives had ended up there. As educators working with youths who are at risk of becoming involved in violence, we need to understand students' perceptions of the insignificance of school to their future lives. If the only opportunity students see for themselves is incarceration, they will have no incentive to follow the rules of the school or of society. We need to create better opportunities for alienated young people.

Violence was an important part of life for these students, and self-protection was a factor in many of their minute-to-minute decisions. Often, "frontin it" seemed essential to their safety. This chapter has described some ways that these and other youths attending the alternative school came to make sense of the violence and drug use that surrounded them every day. These findings may help educators and community leaders understand better the culture of violence some students experience, as we attempt to create violence prevention and intervention programs. We need to understand the role that drugs and violence play in young people's lives before we can keep them off drugs and safe from violence.

REFERENCE

Williams, K. M. (1998). *Learning limits: College women, drugs, and relationships*. Westport, CT: Bergin & Garvey.

7

Interrupting "Good" Girlness: Sexuality, Education, and the Prevention of Violence Against Women

Kristen V. Luschen

Hampshire College

CONFESSIONS OF A "GOOD" GIRL

It was a sunny fall day. I was spending another afternoon writing in my windowless library carrel. I had been organizing my thoughts about how youth come to think about, and make sense of, adolescent female sexuality. Interviews with students and their comments from an urban high school health class suggested that both boys and girls organize adolescent female sexuality around the oppositional construct of "good"-girlness/ "nasty"-girlness. My field notes indicate how school practices also upheld this false dichotomy. Until this point I had been writing a self-removed, academic piece about schooling and adolescent female sexuality. However, in the afternoon I decided to take a coffee break and it was during my break that the connections between gender, school-based sexuality education, and violence prevention became very real to me.

I had finished my afternoon jolt of caffeine and was walking back across campus to the library. At the intersection of two main roads on campus, I waited alone for the cross-walk signal to change to "WALK." A white Ford Taurus rolled up to the stoplight with two college-aged White men in the front seat. Their windows were open as they, like I, enjoyed the warm fall afternoon. They laughed as they listened to music that resonated loudly from their car stereo. The "WALK" sign appeared, and I crossed in front of their car. When I got to the other side of the one way street, the driver loudly yelled to me, "Hey girl!" I turned around with my eyebrows raised and said "Excuse me?" I stepped a bit closer to the car but still maintained a safe distance. The man was of average build, with brown, wavy hair and an arrogant smile. His tone spoke a challenge to me as he yelled again, "Hey girl—have you ever heard this song before?" He turned up the radio so loud that it dominated all competing sounds in the near vicinity. As I scanned the taunting confidence on his face, my anger boiled at being the object of his frivolous inquiry. Through a clenched jaw and with all of the attitude I could muster, I muttered, "I've got to go." I felt his gaze on my back and sensed his laughter as the car turned left and rolled past me.

"I've got to go?" I feel disrespected and belittled and all I can think to say is, "I've got to go?" Why didn't I scream angry obscenities at him? Why didn't I tell this young man that I am not a "girl"? I am a 28-year-old woman who is an instructor at this university, and he should hope that he doesn't end up in my class next semester. In the space of five seconds, because of the actions of this man I felt disrespected and vulnerable.

On the way back to the library I questioned why this man felt free to "catcall" me in that manner, for indeed he did catcall me. He certainly was not trying to woo me, make a date, or compliment me. Rather, the image of this man shouting from his car to me, a woman walking in a public space, instantly brings to mind a history (both personal and public) of men calling harassing remarks to women who dared to venture into public arenas. In this situation the man did not comment on my body or whistle, but his use of the word *girl* and the arrogance he displayed in invading my space and wasting my time to suit his folly was effective. Catcalling is one mechanism by which women are reminded that they do not have authority, or even belong in public spaces. The words, "Hey girl," and the history of harassment they recalled in my memory immediately resulted in a renewed consciousness of my own femininity and my related vulnerability in a patriarchal society.

This unwanted attention is a normal, everyday occurrence for women. We are surveyed and commented on if we are deemed too heterosexual or not heterosexual enough, too feminine looking or not quite feminine enough. The standards of evaluation vary in different communities, but the reality of the surveillance does not. Men also are evaluated, but the evaluation typically involves whether they are deemed masculine enough to avoid comments such as, "fag," "poof," and "wussy." These evaluations are predicated on whether a man looks sufficiently different from a woman. Femininity still remains the standard of weakness based on which men and women are considered available for taunting.

The monitoring of women is a routine and everyday practice (Fox, 1977). It is made natural and taken for granted in American culture. It is not, however, natural. Yet, rather than upsetting the "naturalness" of the situation and challenging the arrogance the man in the white Taurus displayed in catcalling me, I instead took responsibility for his behavior. I questioned myself, "Were my mid-thigh shorts too short? Did I give off the appearance of someone easy to intimidate?" I reinscribed what has been referred to as being "nice"—or "good"-girlness.

"Good"-girlness is organized around a construction of femininity that is embedded in heterosexuality. More specifically, dominant cultural rules posit that "good" or "appropriately feminine" girls are supposed to act as if they do not experience desire. Further, in order to avoid the labels of "nasty," "bad," and "slut," and because they presumably do not feel sexual desire themselves, girls also are held responsible for controlling male sexual desire (Tolman & Higgins, 1996). The man in the white Taurus, in the space of five seconds, stripped me of the confidence and authority around which I have organized my identity—that of a "good" girl. In that moment, "Hey girl," I internalized the brand "bad" girl, "slut," "whore." My mind told me that I somehow had not observed the cultural rules of femininity which require that "good" girls remain outwardly asexual, this means among other things, that they do not attempt to draw attention to themselves and their bodies (Lees, 1993).

I tell you this story because it reminded me that as long as the interwoven construction of gender and sexuality are not interrogated in schools, as well as in larger society, there will continue to be repercussions for women as victims of harassment and violence both in and outside the schools. When discussing violence prevention, gender inequality and sexuality must be part of the conversation. Women are at risk for violence at the hands of both men and women because of the ways that femininity and masculinity are constructed in American culture. My experience is not unusual. Yet how is it that women generally at a young age learn to negotiate their behavior, anticipating surveillance of their enactment of dominant gendered ideologies? For example, how do they choose what to wear on a daily basis, knowing that they are subject to disrespectful treatment if their selection is deemed too risqué by people with more social power? Further, how does conforming to ideologies of appropriate femininity—specifically by upholding the imaginary boundary between "good" and "bad" girls—place women at a disadvantage to men in our daily lives and hence open us up to violence in a variety of ways?

The remainder of this chapter emerges from my work with youth, sexuality and schooling practices over the last four years. The story I have just told illustrates how gender, sexuality, and harassment intersect in "the real world." My harassment was by no account a serious or long-term, personally damaging experience. However, gender harassment, defined as "everyday verbal harassment along with touching, patting, pinching, leaning over, and cornering, provides persistent support for related acts of physical sexual terrorism." (Kramarae, 1992; p. 101). In other words, the harassment that I experienced lays the groundwork for an environment in which related, and more serious, acts of sexual violence are deemed possible, if not acceptable. This chapter explores how my experience, and others much worse than mine, are made possible and normalized, both by the ways that young people envision gendered sexual relationships and the ways that schools help them to make sense of these relationships.

My analysis emerged from a year of observations in a working-class, urban high school health course, informal discussions with twenty students in the class, and in-depth interviews with nine of those students. This chapter will examine the ways that young people think about adolescent female sexuality. How do young people define and enact "appropriate" female sexuality, given the boundaries of "good"-/"nasty"-girlness?[1] The chapter will also explore how school practices are involved in maintaining and challenging the oppositional dualism of "good"-/"nasty"-girlness. Finally, I will discuss the importance of young people's knowledge and education about adolescent female sexuality for young women's health and safety.

THE OMNIPRESENCE OF "NASTINESS"

Girls' sexual reputations are important to society. For example, they matter to parents, who do not want their daughters to wear too much makeup for fear that they will look "too old" (read; too sexual). They matter to

---

[1] Much of the theoretical literature I have read discusses a "good"/"bad" girl construction. Other literature, primarily emerging from ethnographic work, uses the language of the culture in which the study was conducted. The students with whom I worked talked about "bad" girls as "nasty" girls so I will use the term "nasty" throughout this chapter.

schools, which enforce dress codes that do not allow girls to wear current mainstream fashion, like form-fitting shirts and pants or miniskirts, because they distract fellow students, and such distractions supposedly are not "appropriate" in a school setting. Girls' sexual reputations matter to boys, as they are hesitant to date girls who are rumored to be "sluts." They matter to the ways that girls see each other. Girls taunt and fight other girls who supposedly are after their man or who do not maintain the code of controlled desire that is expected among girls (Artz, 1999; Lees, 1993). Most important, they matter to how girls see themselves. Leora Tannenbaum's book, *Slut! Growing Up Female with a Bad Reputation* (1999), demonstrates this as she highlights stories of pain and vulnerability that ensue when girls are branded "sluts."

"Good"-girlness is a central tenet of girls' identities. Yet, in my own observations, it was the deviance from this norm that young people talked about most easily. Often students talked about female sexuality that crossed the line to "nasty." However, I had to prod them to talk about what was appropriate behavior for girls. "Good"-girlness was the assumption, the unsaid center of female sexual identity. The norm of "good"-girlness, marked through the control of female desire in a heterosexual relationship, was preserved by young people through the identification of those young women who deviate from that norm; for example, girls who reject the attention of heterosexual male desire or those who treat it carelessly by becoming involved with more than one young man, lesbians who are "out," teen mothers, and girls with sexually transmissible infections.

How the terms "slut" or "nasty" girl are constructed in everyday practice is not as significant as the presence of the category itself (Lees, 1993). The organization of adolescent female sexuality around the silent norm of "good"-girlness and the marginalizing distinction of "nasty"-girlness thrives in the voices of young people. For instance, Tyson, a young Black male student, described how young men talk about some girls with whom they have had sex:

> *Tyson*: They know about it [sex]. They hear about it. They talk to their friends. That's like the main topic. Like people talk around when they in a group.

> *Kristen*: How do they talk about it? Like, what kinds of things do they talk about?

> *Tyson*: If there is a whole bunch of dudes, right? "Hey you know such and such, she nasty, she did this. I had sex with her." (Interview, 6/7/98)

Tyson, and the other young men with whom I spoke, discussed instances of male conversation structured around the identification and denigration of "nasty" girls. This type of talk situates male bonding as an exercise in sexism (see Lees, 1993, p. 31; Mac an Ghaill, 1994). Tyson's comment illustrates this well as he mentions that young men feel they gain status if they have "had her" (i.e., the "nasty" girl). The young woman's desire and behavior in a sexual relationship serve as the crux of why the relationship is "nasty." In the conversations Tyson spoke about, the "nasty" girl is constructed as an object to be "had" rather than an agent whose involvement with young men emerges from her own desires. Furthermore, whereas the young man's participation in the relationship is naturalized and status inducing, the young woman is failing to fulfill her gendered responsibility of controlling male desire. Hence, she is "nasty."

"Good"-girlness also is organized around young men's sexual attention to young women. In other words, one way in which young women become marked as "nasty" is by breaking the code of femininity that prescribes that each young woman needs to be associated with only one young man. For instance, the young people whom I studied argued that if a young woman is manipulating a young man into a relationship, she subsequently no longer is considered desirable for a committed relationship. Hence, she is at risk for being labeled "nasty."

Gender ideologies have material, everyday consequences in young people's lives, as they do for us all. Ideology helps us to make sense of our actions as "normal." It does this by naturalizing behavior and making invisible the power from which it emerged. Therefore, the concepts "nasty" and "slut" not only are ideologically powerful in shaping gender relations, they also structure girls' (and boys') understanding of how to act in everyday life.

Language is one venue that is shaped by gender ideology. Differences in how a young woman speaks to students versus parents or at home versus in class all enter into how she is perceived sexually. In an interview, Serena stressed that it was important to know "proper terminology" to use in sex education class. I asked why it was important to know the more "medicalized" vocabulary:

Serena: In situations it can be important because when you're talking to your friends, you're not going to say intercourse. You will say sex. But when you're talking with an adult, it's proper to say intercourse.

Kristen: Now why is that?

Serena: If you come out and say sex, they're going to look at you like, what you doing? But if you say intercourse, I think it's just . . . it's more respectful (Interview, 6/5/98).

The danger Serena wishes to avoid is the potential for her being identified as "nasty." Using "proper terminology" is a self-protecting linguistic strategy. Talking in less personal, less familiar, less embodied ways about sex and sexuality allows young women to speak of sex without being labeled "nasty." Using medical or "proper" terms like *penis, vagina,* and *sexual intercourse* permits young women to show their academic familiarity with the subject without attesting to any personal experience or embodied knowledge. Young women who incorporate sexual slang into their daily language broach the risk of being thought too comfortable and too familiar with sex and intimacy. This comfort may suggest to others that they are sexually active, unable adequately to hide their activity, and hence, "nasty."

Similar to how the "nasty"/"good" girl ideology helps young women make sense of how to speak in acceptable ways with the proper lack of sexual desire, the ideology also enters into how young women understand what is the appropriate way to act in class to avoid the "nasty" label. During a class on contraception, I watched as many young women of color refused to inspect the forms of birth control that were passed around the class:

Donovan passed the foam and applicator around to students. As it got to Carmen and Kezia they said, "I don't want it, I don't want it."

The foam and applicator [were] passed to where Tyson was sitting. Initially he jokingly said, "I don't want to see that till I get married," but then he inspected it for a minute.

Tyson then passed the materials to Serena's desk and she wouldn't touch them. She looked at them with her nose crunched up and with a skeptical look on her face. She yelled to the guest speaker, "Miss, come get this. Miss, come here!" The guest educator went to Serena's desk, picked up the contraceptive and continued passing it to the next desk. (Field notes, 2/26/98)

As illustrated here, young men and women tend to have different access to knowledge about sex, sexuality, and the prevention of pregnancy and diseases. Whereas young women must constantly be vigilant about the cues they offer regarding their sexual activity, young men have greater freedom to experiment with, and learn about, contraception. This is because it is expected in American culture that young men are sexually active and, therefore, gaining familiarity with contraception has little, if any, negative implication for their sexual reputations.

Chicana adolescents in Dietrich's (1998) observations of sex education displayed contraceptive avoidance strategies in the classroom similar to those of the young women of color in my study. The young women in Dietrich's study explained that they were protecting themselves from rumors. Girls avoided asking about birth control because they felt that other students would assume they were having sex. Yet, as in Dietrich's findings, during my observation in the class, the young men confidently made jokes, asked thoughtful questions, and touched and played with various forms of contraception, particularly contraception that is intended for use by young women. However, because of the ways in which young women must constantly monitor their sexual reputation, they do not have a place to enter into the conversation about sex, the prevention of unintended pregnancy, and their own bodies.

For young women, discussions of sexuality and sexual desire are not "safe" because they must monitor their actions and language so as not to be thought of as "nasty." The young women who participated in my research learned that they could not share many of their thoughts and experiences, particularly those having to do with sexuality, with other people because those experiences might position them to be labeled as "nasty" or "sluts." This identification gives the green light to young people of both genders to do violence to young women (Artz, 1999; Lees, 1993; Tannenbaum, 1999). Young women justify their verbal and physical assaults on "sluts" by suggesting that girls identified as such have transgressed the codes of femininity (Lees, 1993). Among other things, young women labeled as "sluts" supposedly have sex with men outside of caring, committed relationships. Hence, female to female violence is a way of exacting retribution for the "sluts'" presumed failure to adhere to appropriate codes of femininity (i.e., controlled desire), but also a way to neutralize any potential threat to a female victimizer's own relationship (Artz, 1999; Lees, 1993). This dynamic was demonstrated to me in another research setting. In late fall 1998, a young woman who was seven months pregnant discovered that her boyfriend, who was also the father of her baby, had been seeing another girl. In our group discussions, she talked openly about this "slut." On one occasion she announced that she was going over to the "slut's" house that night "to have a talk with her." On my next visit, following the "talk," I asked what had transpired. The young woman described how she had yelled, chased after, and spat on the "slut." She laughed confidently as she related this story to me and another pregnant young woman. She appeared satisfied that she had exacted retribution on the "slut," who had dared to interrupt and devastate her committed relationship. The young man in the situation did receive multiple tongue-lashings from the pregnant young woman, but he was not the victim of violence in the same way or faulted for the same reasons as the young woman.

In the next comment, Beckie illustrates the lack of security felt by young women in regard to their sexual reputation. Beckie is a White female who, in her own words, acted as a mother to the baby daughter of a friend who did not attend school. When the baby was eighteen months old, she became ill and died, causing Beckie a great deal of pain. I asked her if she was able to share her pain with anyone during the time of the infant's illness and subsequent death. She replied that she could not speak to people at school about it:

Kristen: At school, you didn't tell that many people?

Beckie: Yeah at school.

Kristen: What were you worried about?

Beckie: Being judged.

Kristen: Really? That surprises me, why?

Beckie: Because, a lot of people are judged for what they do in school. You're judged on the way you dress, the way you act, you know. And girls who do have kids are judged because of that. They'll be called sluts or you know. So I didn't feel like being judged.

Kristen: Even though it wasn't your child?

Beckie: Even though it wasn't mine.

Kristen: You didn't feel comfortable telling people about losing this child who was close to you because you thought that people would automatically run around—

Beckie: And automatically think it was mine. (Interview, 6/24/99)

In interviews, young men and women often alluded to the fact that a protruding abdomen codes a young woman as a "slut." As Beckie's words indicate, a baby (and in this case, the mere discussion of one) visibly identifies a girl as a teen mother and marks her as "nasty." Student narratives are embedded strongly in dominant cultural assumptions about pregnant teen girls such as: pregnant teen girls are ignorant because they did not use birth control, they are not in committed relationships, they sleep with multiple partners, they are manipulative and alone, they have been sexually abused, and they have low self-esteem. In all cases, teen pregnancy becomes pathologized or is seen as a character flaw.

Nathanson argued that the transgression of unmarried teen pregnancy is not reproductive, but sexual. "Pregnancy makes sex visible" (1991, p. 4) at a time when young women culturally are expected to be asexual and "in control" of the desire of their male partners and themselves. Therefore, nonmarital teen pregnancy signifies

> ultimate loss of control: by a man driven by his lust, by the girl's mother who failed in her job of supervision, by the young woman who was overcome by passion (or drugs or alcohol or ambition), or by the community in which early sex and childbearing were insufficiently stigmatized." (1991, p. 7)

The unmarried pregnant teenager is the ultimate "nasty" girl. In Beckie's situation, she technically was not a teen mother, but her connection to a young child placed her at risk for the judgment and condemnation that accompanies teen pregnancy. Again, the label of "nasty" did not need to be applied to Beckie, the presence of the category alone publicly silenced her.

Many of the teen mothers I interviewed were frustrated because they felt that they were involved in loving relationships or had used birth control to prevent pregnancy.[2] Regardless of what they felt, once they became pregnant, the teens were coded as sluts by family, friends, and classmates. Many young women explain that sex is acceptable (meaning they do not need to fear the "nasty" identification) if they are involved in a mature, loving relationship. However, as the next comment shows, mature love is a contested concept for youth:

> *Serena*: It's okay to have sex but when you're mature and you're mentally and physically ready for it. Now is not the time. Some people maybe, but you

---

[2]Here I refer to the interviews I conducted as part of my larger study. I made observations in two classrooms solely for pregnant and parenting teens. I held focus groups with the young women in one class and interviewed all the five girls who consistently attended the second class.

should go to school and worry about school instead of worrying about having sex, who you are going to have it with, then what happens afterwards, what happens before, in between, all that stuff.

Kristen: Now what does that mean, a mature person?

Serena: Mature, well, well mature enough to when . . . if say you're a teenager my age and I was having sex, to me, mature would be where it be kept between the two of you, something the two of you will share, so, you know what I'm saying, if you all really, really, got feelings for each other, for love, something like that. . . . You're going to be woman enough to ask a man: "Do you have a condom? Put it on." You going to be woman enough also to take yourself to a clinic to get some pills so you can protect yourself from getting pregnant. I say that's mature of you. (Interview, 6/5/98)

The discourse of mature love was recounted by all the young women with whom I spoke, although each spoke of it in a different manner. As I mentioned, the teen mothers I interviewed felt betrayed by friends, family, and classmates because, even though they had been engaged in committed relationships when they became pregnant, they were still ostracized. They were coded as "sluts," and yet nothing happened to their boyfriends' reputations. However, as Serena explained, there are many components to the discourse of mature love. First, the young woman must be engaged in a committed, loving relationship versus an infatuation. This presents an interesting paradox. People who are in love see themselves as being "in love" (considered mature love) and not "in infatuation" (considered immature love). It is only after the relationship ends that they rewrite their feelings and label them as "infatuation." Hence, the distinction between mature and nonmature love is not useful given that, while involved in the relationship, most strong emotions are read as mature love. Second, a committed, loving relationship is, by Serena's definition, private. Last, women protect themselves against unintended pregnancy in a mature relationship.[3]

Pregnant teenagers, regardless of their involvement in committed relationships, break two rules of mature love, and thus are marked by others as

---

[3]I am conscious that a discussion of prevention for sexually transmitted diseases should be included in a discussion of "mature love." However, the women in this study did not mention protection against diseases; they only mentioned unintended pregnancy. This is likely because people with sexually transmitted diseases often are coded as "nasty," and students would not want to see themselves in a committed relationship with a nasty person. Therefore, the prevention of sexually transmitted infections was not mentioned in the context of their own committed relationships.

"nasty." First, people assume they did not seek out and use a form of birth control to prevent pregnancy. Second, mature love is premised on public silence. Girls explain that when one is in a mature relationship, sex is private and not discussed outside the relationship. A pregnant girl's protruding abdomen signals to the world that she has had sex. A pregnant body betrays the gag rule implicit in teens relationships organized around a concept of mature love. In effect, by becoming pregnant, a young woman demonstrates that she is not in a mature relationship; she is then simply considered nasty. In contrast, a young woman who engages in sex in a committed relationship and does not become pregnant keeps her relationship private; thus, she may engage the discourse of mature love to make sense of her sexual actions.

However, buying into the discourse of mature love is complicated. As you see from Serena's comment, love is dependent on maturity, and maturity is a slippery construct in reference to adolescence. The concept of maturity is embedded in developmental theory, a discourse through which we have come to think about adolescence (Lesko, 1996). Adolescence is constructed as a contested period between the poles of childhood and adulthood. It is an "in-between" space wherein youth are not quite adults, and therefore not quite mature, but they also are no longer children, and therefore should not act immaturely. Further, adolescence, as embedded in a developmental discourse, is strongly associated with age (Lesko, 1996). For instance, when we say that Sarah is sixteen, we can envision many things about Sarah other than her age. However, we have come to know what it means to be an adolescent through the signifier of age. Serena's comment speaks to the ambivalent construct of adolescence. Young women narrate that it is okay to be sexually intimate when they are in love. Yet, specifically in their sex education class and more generally in culture, they are told that mature love (versus infatuation) is something that adolescents do not experience. While "good"-girlness, on the surface, can exist alongside sexual activity—as long as one is involved in a mature, loving relationship—young women are also told that this type of relationship is never, or rarely, a possibility for them. The implication is that sexual activity, also, is not an option; unless, of course, they want to risk the label of "nasty."

Many young women understand the discourse of mature love to be combative of the "nasty" identity (Lees, 1993). Yet this understanding is problematic, given that the discourse of mature love permits a young woman to engage in sexual activity without a "nasty" reputation only if her desire remains controlled and connected to one young man and her sexual activity does not become visible through pregnancy. If she does become pregnant and her sexual activity is publicly advertised, then, immediately, she is nasty. In effect, the discourse of mature love works to hide sexual activity by keeping it unseen, unacknowledged, and private. Hence, it bolsters the dichotomy between who is good and who is nasty, maintaining the representation that "good" girls are those who effectively conceal their sexual activity, as well as any sexual desire.

Representations of sexual relationships, as predicated solely on love rather than on desire, continue to lead girls to covertly negotiate a culture of mixed messages about sexuality while finding few meaningful options through which to act as sexual agents. Furthermore, Thompson's research (1995; see especially the chapter, "Victims of Love") describes girls who entered into sexual relationships based on love (as opposed to sexual desire) as being devastated when the relationships ended. Once love dissolves, girls often are left feeling used, depressed, and questioning their own judgment rather than feeling that they had some power and agency in making decisions about the relationship. Hence, the standard of mature love, by which many girls choose to enter into sexual relationships, very often leaves them emotionally battered and distrustful of men.

A final problematic with the discourse of mature love involves its significance in school-based sex education. Engaging the discourse of mature love in sex education is problematic in that it clashes with the dominant representation of romantic love. Romance often is portrayed in popular culture as a phenomenon in which women (especially young women) are "swept up" in emotion, so much so that "their heart guides their head." This discourse, in which many young people are invested, becomes, as I will argue further, an issue in school-based sex education, particularly concerning contraception and the prevention of pregnancy and sexually transmissible infections.

American school-based sex education primarily is organized around a prevention model. It examines and tries to educate students to prevent unintended pregnancy, sexual assault, child abuse, sexually transmitted infections, birth defects, ineffective discipline of children, and harmful parenting. Particularly concerning sex, young women are the targets of prevention discourse, as the following quotations from interviews demonstrate:

> *Kristen*: Regarding the class itself or how the topics were addressed, do you think it spoke to women and men in different ways?

Scott: Yeah, when we were talking about birth control, like a lot of the kids that were there and a lot of the guys that were there, "Oh no, this doesn't involve me, I don't have to worry about it." And the girls are going, "Okay, this definitely involves me." (Interview, 6/9/98)

Just as young women are held accountable for stopping sexual assault by constraining male sexuality, they also are expected to plan for male desire when they enter into a consensual relationship:

Kristen: Do you think it [the parenting class] was talking mainly to girls?

Tyson: Yeah. 'Cause there ain't no dudes out there having a kid. There ain't no dude out there that wanna have a kid now. She just talking basically to girls.

Kristen: Okay, talk to me more about that. What do you mean?

Tyson: Girls they know what they have to do. They know if they do have sex they have to wear a condom. They know that. If they don't, something wrong with them. [He smiles.] I don't know. (Interview, 6/7/98)

Birth control increasingly is becoming feminized (Luker, 1996). This is particularly poignant given Tyson's slip, in which he assigns the wearing of condoms to young women. I am confident that he was not referring to the minimally utilized, female condom. Rather, young women and young men learn that it is the responsibility of the female to become familiar with and have access to birth control. However, the discourse of romantic love, as opposed to mature love does not allow for planning or prevention (Thompson, 1995). Young women often do not plan for first heterosexual intercourse because to do so would mean that they wanted to do it. Desiring to have sex is an admission of sexual desire and hence, a clear indication of "nastiness." Planning for pregnancy and the prevention of sexually transmissible infections would mean that a girl was not simply swept away by romance, the only condition under which she can become sexual without reputational repercussions.

Therefore, the competing discourses of romantic love and mature love, in an environment organized solely around prevention, place girls in a catch-22. To plan for sex by obtaining contraception means that young women are not checking their desire and rather are intentionally engaging in sex, the very thing they are held responsible for stopping. To plan is to give oneself over to being a "nasty" girl. Evidence of this is illustrated by girls' hesitancy or refusal to become familiar with contraception in class. Yet, if they do not obtain contraception and instead become pregnant or contract a sexually transmissible infection, as Tyson states, the young women will be held responsible for the "mistake" and condemned as "nasty" anyway. Hence, it is important that sex education be organized around the interplay of desire and danger (Fine, 1988) and that it suggest multiple ways of being sexual, including, but not limited to, sexual intercourse. A predominantly prevention-oriented model that only discusses the dangers of sex does not provide space for young women and men to broach the idea of young women's sexual desire. Instead, it classifies female sexual identity as either good or nasty, when, in practice, most young women occupy the tenuous space in between.

EVERYDAY VIOLENCE
AND THE CURRICULUM
OF INDIVIDUAL RESPONSIBILITY

In the previous section, I discussed the power of the "nasty"/"good" girl construct in organizing young people's understanding of adolescent female sexuality. I argued that a prevention-oriented curriculum targets young women to act as the responsible, constraining subjects in heterosexual relationships. In this section, I argue that a sexuality curriculum ideally should construct an interplay between the framework of individual empowerment and broader power dynamics, particularly in regard to sexual violence. For instance, sexuality education *solely* emerging out of a framework of individual empowerment naturalizes violence endured by women by portraying it as resulting from their lack of character or aptitude. In contrast, sexuality education organized *solely* around broader power dynamics (or social forces) removes all agency from the victims and constructs them as passive objects who are entirely acted upon. Since women are neither at fault for their own victimization nor merely passive objects of sexuality, sexuality education must recognize the interplay between social forces and individual agency.

To examine this dynamic more closely and explore what it means for violence prevention and sexuality education, I will look at two instances concerning sexuality and gendered violence that were discussed within a high school health education classroom in an urban school district. The class generally consisted of sixteen students (six Black, eight White, and two Vietnamese) and an experienced, White, middle-class teacher in her early forties. The first example takes up a teacher-generated discussion about sexual limit setting. The second, and lengthier, example explores how female sexuality was constructed within a class on sexual assault.

While the students, the teacher (Ms. Wheaton), and I all acknowledged the existence of a prevention structure to the sex education course, Ms. Wheaton also strongly understood it as being concerned with empowerment. In her view, her course was about giving "tools" to students who might not feel they had many choices in their life. Her hope was that the "tool kit" would help them to make healthy choices and open up opportunities for them. This curriculum of empowerment especially extended to the young women in the class. Ms. Wheaton engaged issues defined by students as female oriented, like birth control, pregnancy, and sexual assault. She frequently informed students in her class that they had the choice to say no to sex. However, she did not often acknowledge the choice to say yes. Rather, she sought to give students the support that would allow them to resist peer pressure to become sexually involved or, if they did have sex, to be "safely" active (a term that was defined by the school, teacher, and students as having no pregnancies, sexually transmitted infections, and sexual assaults). Her curriculum of empowerment organized the class to focus on the discourses of choice and responsibility. For instance:

Ms. Wheaton said, "I want to talk to you about setting limits. What's that about?"

A few students said, "having sex" and "being pressured."

Ms. Wheaton responded, "Yeah right. You need to make your limits clear, so when you get into a relationship you know what your limits are. It's really important to know what your limits are so when you get into a relationship and someone's pressuring you to have sex, you can comfortably tell the person no. So you need to get in your mind what your limits are now, so we need to think about that."

Ms. Wheaton talked a little bit more about the importance of setting limits and "if you're not comfortable with somebody going beyond your limits" then "you have the right to say no." She commented, "You should be okay with saying no and not worrying that you're going to disappoint them. If you're not able to tell the person your limitations, you may not be ready for a relationship. Do you agree with that?"

Carmen, like most people, had not been paying attention to Ms. Wheaton. . . .
She perked up at the end of Ms. Wheaton's comments and said, "If what?"

Ms. Wheaton repeated, "If you're not able to tell a person what your limitations
are, then you might not be ready for a relationship."

Carmen said, "Yep, yep."

Ms. Wheaton again emphasized, "Don't be uncomfortable telling people in any
relationship. If you're not able to verbalize your limits, then you may not be
ready to date." (Field notes, 2/13/98)

At the beginning of this lesson, Ms. Wheaton reminded students of
their right to make decisions about their own bodies. Yet the students'
sense of empowerment seemingly emerged from decisions about what
they did *not* want to do with their bodies rather than what they *did* want to
do. Ms. Wheaton prodded them to consider the limits they might choose
to set for themselves. However, the conversation did not enter into the
complexities that often prevent youth from making "healthy choices";
namely, how culture, class, gender, and race shape sexual limit setting. In
the absence of this discussion, her last comments instructing students that
they might not be prepared to date if they could not set verbal limits
removed the discussion of empowerment from its cultural, political, economic, and gendered nexus and laid the responsibility squarely on the
shoulders of each individual.

As I already discussed, because, in our culture, the individual who is
accountable for setting limits is the young woman, the responsibility for
transgressing limits lies with her. What begins as an empowering discourse doubles back on young women. Young men and young women
both are led by the class discourse to understand that if something dangerous happens in a heterosexual relationship, the young man is not accountable for his behaviors because the female partner should have prevented
it, preferably by not entering into the relationship in the first place. Young
women who were not fully comfortable would verbalize their "no's," and
"shout their resistance." Yet I remember my own harassment at the cross-
walk when I could not construct a strong retort to a troublesome comment
in a moment of vulnerability. Limit setting is not easy when you feel you
are in a disempowered position.

Although students describe sexual limit setting as a female responsibility, in this class Ms. Wheaton spoke to all students as if they had the

same power when it came to sexual advances and limit setting was an equal responsibility shared by both men and women. However, students' comments, as well as cultural and legal precedents, tell us otherwise. They teach us that it is the "nasty" girl who fails to set strong enough limits and "gets what she deserves" (Tolman & Higgins, 1996). Ms. Wheaton spoke to her students in an inclusive manner, teaching them that everyone ("you") should share responsibility with their partners in sexual limit setting. However, by not addressing the environment of inequality in which young women and men negotiate their sexual relationships, she allowed the facade of equal power in sexual limit setting to be maintained. Hence, when an assault occurs, students may presume it is the fault of the "nasty" girl for not saying no, since, as they have been taught, any woman can say no if that is her desire.

The pockets of empowering discourse, where young women hear strong messages about their rights and the kind of respectful treatment they are entitled to, are often overshadowed by the "patriarchal voice" in the classroom. The patriarchal voice to which I refer comes from both female and male students and, at times, as in the previous instance, from the teacher. Therefore the patriarchal voice is not a "male" voice, but one that speaks in order to maintain women's oppression and uphold a patriarchal structure in society. With a few exceptions, this voice is a constant companion in the lives of young men and women. It accompanies them into the sex education class.

On the day the class talked about sexual assault, the patriarchal voice emerged loudly. Reflecting on the way gender operates in this context provides a window to see how power works to position young women in a situation where they have little agency. Young women, for whom it is second nature to attempt to avert the identification of nasty, have little agency to interrupt the patriarchal discourse that locates them at fault for their own victimization. The following data excerpts create a landscape of what learning about sexual assault is like in a diverse environment that leaves male privilege intact. The class began with Ms. Wheaton explaining that there would be a speaker from Rape Crisis Services:

Ms. Wheaten told the students to, "act maturely" as rape was a sensitive issue and that some people in the class might have experienced it.

Serena, a Black, female freshman, shouted jokingly, "I did."

Tyson, a Black, male junior followed immediately with, "I have."

Students laughed when Serena made the remark. When Tyson said it, nobody said anything. Ms. Wheaton got up and introduced Adrienne, the speaker from Rape Crisis Services. Adrienne is White and in her mid to late 20's. She began walking around the room and said, "I'm going to start out by passing out this pamphlet which is some information on sexual abuse."

As she was handing out the pamphlet, Tyson said, "I don't need one because I ain't going to get raped."

Kiana, a non-traditional (older), Black student who is pregnant, challenged him. "Why because you're going to want it?"

Serena, sitting a seat away from Kiana starting laughing and quietly said, "you know guys." (Field notes, 5/21/98)

As with many sensitive issues, the class opened with Tyson and Serena trying to add humor to lighten the mood set by Ms. Wheaton. Humor is a common way to negotiate tension and, as odd as it may sound, it did ease the mood when Serena made light of being the survivor of rape. However, the joke did not work in the same way for Tyson. Whereas Serena, a young woman, could poke fun at a situation in which women are identified as being particularly vulnerable, Tyson did not have the same access to such humor. His second attempt was met with increasing hostility by one of the few women in the room who could challenge him relatively safely. Kiana, a nontraditional (older), Black student who had returned to high school, was one of two visibly pregnant young women in the class and the only one in attendance on that day. By virtue of her pregnancy, Kiana was identified as marginal at best and, more likely, as a "nasty" girl. The challenge to Tyson was uncharacteristic of Kiana, and subsequently it was neutralized by Serena's enactment of "good"-girlness, as she again negotiated the tension in the class.

Later in the class, a film was shown that highlighted the stories of three women who were raped. They told their stories with emotion and detail. As a backdrop to the stories, the film showcased separate groups of men and women discussing communication and gender issues surrounding sexual assault:

At one point in the film a Jamaican woman in her late 30's told her story of rape. . . . While the film continued playing, Tyson spoke over the woman's story and commented loudly to the class, "Look how big she is."

Ms. Wheaton commented, "Tyson, we'll talk about it later." . . . The issue was not raised again.

[Later in the film] The same woman was talking about the difficulty she had proving her case. Tyson again spoke over the film and said something about, "but she should have fought."

Ms. Wheaton said: "Yeah, she did. She was kicking and screaming and everything."

Tyson responded, "Oh, she did?"

Ms. Wheaton confirmed, "Yeah." (Field notes, 5/21/98).

On this day, the patriarchal voice often was embodied by Tyson. Initially he spoke over the movie to comment on the weight of the survivor. He implied that the woman could not have been raped because no one would desire her because of her weight. In effect, he argued that rape is about sex, not power, and that only people who culturally are defined as "beautiful" can be raped. Also, if this woman were given sexual attention from a man, he presumed that she would welcome it. Hence, the claim of rape must be a lie.

Tyson commonly made oppositional comments in class, which often disparaged women. In an interview I had with him later, he claimed he did this because he "just be playing around." In fact, he believed that he and Ryan, a White male student in the class, often tried to tell Ms. Wheaton "what they heard out on the street" but that "most of the time she don't want to hear it."

Tyson: It's like me and Ryan basically always have something to say, but she like "I don't want to hear it." She like, "Ryan be quiet." So we just forget it and stop talking about it and just listen to what she has to say. (Interview, 6/7/98)

As when Tyson challenged the film, Ms. Wheaton chose to silence Tyson's interruption rather than use his comments as a way for students to think through who they imagine can be victims of rape. Certainly Ms. Wheaton made a strong statement when she implied that Tyson's comments were not valuable to the class's education about sexual assault. Yet Tyson's comments, if taken up by either the teacher or other students, could have been a significant avenue for exploring students' understanding of sexual assault, perhaps more so than the substance of the film. Tyson's unsolicited comments could have been thought of as a "teachable moment." The benefits for examining, rather than silencing, Tyson's interruptions would have been twofold. First, he would have felt validated as having had something valuable to say. Second, he and other students would have had the opportunity to reflect on how attitudes like his are constructed and what they mean, both culturally, for the definition and prosecution of sexual assault, and interpersonally, for how young men and women negotiate sexual situations. What might have been an occasion for students to reflect on their ideas about sexual violence and how assault becomes defined through gender, race, class, and cultural considerations instead continued on as another lesson, via the film, about how difficult rape is to both prove and overcome.

In the second comment, we again can see the interplay between empowerment and personal responsibility. Although Ms. Wheaton took up Tyson's comments about what the survivor "should have done," she strengthened the notion that women have the option to escape when they are being raped. Both she and Tyson talked about sexual assault as something one should respond to with forceful resistance. Certainly this is one option that can be used by young women. However, a discussion about why a young woman might not be able to scream or fight and about how gender, race, or cultural dynamics might result in a silent response to sexual assault was not raised. The unspoken discourse, one that is supported strongly in American courts, remains: if a person who is sexually assaulted does not forcibly resist, she must have consented.

Women's culpability in their own victimization was emphasized further by the following two situations. The first was a conversation that occurred among the female discussion group in the film itself. The second example reflects a female student's response to a rape survivor whose story was depicted in the film.

> In the film, between slices of the survivors' stories, women in the focus group said, "You need to watch yourself." What they didn't accept was "Women who lost control and then are raped. Like when you go out and you get totally wasted and then the next day you call it rape. Yeah, that's your fault. It was your responsibility to not get like that, to not be totally out of control, and when you do and you get raped, that's your responsibility." (Field notes, 5/21/98)

Female culpability also resonated in the class when Serena responded to the story of rape told in the film. As I reported in my field notes:

The white woman in her early twenties talked about how she was invited to a pool party. A guy invited her over to a pool party and she thought, "Oh, cool, pool party." When she got there, there were only males and she nervously thought, "I was in the company of no females. There was only males around."

Serena said, "That was stupid."

Ryan, who was sitting over in the corner, commented in agreement. (Field notes, 5/21/98)

In both situations, women are blamed for their stupidity or carelessness. Because of their actions (or inaction), they are responsible for their injury. The sense students made of these situations emerged from an ideology of victim blaming that is naturalized in American culture. Sexual assault discourse constructs "true victims" as fully innocent and in no way involved in the violence enacted on them. Likewise, perpetrators are fully guilty and are "evil" human beings (Lamb, 1999). This is a particularly dangerous ideology in that the maintenance of the strong dichotomy between victim and perpetrator, and the purity of the victim category often results in the perception that women who are victims of sexual assault are responsible for their own victimization. This is evidenced by Serena's reaction to the woman who did not remove herself from what she suspected was a dangerous situation. According to Serena, the victim's poor judgment or lack of foresight made her culpable for her own assault. She was not fully innocent; therefore, she was not fully a victim.

The ideology that victims must be "purely" innocent and devoid of sexual desire also strengthens the "good"/"nasty" organization of girls' sexuality. For instance, if a young woman shows any desire for a young man prior to her assault, then the nonconsensual sexual encounter may well be understood in American culture, particularly in the legal courts, not as an assault, but as mere miscommunication between two people (Tolman & Higgins, 1996).

In the case of sexual assault, victims typically blame themselves for the attack (Lamb, 1999). This is not a natural response to their victimization. Rather, it is a naturalized response. When women are enmeshed in an environment where the discourse of sexual assault identifies victims as "true victims" only if they in no way contributed to the circumstances surrounding their assault, very few women will view themselves as victims of sexual assault.

This problematic discourse of sexual assault and its implications is present in the schools. In a sex education course saturated with the discourse of individual responsibility, girls are hurt when patriarchal comments in the film and from students go unchallenged. These lessons shape students' understanding of adolescent female sexuality. The structure in which "good" girls successfully stop sexual desire and "nasty" girls do not, remains intact. The women in the film initially were not devoid of sexual desire, and that component contributed to students' doubt of their injury. The classroom environment allowed and validated the idea that females are in control of sexual desire, resistance should be verbal and aggressive, and, ultimately, young women are responsible for their own victimization.

I want to emphasize that my goal here is not to blame the teacher for inappropriate remarks. On the contrary, Ms. Wheaton addressed each comment with various pedagogical techniques. Her responses reflected an attempt to speak in the interests of women that emerged out of an empowerment discourse, that foregrounded individual agency and potential. Rather, I am arguing that the responses of Ms. Wheaton and others in the room (the students' silence was also a response) to the patriarchal voice were incomplete. They lacked attention to the complex power issues that helped shape various attitudes and behaviors that the voice embraced.

Ms. Wheaton attempted to empower her students by telling them they could feel confident enough to make decisions about their own sexual limits and relationships. Yet, ironically, the class, consisting of the students, guest speaker, teacher, and myself, did not resist the harassment of the rape survivors. Instead, we all allowed the patriarchal privileged voice to emerge and strengthen in the classroom the class's analysis of the film developed as follows:

> In the end of the film, the Jamaican female who is a rape survivor discusses how since she's been raped, it has really affected her sex life. She "just doesn't want to do it anymore." She "can't do it."

> When she got to the part explaining how she feels when she does have sex, Tyson yelled incredulously, "She's lying!"

> Adrienne, the guest speaker, said," What do you mean?"

> Tyson said "That lady, she says she can't have sex no more but then she said, when she does have sex, it don't feel good anymore. So she's lying because she is having sex."

> Ryan said, "Yeah, that's a lie."

Adrienne said, "Well, no, it's not. It's just that maybe it's not good for her since she was raped."

When the video ended Adrienne said, "So what did you think about it?" A conversation started about rape being about power not sex.

Serena said, "It's about respect."

Adrienne said, "Yeah, right."

Carmen, with an uncertain smile on her face, looked over at Tyson who was sitting in a seat across the room. He was smiling and laughing. Carmen said, "He's sick. He's over there laughing."

Adrienne looked over at him and continued talking. (Field notes, 5/21/98)

It has been more than a decade since Michelle Fine's (1988) prominent research established that critical efforts in the prevention of sexual victimization were not being made in public schools. Schools evidenced their lack of seriousness about preventing victimization as they avoided or silenced discussions that explored the relatively few risks for unintended pregnancy and sexually transmitted infections associated with lesbian relationships, masturbation, or protected sexual intercourse (Fine, 1988). My research supports that even though they are embedded in an empowerment discourse, schools' current efforts at preventing sexual victimization have not progressed much. Although the urban district where I conducted research did permit discussions about contraception and using latex barriers to prevent infections as well as unintended pregnancy, it failed to address safer-sex practices outside a heterosexual framework or questions of sexual pleasure.

The example just presented further supports my claim that schools continue to avoid critical efforts at preventing victimization. The patriarchal voice, represented by Tyson and Ryan in the example given here, attempted to position the rape survivor as a manipulative, lying woman. Earlier, the voice was represented by Serena when she identified another rape survivor as "stupid." In effect, the students made sense of the women in the film as "nasty" girls who either were desirous and then lied about their victimization, or who, stupidly, were not able adequately to control male desire. In both cases, young people came to learn that women involved in sexual relationships are physically and emotionally at risk and, if harmed, have no one to blame but themselves.

Sex education that does not explicitly take up issues of power and gender is likely to reinforce male privilege and the absence of female desire. For instance, Brian, a White male who was a senior, told me in an interview that sex education erroneously is organized around the concept of peer pressure. He claimed that "if you have any self-esteem, no one can push you into anything." His lens of male privilege allowed the view that if young women enter into a dangerous situation, it is their lack of confidence that is the culprit. He argued that issues like date rape are "common sense . . . don't go somewhere unsafe. . . . Go out with people you trust." The sex education environment currently fails to facilitate discussions that challenge this form of local analysis of violence issues. Sexual violence prevention is not fully about common sense. Yet in the absence of talk about the power dynamics that structure the organization of male and female sexuality, particularly sexual desire, blame for sexual violence will continue to be attributed to those least able to prevent it.

TAKING THE ROAD LESS TRAVELED

Adolescent female sexuality is a contested site. Although girls physically experience sexual desire, young people learn that girls should not feel or demonstrate sexual desire, at least not to the same extent as boys. The messages they hear are multiple and conflicting. First, because girls presumably are less invested in sex, unlike their male counterparts, they are responsible for stopping it. Second, they also should plan to prevent pregnancy if they do have sex, but they should only have sex if they are in love. Third, because they are young, they do not really know what love is, so they should not be sexually active. Fourth, if they do show any sign of desire, either in action or appearance, and it is misconstrued as sexual consent, they should have known better and acted differently. Fifth, and finally, they need to protect the "goodness" around which their identity is organized. Therefore, they should ostracize or physically or verbally punish any young woman who threatens the "goodness" of their identity, otherwise they might be suspect and punished for colluding in being "nasty."

Young women live in the center of these mixed messages. They constantly negotiate, enforce, and resist the dualistic oppositions around which their sexuality is organized, namely as "good" or "nasty." Yet society does not support interrogating the tense spaces between the poles. Rather, educational practice, social policy, and students' own narratives position girls into either one category or the other. I, and others before me (Artz, 1999; Tannenbaum, 1999; Tolman & Higgins, 1996), have argued that girls are punished physically, verbally, and emotionally when they resist "good"-girlness. Hence, for young women, enacting "good"-girlness is, in many ways, the safest path.

Paradoxically, being "good" generally is not good for girls because it maintains the false dichotomy of the "good"/"nasty" girl and denies women's feelings of desire (Tolman & Higgins, 1996). Therefore, young women need a public space in which to explore the tension between good and nasty. They need a place in which to talk about the interplay of sexual pleasure and danger (Fine, 1988), individual responsibility, and power structures. The best location for these conversations may not be in the schools, which attempt to stifle signs of sexuality at every turn and focus all discussion of sex and sexuality into one class, sex education. Given the context of school regulations, school-based sex education, as it is currently organized, likely is not the space most conducive for holding challenging and reflective conversations about sex and sexuality (Epstein & Johnson, 1998).

Students also learn a great deal about sexuality when they venture beyond the school walls. Indeed, sex education outside school shapes and informs how students make sense of sex education in school, and vice versa. The students with whom I spoke talked of parents, alternative education programs, and media that had engaged them in discussions of sexuality. Yet school still is a place where youth spend a great deal of their time. Hence, it is not enough that students challenge their thinking about the powerful good/nasty framework oppressing young women once they are outside school walls. Schools must address the tension existing between good and nasty that shapes girls' sexual identity. Schools have a responsibility to care for girls. Interrupting "good"-girlness, in the halls, in the curriculum, in policy and in everyday practice, is essential in caring for girls.

As it stands, sex education is valuable, but if it truly is going help girls it must expand beyond the discourses of prevention and individual responsibility to encompass gendered power relations. Teachers are integral to this practice. Weis (2000) highlighted a teacher who facilitates empowering discussions concerning female sexuality in an abstinence-based sex education program. In what one might assume would be a sexually conservative class, young women's understandings of good and nasty female sexuality often are challenged by the teacher. In contrast, Ms. Wheaton, a genuinely concerned teacher, attempted to empower young women by making girls' bodies and girls' potential victimization central to the class. However, because the patriarchal voice remained prominent, validated, and relatively unchallenged, conversations emerged in a way that erased the teacher's intentions to empower.

Sexuality education cannot be solely focused on prevention and victimization and still be useful to girls. Making space for women's right to admit their sexual needs and supporting young women who do so are also necessary. In order for young women to feel empowered to act on their own needs and desires and avoid the victimization that they encounter daily, both they and young men must push to interrogate how gendered power relations assist in organizing their lives.

Tearing down the confines of male and female versions of sexuality that are premised on male aggression and female compliance is not safe work. It also is work that does not belong, or occur, solely in schools. It can happen over dinner, in a church or synagogue, while watching television, while babysitting, or when someone tauntingly yells "Hey girl!" to you or to a woman standing near you. It is a task that is threatening, challenging, and painful, and it requires the strength and vulnerability of all involved players.

Violence prevention, particularly in regard to interrupting gender oppression, is not just about creating the right program or flagging the appropriate indicators of risk. Rather it involves encouraging a general shift in philosophy to one of tolerance, social justice, and the critical interruption of everyday oppressive practices. Educators, especially, need to be strong facilitators. They need to be invested in this project. Yet to do so, they need institutional support. This task certainly does not deviate from the mission of most educational institutions. After all, are educational spaces not sites where all of us should be challenged to learn about the way the world is organized, how we are implicated in it, and what we could do to make it more peaceful?

REFERENCES

Artz, S. (1999). *Sex, power and the violent school girl*. New York: Teachers College Press.

Dietrich, L. C. (1998). *Chicana adolescents: Bitches, 'ho's and schoolgirls*. Westport, CT: Praeger Publishers.

Epstein, D., & Johnson, R. (1998). *Schooling sexualities.* Philadelphia: Open University Press.

Fine, M. (1988). Sexuality, schooling and adolescent females: The missing discourse of desire." *Harvard Educational Review, 5*(1), 829–853.

Fox, G. L. (1977). Nice girl: Social control of women through a value construct. *Signs: Journal of Women in Culture and Society, 2*(4), 805–817.

Kramarae, C. (1992). Harassment and Everyday Life. *Women making meaning: New feminist directions in communication.* L.F. Rakow. New York: Routledge.

Lamb, S. (1999). *The trouble with blame: Victims, perpetrators and responsibility.* Cambridge, MA: Harvard University Press.

Lees, S. (1993). *Sugar and spice: Sexuality and adolescent girls.* New York: Penguin Books.

Lesko, N. (1996). Past, present and future conceptions of adolescence." *Educational Theory, 46*(4), 453–472.

Luker, K. (1996). *Dubious conceptions: The politics of teenage pregnancy.* Cambridge, MA: Harvard University Press.

Mac an Ghaill, M. (1994). *The making of men.* Philadelphia: Open University Press.

Nathanson, C. A. (1991). *Dangerous passage: The social control of sexuality in women's adolescence.* Philadelphia: Temple University Press.

Tannenbaum, L. (1999). *Slut! Growing up female with a bad reputation.* New York: Seven Stories Press.

Thompson, S. (1995). *Going all the way: Teenage girls' tales of sex, romance and pregnancy.* New York: Hill & Wang.

Tolman, D. L., & Higgins, T. E. (1996). How being a good girl can be bad for girls. In N. B., Maglin, & D. Perry, (Eds.), *"Bad girls"/"good girls": Women, sex, and power in the nineties.* New Brunswick, NJ: Rutgers University Press.

Weis, L. (2000). Learning to speak out in an abstinence based sex education group: Gender and race work in an urban magnet school. *Teachers College Record, 102*(3), 620–50.

Part Two

Appraising Strategies to Counter School Violence

8

Involving the Whole School in Violence Prevention

Joan N. Burstyn

Syracuse University

Rebecca Stevens

University of South Carolina Spartanburg

WHY TAKE A WHOLE SCHOOL APPROACH TO VIOLENCE PREVENTION?

Televised pictures of students who have killed their school fellows with handguns; newspaper stories of a teacher disarming a student in the classroom; and telephoned bomb threats that close down schools for searching, while students shiver on sidewalks and in parking lots, watching; all these foster a belief that public schools are no longer safe. What has happened to cause these events? In 1993, John E. Richters of the National Institute of Mental Health wrote: "In a few short years the widespread availability and use of handguns has transformed childhood into something quite foreign to what most adults can recall of their own childhoods" (Richters, 1993, p. 3). By 1993, those who lived in the cities understood the effect of handguns on adolescents, especially those drawn into the traffic of illegal drugs. However, it was not until 1997–1998 that the nation at large became aware of just how far childhood, for all children, had been transformed by them.

An earlier version of the ideas developed in this chapter was published as Burstyn, J. N., & Stevens, R. (1999). Education in conflict resolution: Creating a whole school approach. *NeXus: Journal of Peace, Conflict and Social Change*, *1*(1), 56–70. Copyright © by *NeXus*.

During those years, headline news on television and in newspapers across the country announced that, in a series of incidents, boys had shot to death several people at schools in Pearl, Mississippi, West Paducha, Kentucky, Jonesboro, Arkansas, and Springfield, Oregon. The killing did not stop in 1998. Similar incidents, some perpetrated by even younger boys, have occurred since then each year.

Yet, even after these high-profile killings and even in neighborhoods known for their violence, schools remain relatively safe places for children. They are safer, that is, than their homes and the streets. There, children are in danger of violence, not only from their peers, but from adults as well. Nevertheless, it is school violence that has persuaded parents and educators to intensify their efforts to teach all children how to handle disputes nonviolently. This is a national issue because violence threatens the democratic principles of our multicultural society. If we, the citizens of our country, cannot handle disputes non-violently, we will soon destroy the fabric of democracy in the United States.

Often administrators and teachers need immediate help with crisis situations; and those of us who offer education in violence prevention and conflict resolution do provide information on crisis management (Raider, 1995). However, our main work has to be with administrators and teachers and must focus on ways to prevent crises from arising in the first place, through a curriculum that builds civility by teaching tolerance for others unlike ourselves and skills such as anger management, active listening, the sophisticated use of language, negotiation, and mediation. These are skills that individuals need in order to sustain a democratic community.

For more than a decade, many onetime or one-grade-level interventions have been offered in schools, as though by inoculating students we could provide them with protection against violence and teach them how to deal with conflict peacefully. Often these interventions have languished because they have been add-ons to the regular curriculum, given to no teacher's or administrator's protection and nurturance. This chapter develops a plan for integrating violence prevention and conflict resolution education into the fabric of a school.

To do this, we have not only to offer add-on education in the skills already referred to, we must, also help teachers draw inferences about ways to handle conflict from the material they teach every day, such as the stories they ask students to read and the history or the science they teach. We have to ask them to explain to their students how cooperative learning in the classroom is part of learning to work together in a community without resorting to violence, that conflict is a process that can be either creative or destructive, and that violence (either verbal, psychological, or physical) is the most destructive outcome of conflict. The classroom can become an important site where students can learn positive ways to handle conflict. Such education is needed now in all schools, whether or not they have experienced outbreaks of violence.

A whole school approach to violence prevention aims at changing people's beliefs, attitudes, and behaviors so that violence will be reduced. It calls for a commitment to change on the part of everyone associated with the school. In the city where our research was conducted, we worked, not only with the schools, but also with the students' parents and other members of the community. We did so because we perceive that school, family, and community all have roles that impact on one another in shaping children's behaviors and attitudes. We have found the contextual systems model, formulated by Pianta and Walsh (1996), to be a useful tool for understanding how the family-and-child, as one system, and the school, as another system, interact. We perceive, also, that within a school there are subsystems, each with its own set of rules and sphere of influence, that interact with each other.

Within the academic curriculum, a whole school approach to violence prevention commits teachers to teach, and students to learn, ways of handling conflict constructively at all grade levels. The whole school approach enables students to build their skills in this area from one grade to the next. It encourages teachers to incorporate knowledge about conflict resolution into all subjects and to establish democratic processes for resolving conflicts peaceably in their classrooms.

Beyond the classroom, a whole school approach to violence prevention involves all school personnel in developing new skills of communication. Ideally, people in all roles, such as schoolbus drivers, teachers, secretaries, and administrators, meet in heterogeneous groups to discuss ways to reduce conflicts and to refresh their communication skills through a greater understanding of cultural differences and knowledge of anger management, negotiation, and mediation. By doing so, they will be better equipped to reinforce positive behaviors among the students and, incidentally, also among themselves. Because it commits all those in a school to learning new ways to handle conflicts, a whole school approach to violence prevention has the potential to change the entire environment. All become involved with learning new forms of knowledge and new ways of behaving. Thus, a whole school approach, based on teaching civility through a democratic process, can transform the ecology of the school.

ANSWERING THOSE WHO MAY OPPOSE
A WHOLE SCHOOL APPROACH
TO VIOLENCE PREVENTION

Opponents of a whole school approach may argue that for too long in the past, schools were concerned with the socialization of students, to the detriment of their scholastic achievement. An increase in achievement was the goal of the reform agenda of the 1980s and 1990s, and rightly so, they feel, because the prime concern of education should be academic achievement. An emphasis on violence prevention and conflict resolution, they argue, may oust academic excellence from being the prime concern of education to the detriment of our nation's economy.

We agree with the argument that academic achievement should be a major concern of public education. We claim, however, that it is only one of several major concerns. Just how far some public schools have ventured away from teaching students how to create community is indicated by James Giarelli and Ellen Giarelli (1996):

> The public school system where we live in the suburban Northeast United States is . . . considered effective because it prepares children for successful individual competition in the private economy; in substance and aims, it is *private* schooling [emphasis in original].

> We wondered, then, where we might find what could be counted as public education? As we looked further, we identified a school, the Friends School, a private school. . . . This school's effectiveness is assessed against an ideal of full, free, communal sharing of knowledge, interests, and materials in service of associated development. In aims and substance, it is public education. (p. 11)

We believe violence prevention should become a focus in our public schools because academic excellence for the individual flourishes within a civil society where citizens demonstrate concern and compassion for one another, and not in an atmosphere of violence. Each child has to learn how to function as a member of a community, and those skills, as well as the skills involved in academic subjects, have to be taught and practiced in our public schools. Teaching and learning the skills of how to build and maintain a community have been downplayed over several decades, which is why schools must focus on them now.

A school can become free of conflict as the result of coercive management and coercive discipline. In such a school, there is zero tolerance for any form of misbehavior, inside or outside the classroom, with consequences ranging from suspension to expulsion. All students may have to show identification and walk through a metal detector to enter school (or guards may search each student with a handheld metal detector), lockers may be searched regularly, armed guards patrol the corridors, and lockdowns take place in the classroom each time a fight occurs. We know of schools that employ these methods. Though many conflicts are repressed or avoided in that type of environment, it represents a prison, not a school.

Coercive management and coercive discipline are incompatible with our goals. A whole school approach to violence prevention is a model of education where all students, as well as adults, learn to practice skills of non-violence and civility, where care, cooperation, and democratic human relations create an environment in which conflict is not repressed, but becomes constructive, and a site for individual and collective growth (Bodine, Crawford, & Schrumpf, 1994).

Up to now, our discussion has focused on students and their development as a reason for schools to engage in violence prevention and conflict resolution education. Now, we turn briefly to focus on the adults in the school as a reason for establishing a whole school approach. Adults face a new challenge to resolve conflicts creatively because few classes are now taught by one teacher, alone. That model is being replaced, particularly in inclusive classrooms, by a class where several teachers, teacher's aides, and parents work together. In some cases, teams of professionals work with one particular child. Disputes sometimes arise over the roles of the various professionals and the roles of professionals versus nonprofessionals. Such conflicts erupt among the adults, not the students, in the classroom. Because we cannot assume that all adults who work in a school know how to cope with conflicts that arise in these new situations, we should provide them with the opportunity to learn new skills of conflict resolution.

In our increasingly diverse society, friction also grows out of conflicts over ethnic, religious, socioeconomic, and physical differences. American schools include students of many ethnicities and of varied physical and mental abilities, differing sexual orientation, and increasingly disparate socioeconomic status (Kozol, 1991, 1996). Intolerance of these differences, though it may not surface as the proximate cause of a particular dispute, may lie behind the animosities that lead to it. Both the adults and the students in schools have to learn how to negotiate relationships so that violent conflicts do not arise from such differences. In this regard, educators have to teach students how to live harmoniously among people of different backgrounds and how to use a democratic political process to rectify what they perceive to be injustices. Both these tasks have to be integral to the school's approach to violence prevention.

ESTABLISHING A WHOLE
SCHOOL APPROACH TO VIOLENCE PREVENTION

The following issues have to be addressed in developing a whole school approach to violence prevention.

A whole school approach to violence prevention is a multiyear undertaking that needs the full support of the school's administrators. A variety of obstacles will undoubtedly arise as plans are instituted. Public education is subject to pressures that make multiyear undertakings difficult to sustain. Nevertheless, these pressures have to be resisted for a whole school approach to violence prevention to be successful because, as Pianta and Walsh (1996) pointed out, "Change of complex systems takes time and does not usually come about by large, one-time reorganizations following large external challenges . . . but by incremental changes within subsystems that are constantly adapting to the demands of contact with other systems" (p. 91). Because we are looking at systemic change, the support of the local school board and the superintendent, as well as the personnel running the school, are important assets for those instituting a whole school approach to acquire.

All groups within the school need to become integral to the school's efforts. Discussions about school policies and the possibility of changing them may become necessary because, according to Crawford and Bodine (1996), "typical school academic and disciplinary policies and practices often contradict the peaceful resolution of conflicts" (p. 40). Effective violence prevention efforts depend on the collaboration of everyone in the school: teachers, teacher aides, secretaries, psychologists, nurses, librarians, lunch room attendants, janitors, hall monitors, counselors, bus drivers, students, and administrators. Communication among members of each group must be open and fluid, and each has to be aware of the role of the others in the prevention of violence. Organizing work groups composed of people with varying tasks within the school may be desirable as a means to focus on ways to change a school's environment in order to develop violence prevention efforts.

Implementation plans have to be carefully designed, whether these are plans for the school buses or the classrooms, and for adult personnel or students, and the plans have to be acceptable to all the stakeholders. The effectiveness of these plans needs to be assessed through various means such as teamwork, reports of progress, surveys of employee and student satisfaction, and interviews and observations of what is going on in the school and its neighborhood.

A benefit of involving parents with a school's violence prevention activities is that families can become sites for the practice and refinement of skills. Parents may also provide feedback to the school on the effectiveness of its activities and suggestions for changing them.

Teachers need substantial long-term support to learn about violence prevention and conflict resolution theory and practices so that they become comfortable using them daily in their interactions with each other and with their students. Such support could consist of weekly team meetings for reflection, refresher courses on skills development and their integration into the curriculum, and peer observations of classroom practices.

Any new influence on a school's environment takes time to establish. Therefore, when one wants a change to be maintained, one has to provide newcomers with the understanding and the tools that those they are joining already possess. A hindrance to sustained change in schools is the constant turnover in personnel, through the annual graduation of students, students' moving into or out of a district, and members of the teaching staff or administrators changing jobs. Because institutional memory is vested in specific individuals, when they move, their memories are lost to the institution. Thus, newcomers, both students and teachers, need to learn about the approach to violence prevention in the school. For instance, orientation programs can provide an introduction to the ethos of the school, while follow-up sessions for newcomers can provide the same training in violence prevention and conflict resolution had by those already in the school.

The effect of violence prevention and conflict resolution on a school's environment depends on the overall integration of the programs chosen. Many programs on violence prevention and conflict resolution have been developed, some with a multicultural focus, some with a behavioral focus, and others with a humanistic focus on world peace. However, few of them consider how to develop a child's use of violence prevention and conflict resolution skills over a number of years. Fewer still consider how the knowledge acquired in them may augment student learning in such areas as literature, social studies, science, and mathematics. Those implementing a whole school approach need to decide what skills and knowledge are most appropriate for the particular setting and which programs will provide a seamless learning experience to the students.

ASSESSING THE EFFECTIVENESS OF A WHOLE SCHOOL APPROACH TO VIOLENCE PREVENTION

Although their number is growing, few reliable studies of the effects of violence prevention and conflict resolution education programs have yet appeared. Moreover, few of the existing programs affect a whole school; therefore, they don't provide entirely useful models of assessment for a whole school approach. For instance, assessment studies have been conducted on the use of Arnold Goldstein's Aggression Replacement Training and his Skillstreaming training among various populations, but not on the application of either to a whole school (Goldstein & McGinnis, 1997).

However, Barbara McEwan has written about the effects of adopting *judicious discipline* (McEwan, 1996). While not usually referred to as a violence prevention and conflict resolution program, Judicious Discipline, designed by Forrest Gathercoal (1990), has many of the aspects of one. In it, students and teachers learn to discuss interpersonal issues and conduct themselves in school using language provided by the U.S. Constitution, especially its First, Fourth, and Fourteenth Amendments. McEwan (1996) stated:

> On a school-wide basis, in all settings, typically the first change is a reduction of office referrals. In interviews I have conducted, educators report feeling more confident about their decisions, because the language they use with students is legal, fair, and rational. Hence they are more willing to solve problems in their classrooms and not seek outside interventions. . . .
>
> Attendance rates tend to increase with Judicious Discipline. Students report that they see the schools as safer places to be, which may help account for the increase. (p. 112)

McEwan painted a dismal picture of the nondemocratic attitudes of many teachers whom she interviewed, who didn't seem to understand our governmental system. Thus, she said, they could hardly be expected to pass democratic values on to their students:

> I have discovered, also, that the fundamental concepts of constitutional rights and responsibilities, so elemental to the structure of democratic society, are the very concepts many educators have trouble understanding and practicing. (p. 109)

Ideally, a whole school approach to violence prevention and conflict resolution entails the establishment (or reestablishment) of a democratic environment in a school. However, one has to be careful not to raise expectations about the results of particular programs. Each program has limitations. Those introducing them should learn the limitations of each and not promise what is beyond their ability to deliver.

VIOLENCE PREVENTION AND THE CLASSROOM ENVIRONMENT

Creating a Safe Space

A democratic classroom is important for establishing a safe environment in which to practice violence prevention and conflict resolution. Judicious discipline is but one way to create such a space. Another may be found in the introduction to *Creative Conflict Resolution* (Kreidler, 1984), where William J. Kreidler, of Educators for Social Responsibility, identified the main causes of classroom conflict. Kreidler placed each cause in one of six categories: competitive atmosphere, intolerant atmosphere, poor communication, inappropriate expression of emotion, and misuse of power by the teacher (pp. 4–5). Later, he devoted a whole chapter to "resolving student vs. teacher conflicts," in which he described the power games that teachers play, usually because "they confuse authority with authoritarianism." He then outlined ways to establish goals that are mutually satisfying for the students and the teacher, as well as ways to establish effective rules that "prescribe positive behavior and list a range of consequences for not behaving that way" (p. 37).

Creative Problem Solving

Among the techniques that can be practiced in a safe, democratic classroom is creative problem solving. Edward De Bono (1967, 1985) claimed that creative problem solving is an important component that is often left out of conflict resolution strategies. He advocated teaching adults and children, especially those of high school age, a variety of problem- solving skills, including what he called "lateral thinking." Lateral thinking calls for participants to interrupt the accepted way to proceed by suggesting new pathways, shortcuts, or alternative routes—solutions to a problem that overturn the accepted "givens." All ideas, including those considered far-fetched, are examined by a group calmly and without judgment. Those problem-solving skills would serve people, not only in interpersonal relations, but also in their academic work.

The use of creative problem solving for facilitating group activities has a long history in industry. For example, Synectics was introduced in the 1960s (Prince, 1970). It called for a cooperative structure for team meetings and new roles for team leaders as facilitators of creative problem solving. Prince's technique takes would-be problem solvers on a vacation from their task by asking them to develop an intricate series of analogies. After the analogies have led the problem solvers far afield, the facilitator guides them back to their task through a series of planned activities. Groups usually generate a greater array of solutions through this process than through conventional problem solving. In the 1970s, Synectics materials were adapted for various school subjects, such as social studies. The techniques suggested by Prince and De Bono can help students, both inside and outside the classroom, visualize new, and less confrontational, ways to interpret people's actions and motives.

There are, however, some inherent contradictions in traditional schooling that make experimentation with creative problem solving difficult. The first contradiction is that between teacher-centered education and student–centered education—between an emphasis on teaching and an emphasis on learning. At the root of this contradiction is the question: Who is to maintain control over what is learned and how it is learned? If the people designing a whole school approach decide to encourage students to think creatively, then teachers in the school may have to relinquish some of their control over the students' learning.

A second contradiction is between learning that is individual and individually assessed and learning through group interactions that is assessed by both the product of the group's activities and the process of collaboration among the group. How is such work to be graded? If teachers wish students to embrace group activities and function amicably while undertaking them, they may have to reconsider their grading system in order to reward group work appropriately.

Multicultural Education

Children and adults carry attitudes and beliefs from the wider society into the classroom. Ours is increasingly a multicultural society, where the conflicts we encounter often arise from differences of race and ethnicity. Such conflicts may result from differing cultural values and traditions. They may also arise, as may conflicts over gender, class, and disability, from differing amounts of access to power and influence. Christine E. Sleeter and Carl A. Grant (1991) mapped the different forms of power that accrue to students from their own cultural knowledge and classroom knowledge. Subsequently, they identified five approaches to multicultural education (Sleeter & Grant, 1994). Individuals designing violence prevention programs need to consider the outcomes they wish to achieve before adopting one of these approaches.

The *teaching the exceptional and the culturally different approach* is designed to build bridges between the students and the school. The strategy is to get those not already aligned with the school to fit into the system.

The *human relations approach,* based on the ideals of tolerance and acceptance, is realized through the promotion of positive feelings among all students. Differences are confronted on levels that are affective and relational, not cognitive or intellectual.

The *single group studies approach* to multicultural education targets a particular group to empower its members; to inform and educate them about the group's culture, including its history of victimization, and to lead members to understand the group's perspective. The orientation of this approach is to empower group members to act on their own behalf.

The *multicultural education approach* promotes equality and cultural pluralism. It focuses on both structural and personal issues. Structurally, its goal is to obtain power equity through institutional accessibility and equal opportunity. Personally, its goals are to use respect, understanding, and critical thinking to teach about differences.

The *education that is multicultural and social reconstructionist approach*, which is favored by Sleeter and Grant, differs from the multicultural education approach by its greater emphasis on preparing students to change the social structure in order to achieve equality. Differences are explored at political and institutional levels. By a social reconstructionist education, Sleeter and Grant mean one that envisions a society that empowers every group and individual within it to effect change.

Sleeter and Grant's typology of multicultural education spans issues that are relational and interpersonal to those that are structural and involve social justice. Thus, they offer a range of ways to think about differences among people and how they may be reconciled through education.

VIOLENCE PREVENTION AND THE CURRICULUM

How can preventing violence and learning how to resolve conflicts creatively become an integral part of the curriculum in schools? One answer would be to revolutionize the curriculum. Nel Noddings (1992) suggested that the curriculum we know should be replaced by one with caring at its center. Noddings suggested the following centers of care: self; inner circle; strangers and distant others; animals, plants, and the earth; the human-made world; and ideas. Educators may agree with Noddings that, ideally, teaching students to care is what schools should emphasize, especially public schools which protect the welfare of the community as well as the achievement of individuals. Nevertheless, many may doubt that such an emphasis will be adopted in their lifetime. So, short of a revolution in educational thought, what can be achieved? Noddings herself provided guidelines for introducing some components of her centers of care while retaining the curriculum as now structured. Those components could form part of a whole school violence prevention program.

Add-on Programs

As of now, many violence prevention programs are introduced as an add-on to the existing curriculum. Outside consultants provide one or two-day courses on conflict resolution strategies, anger reduction, or negotiation skills, sometimes for staff or students only, and sometimes for both. As add-ons, these courses tend to be marginalized. The curriculum in most schools is already full of requirements that cannot be laid aside. Teachers, therefore, may acknowledge the importance of violence prevention but be hard put to find time to teach it, unless gun violence has already taken place in their school or their district.

More elementary than middle or high school teachers may find time to add such programs to the curriculum. However, as Stevens (1998) pointed out, elementary teachers, as well as their peers in middle and high schools, need reassurance that the violence prevention and conflict resolution skills they have acquired through their previous training and experience as a teacher are acknowledged and incorporated into any new program they are expected to teach. This is a serious issue because some programs insist on using a specific vocabulary or structure to achieve the very same goals that some teachers have achieved for many years through less formal means.

Some middle and high schools have found time to experiment with one form of violence prevention: peer mediation. These programs may be particularly acceptable because they appear to have the potential for reducing the time that teachers and administrators spend mediating conflicts among students. We are puzzled that, in the schools observed by members of the

Syracuse University Violence Prevention Project, peer mediation was considered an extracurricular activity by students and staff; no time in the school schedule was provided for adult and student mediators to meet and reflect on the learning that takes place during the mediation process. (This issue is discussed further in this volume in the chapters on mediation: chapter 9, by Ronnie Casella, and chapter 11, by Kimberly Williams.) We believe that the skills learned in mediation may be applied to academic subjects, as will be described later. We recommend that time be provided, weekly, for adult and student mediators to explore the learning that has taken place. (Ideally, the discussion group would include those being mediated, also.) We recommend as well that regular monitoring be built into every school peer mediation program to ensure that both peer mediators and adult facilitators fulfill the spirit and the steps of the mediation process.

Curriculum Infusion

Another way to address violence prevention is to incorporate it into the existing curriculum. This calls for more extensive teacher preparation than the add-on programs but is also more likely to ensure that teachers will incorporate violence prevention into their day to day work. This approach includes pedagogical methods, such as cooperative learning, that provide the opportunity for students to practice the micro skills needed for resolving conflicts, including turn taking, active listening, negotiating, and problem solving. Extensive practice of these skills is essential if individuals are to integrate them into their repertoire (Raider, 1995). Constructive controversy is another pedagogical process that builds on the skills developed in cooperative learning. In this approach to violence prevention and conflict resolution, students take turns developing the argument for each participant in a controversy. This provides them with the opportunity to understand their opponents' viewpoints in a non-threatening situation (Deutsch, 1993a). Other research by Deutsch suggests that children who learn the skills needed for the peaceful resolution of conflicts improve academically as well (Deutsch, 1993b).

We suggest that skills related to violence prevention need to be practiced in a variety of subjects and be built upon in each successive grade. Because such an approach has only recently begun to be instituted, we can only hint at the ways it can be achieved by providing the following examples

An example of how to introduce violence prevention into the high school curriculum is the "Peaceful Resolutions to Conflict in a Multicultural

Society: A Pilot Program Integrating Conflict Resolution Skills in the High School U.S. History Curriculum." Funded by the Ford Foundation, this began in 1994 as a collaborative project of the Rutgers Center for Historical Analysis, the Rutgers Center for Negotiation and Conflict Resolution, and the New Jersey Center for Law-Related Education. High school teachers met with university faculty to learn the vocabulary of negotiating and mediating and to put that to use in historical disputes that had been constructed as case studies for this purpose. For instance, the dispute over land claims that led to the Mexican American War of 1845 was developed as a case study in which characters from both sides of the dispute had to negotiate, with the help of a mediator, a settlement of the issues. Since that time, high school teachers and university faculty who participated in the workshop have developed more case studies for the U.S. history courses in high schools.

Aiming to expand the use of the case studies that have already been developed, in 1996 the project sponsors (including the Program on Negotiation at Harvard Law School) held a national seminar for a group of university and high school teachers on "Peaceful Resolutions to Conflict in a Multicultural Society." Through hands-on experience, participants learned how to use the case studies to incorporate mediation and negotiation into the teaching of United States history.

An example of how to incorporate conflict resolution education into the teaching of children's literature (kindergarten through second grade) was written by William J. Kreidler of Educators for Social Responsibility. Kreidler (1994) suggested that with some additions of vocabulary and ideas (such as those he provided in his 1984 book on conflict resolution), stories read in school classrooms can be enriched by discussions about the ways conflicts among the characters are handled. Such discussions provide students with new ways to consider their own and their friends' behavior. Kreidler's book provides teachers with a springboard for expanding their own repertoires of pedagogical skills and materials on conflict resolution. The techniques he suggested can be expanded upon for incorporating conflict resolution education into the study of literature in middle school and high school.

As a last example, we have ourselves developed and taught a graduate course entitled "Integrating Conflict Resolution into the K–6 Curriculum," in which students study material on conflict resolution education, participate in conflict resolution activities, including brainstorming on how to incorporate conflict resolution into all subjects, for instance through cooperative activities in science and mathematics. Students then create parts of a curriculum in their own subject area at a grade level of their choice. Ideally, such a course could be attended by, or offered for, many teachers from one school, who would then be able to design an integrated curriculum for the whole school.

VIOLENCE PREVENTION
AND STAFF DEVELOPMENT FOR TEACHERS

A whole school approach to violence prevention is far more advantageous to teachers than having their principal encourage them to adopt a program within their own classrooms. Let's assume the latter takes place. A teacher attends a districtwide in-service workshop for one afternoon or a series of afternoons. Then she or he returns to the classroom with notes taken during the workshops, photocopied handouts, and a manual of activities for use in class. Even if several teachers from the school attend the workshops, they will be unlikely to meet regularly afterwards to reflect on their practice of what was learned there. Essentially, each teacher returns to an isolated classroom with no support. Thus, the odds that any one teacher will continue thinking about the material, let alone place it at the forefront of classroom practice, are slim indeed.

A schoolwide program can address barriers that teachers face when trying to introduce a program in their own classroom. Three significant barriers are, first that teachers often feel incompetent to teach a program after a short immersion in it; second, they may receive no rewards from the principal for carrying it out; and third, the violence prevention program may get lost within the pile of innovations presented to teachers each school year. A whole school approach provides support for teachers who try out a program for the first time. The school schedule is adapted to provide teachers the time to meet and consider the implications of violence prevention education in the classroom and the curriculum. In some cases, school and university partnerships enable school personnel and university faculty to work together to design programs and assess their effectiveness. Such collaboration between schools and universities on violence prevention already exists in many places, and in some, as with an alternative school and the Syracuse University Violence Prevention Project, a version of a whole school approach is being instituted.

A successful schoolwide violence prevention program attends to both the school structure and the development of each teacher in terms of his or her learning. Teachers are encouraged to "examine their own beliefs and understandings, reexamine their premises about teaching and learning and modify their practice" (Richardson & Hamilton, 1994, p. 112). For the teachers, as for the students, "learning is an active process in which students construct and reconstruct concepts, premises, and theories' (p. 112). For the individual teacher, this process involves active participation with a group of colleagues.

The structure and organization of the school have a direct influence on the patterns of relationships among teachers (Hargreaves, 1992). Hargreaves outlines four types of teacher relationships: *Individualism* is characterized by teachers who are isolated from others, within their own classrooms. *Balkanization* is characterized by teachers who associate with small groups of colleagues in similar situations, such as other math or fourth grade teachers. These individuals tend to identify with and remain loyal to, their particular group. *Contrived collegiality* is characterized by procedures mandating particular joint projects. Finally, the *collaborative culture* is characterized by ongoing and continuous help, trust, and openness, which permeate all relationships among the staff. In such a culture, the staff is united. The development of a collaborative culture is the intention of a violence prevention program.

In a school with a collaborative culture, adults recognize that conflicts are bound to occur and that ways to discuss them openly and resolve them creatively need to be encouraged as part of the school's violence prevention. Adults are thus able to model the relationships they are encouraging children to develop.

It seems likely that changes in beliefs, values, and attitudes in teaching parallel changes in the ways teachers relate to their colleagues, that is, in their characteristic patterns of association (Hargreaves, 1992, p. 219). Thus, as well as providing formal times for school personnel to discuss issues, a schoolwide violence prevention program has to provide opportunities for informal contacts. Research suggests that a significant amount of teacher learning takes place on an informal, day-to-day basis (Hargreaves, 1992, p. 217). These more casual interactions can be encouraged with a welcoming and comfortable faculty lounge, faculty lunches, and social events. It is important to give value to, and allow for, a relaxed "down time" when teachers can talk.

Administrators and teachers in the school have to provide examples of care and collaboration. Formal structures need to encourage cross-level working and study groups composed of professionals, semiprofessionals, and nonprofessionals, as well as peer observations and teacher research projects. These schoolwide structural changes may take time to introduce and maintain. They support individual teachers and other staff in developing and implementing violence prevention within their own classroom and practice.

Changing practice and beliefs is a dynamic activity (Richardson, 1994, p. 90) that entails the scrutiny of both. Formal and informal staff development in the school encourages a spirit of inquiry to facilitate the examination of both practice and beliefs. "The inquiry orientation allows for an examination of personally held values, goals, and empirical beliefs as well as student learning and development" (Richardson & Anders, 1994, p. 206). Such an orientation allows for the infusion of new ideas and practices.

However, a whole school approach to violence prevention sometimes meets resistance of two kinds: the first is to the ideals or content of violence prevention and conflict resolution education, and the second, to the need for collaboration entailed by a whole school approach to change. The first may occur because violence prevention and conflict resolution education, which includes cooperative learning, peace education, prosocial development, and social skills training, runs counter to the very lifestyles of many people in American society (Kohn, 1992). Shifting from an individualistic, competitive, teacher-centered focus in schools may be threatening to some parents, teachers, and administrators.

The second form of resistance may be to the collaborative approach to change. This approach assumes that change will occur, not only for students and their curriculum, but also for teachers and administrators, both in their working relationships with one another and in their design and implementation of school policies.

Change is both difficult and exciting. Those who become involved in changing their beliefs and practices will have many questions and doubts. They also will acquire new perspectives and insights to share and test out. Teachers need to feel competent with a new program. Opportunities to discuss the changes they are implementing will enhance their level of competency and expertise concerning any new material. School change and staff development "is time consuming and requires dialogue in a trusting atmosphere" (Richardson & Anders, 1994, p. 211). Time for dialogue is particularly necessary when considering change on the organizational, relational, and individual levels. Individual teachers need complete support in order to bring a conflict resolution program successfully into their classrooms where children spend most of their time.

CONCLUSION

As the comments by Richters (1995; quoted at the beginning of this chapter) imply, violence in schools is related to violence in society at large and to broad social issues such as children's access to handguns. As Pianta and Walsh (1996) reminded their readers:

> Schools cannot change society. They are but part of the larger system and have limited resources to direct towards changing dysfunctional relationships within or between family, community, or culture. But schools play an important role in maintaining health in a cultural system. Furthermore, changes can be made in schools that will positively affect the lives of children who attend them. (pp. 153–154)

We have outlined the means by which schools can make a significant change to positively affect the lives of their students. Schoolteachers and administrators often seek help to stop violence once it has erupted in their schools. In other cases, they want to prevent violence from occurring. However, violence prevention and conflict resolution education offers a vehicle for greater change than they usually envision. By instituting a whole school approach, teachers and administrators can effect a change in the overall ecology of the school.

For our pluralistic society to function civilly, each person needs to learn skills of relating positively to others, accepting differences, and finding creative ways to resolve conflicts. Each child enters school with some interpersonal skills. However, those skills need refining and expanding for the child to grow to adulthood with the ability to resolve conflicts creatively and without ever resorting to violence. We can guarantee that the majority of people will learn the skills needed to participate fully in our multicultural, democratic society only when we teach those skills in our public schools. A whole school approach to violence prevention provides the vehicle for doing that.

REFERENCES

Bodine, R. J., Crawford, D. K., & Schrumpf, F. (1994). *Creating the peaceable school: A comprehensive program for teaching conflict resolution.* Champaign, IL: Research Press.

Crawford, D. K., & Bodine, R. (1996). *Conflict resolution education: A guide to implementing programs in schools, youth-serving organizations, and community and juvenile justice settings* (Program Report). Washington, DC: U.S. Department of Justice, Office of Juvenile Justice and Delinquency Prevention; U.S. Department of Education, Safe and Drug-Free School Program.

De Bono, E. (1967). *The use of lateral thinking.* London: Penguin Books.

De Bono, E. (1985). *Conflicts: A better way to resolve them.* London: Penguin Books.

Deutsch, M. (1993a). Educating for a peaceful world. *American Psychologist, 48,* 510–517.

Deutsch, M. (1993b). Conflict resolution and cooperative learning in an alternative high school. *Cooperative Learning, 13*(4), 1–5.

Gathercoal, F. (1990). *Judicious Discipline.* Ann Arbor: Caddo Gap Press.

Giarelli, J. M., & Giarelli, E. (1996). Educating for public and private life: beyond the false dilemma. In J. N. Burstyn, (Ed.), *Educating tomorrow's valuable citizen* (pp. 9–37). Albany: State University of New York Press.

Goldstein, A. P., & McGinnis, E. (1997). *Skillstreaming the adolescent: New strategies and perspectives for teaching prosocial skills* (Appendix A). Champaign, IL: Research Press.

Hargreaves, A. (1992). Cultures of teaching: A focus for change! In A. Hargreaves & M. G. Fullan (Eds.), *Understanding teacher development* (pp. 216–240). New York: Teachers College Press.

Kohn, A. (1992). *No contest: The case against competition.* Boston: Houghton Mifflin.

Kozol, J. (1991). *Savage inequalities.* New York: Harper Perennial.

Kozol, J. (1996). *Amazing grace.* New York: Harper Perennial.

Kreidler, W. J. (1984). *Creative conflict resolution.* Glenview, IL: Scott, Foresman.

Kreidler, W. J. (1994). *Teaching conflict resolution through children's literature.* New York: Scholastic Professional Books.

McEwan, B. (1996). Assaulting the last bastions of authoritarianism: Democratic education meets classroom discipline. In J. N. Burstyn, (Ed.). *Educating tomorrow's valuable citizen* (pp. 93–118). Albany: State University of New York Press.

Noddings, N. (1992). *The challenge to care in schools.* New York: Teachers College Press.

Pianta, R. C., & Walsh, D. J. (1996). *High-risk children in schools: Constructing sustaining relationships.* New York: Routledge.

Prince, G. M. (1970). *The practice of creativity.* New York: Collier Books.

Raider, E. (1995). Conflict resolution training in schools: Translating theory into applied skills. In Bunker, Rubin & Associates (Eds.). *Conflict, cooperation and justice* (pp. 93–121). San Francisco: Jossey-Bass.

Richardson, V. (1994). The consideration of teachers' beliefs. In V. Richardson, (Ed.). *Teacher change and the staff development process* (pp. 90–108). New York: Teachers College Press.

Richardson, V., & Anders, P. L. (1994). A theory of change. In V. Richardson, (Ed.), *Teacher change and the staff development process* (pp. 199–216). New York: Teachers College Press.

Richardson, V., & Hamilton, M. L. (1994). The practical-argument staff development process! In V. Richardson, (Ed.), *Teacher change and the staff development process* (pp. 109–134). New York: Teachers College Press.

Richters, J. E. (1993). Community violence and children's development: Toward a research agenda for the 1990s. In D. Reiss, J. E. Richters, M. Radke-Yarrow, & D. Scharff, (Eds.), *Children and violence* (pp. 3–6). New York: Guilford Press.

Sleeter, C. E., & Grant, C. A. (1991). Mapping terrains of power: Student cultural knowledge versus classroom knowledge. In C. E. Sleeter, (Ed.), *Empowerment through multicultural education* (pp. 49–67). Albany: State University of New York Press.

Sleeter, C. E., & Grant, C. A. (1994). *Making choices for multicultural education: Five approaches to race, class, and gender* (2nd ed.). Englewood Cliffs, NJ: Merrill/Prentice Hall.

Stevens, R. (1998). Conflict resolution education in classrooms: The intersection of a training program, a curriculum manual and teachers. Ph.D. dissertation, Syracuse University, NY.

9

The Cultural Foundations of Peer Mediation: Beyond a Behaviorist Model of Urban School Conflict

Ronnie Casella

Central Connecticut State University

BACKGROUND ON PEER MEDIATION PROGRAMS

In recent years, throughout the United States, peer mediation programs have gained the support of school faculty and administrators, as well as educational researchers, as a means of combating school violence (Bey, 1996; Reiss & Roth, 1993; Van Slyck & Stern, 1991). The logic of peer mediation is that students who have trained as mediators can meet with fellow students who have disputes to help them solve their problems, thereby avoiding more serious conflict that could erupt if the disputants were not mediated. This logic suggests that violence in school is alleviated when disputants can air their grievances in the presence of trained mediators who are capable of employing mediation and conflict resolution strategies.

The author wishes to thank Joan Burstyn, Kim Williams, Rebecca Stevens, and Domingo Guerra for insightful feedback on this chapter.

Meanwhile, there is another rationale for peer mediation programs that suggests that violence in schools is alleviated not when disputants are mediated, but when mediators learn conflict resolution skills. In this case, the logic is as follows: when students are trained to mediate disputes in their schools, the training teaches these students, not only how to mediate, but also how to solve their own disputes—in school, in their communities, with their families—throughout their lives. The point in this case is to train as mediators as many students as possible and to therefore inundate society with individuals who possess the skills to resolve conflicts nonviolently (Johnson, Johnson, Dudley, Ward, & Magnuson, 1995). Here it is the training itself, not the mediation process, that leads to decreased incidents of violence. Given these two scenarios, we are led to a crossroad regarding peer mediation programs: who should benefit from peer mediation, the disputants or the mediators? When we evaluate a peer mediation program, should we, as educational researchers, evaluate how effective programs are for the mediators or for the mediated?

This crossroad is traversed by suggesting that peer mediations have a lasting effect on both the mediated and the mediators, as well as the community around the school and the families of students who undergo the mediation process (Johnson et al., 1995). This ideal situation is given impetus by "diffusion theory," or what is sometimes referred to as the "peace virus" (Crary, 1992). This theory suggests that peer mediation programs—and all violence prevention programs—have a "spreading" effect. Mediators learn conflict resolution skills that help them in their lives, both within and outside school (Johnson & Johnson, 1995a). In addition, when disputants are mediated, they, too, learn how to solve conflicts non-violently (Stevahn, Johnson, & O'Coin, 1996). According to diffusion theory, students who mediate, as well as those who are mediated, take what they have learned into their communities and households. Thus, families and society, as well as the school and individual students, benefit from the mediation process (Harrington & Merry, 1988; Shook & Milner, 1993).

On the other hand, critics of peer mediation and other violence prevention programs cite several factors that often block this ideal scenario from occurring (Webster, 1993). For instance, based on evaluations of three violence prevention programs—Violence Prevention Curriculum for Adolescents, Community Violence Prevention Program, and Positive Adolescent Choices Training—the authors of one study concluded that violence prevention programs do not produce long-term changes in violent behavior or decrease the risk of victimization (Johnson & Johnson, 1995b). Their ineffectiveness is caused by the following: many programs are poorly targeted; the programs provide materials but do not focus on program implementation; proponents of violence prevention programs confuse programs that work in neighborhoods with those that work in schools; and many programs are unrealistic. The authors argue that schools need to go beyond violence prevention to conflict resolution programs. The difference here is subtle, yet important. Conflict resolution does not aim to eliminate all conflicts. In addition, conflict resolution would require schools to create a more cooperative environment (use cooperative learning, for example), to decrease in-school risk factors (such as competitive, noncaring, and short-term relationships), to use academic controversy to increase learning (they need to show how conflict arises in everyday life and is not always negative), and, finally, to teach *all* students how to resolve conflicts constructively.

In general, the study of peer mediation programs has been a highly contentious undertaking. The research discussed in this chapter will address two areas of debate in peer mediation research: first, the belief that peer mediation should benefit both the mediated and the mediators, and second, the notion that peer mediation is even capable of reducing violence in the absence of other systemic changes regarding students' lives and the structure of schools.

METHODS

In order to examine the impact of culture on peer mediation, a case study ethnographic research design was employed to focus long-term on the workings of one peer mediation program; then, other sites were chosen for less intensive research to test the validity of my conclusions (Erickson, 1973; Spindler, 1997). The case study research was conducted in New York State during the 1997–1998 school year for five to ten hours each week. The research was qualitative, focused on the cultural context of peer mediation, and took seriously the notion that all school activities, including peer mediation, are infused with a "continual process of creating meaning in social and material contexts" (Levinson & Holland, 1996, p. 13; see also Fetterman, 1988; Lincoln, 1988). The data were drawn from four sources: observations of 20 peer mediation sessions; 53 open-ended interviews with peer mediators and staff organizers; observations of the peer mediation training of student mediators and their in-service meetings; and data compiled from school records kept about the mediations and those who were mediated. During observations, field notes were taken and transcribed to a computer program. Once this portion of the research was concluded, I studied other peer mediation programs in an elementary school and middle school in two cities in Connecticut to compare the different programs and to test the validity of my conclusions. Though the data in this article were gathered from the original high school site in New York, my conclusions reflect what I discovered in each of the three schools I studied.

My field notes were coded, and then the codes were condensed according to themes. All interviews were tape recorded, transcribed, and coded. Hypotheses were inductively generated from the coded materials. Also included as data were the booklets, handouts, and articles about peer mediation that the schools distributed. These texts, too, were coded and used to generate hypotheses inductively. In the tradition of school ethnography, the study, not only evaluates the programs, but also focuses on the everyday events and rituals, the assumptions and taken for granted "facts" that undergirded the programs and are, therefore, in many ways invisible to school policymakers, administrators, teachers, students, and, at times, other researchers (Bogdan & Biklen, 1988; Payne, 1994). Unlike most research on peer mediation, which usually evaluates programs through surveys and therefore misses the complexity of interactions between students and mediators, this research focused on the face-to-face dynamics of peer mediation programs in urban schools (Levinson & Holland, 1996).

THE SCHOOL

Brandon High School, where the case study research was conducted, is one of four public high schools in a midsize city in New York State.[1] The school is located on the south side of the city, parts of which are poor and mostly African American and parts of which are affluent and mostly White. The community around the school often gets attention in school and community meetings as an area that is particularly troubled. About half the 1,400 students in the school are African American, some from middle class backgrounds. About 45 percent of students are White, and there are small minorities of Native American, Asian, and Latino students. Many students come from professional and secure families; others do not. Forty percent of the students are eligible for the free lunch program.

---

[1]The names of all individuals and localities have been changed.

Though not thought of as a particularly violent school by community people or by most of the students, faculty, and administrators in the school, Brandon High School does have its share of violent confrontations. For example, between September 1, 1997, and June 15, 1998, 128 students were suspended for fighting in school.

FINDINGS

While researchers argue over the benefits or the ineffectiveness of school-based peer mediation programs, drawing subtleties between "add-on" approaches, whole school approaches, and conflict resolution, as opposed to peer mediation, programs, many policies in schools are misguided because they lack an understanding of what "conflict" means to students in their daily interactions with one another. In schools such as Brandon High, a persistent behaviorist model of conflict, which views disputes as "personal" or "individual" matters caused by disagreements between students, prevents an examination of the cultural patterns and economic disparities that pervade the peer mediation program and students' conflicts.

During the mediation training, students learned to define conflict in particular ways. This definition had consequences on how students conducted their mediations throughout the year. For example, students learned to respect human diversity, but they also learned that conflict was the result of inappropriate behavior, for which various forms of behavior modification techniques were recommended. The focus on the individual and his or her behavior often overshadowed the possibility of examining in detail the complex sexual, economic and racial issues that came to the mediation table.

Furthermore, like most extracurricular activities, the peer mediation program was generally participated in by the most active and high-achieving students. Both the student mediators and school staff who organized the program recognized the importance of being a part of the peer mediation "team," for it brought recognition to the students and the school. It was also used by students to "beef up" their résumés or college applications. Essentially, peer mediation programs like this one are developed to benefit mediators—not those who have disagreements—though some disputants benefit as well. Peer mediation is a conflict resolution service in school; but it is also an extracurricular activity that high achieving students use to better their life experiences and opportunities. In short, it is used by mediators as a résumé booster. Unfortunately, those who could use the résumé booster the most are not involved in the program—except as those who get mediated.

PEER MEDIATION IN CONTEXT

In spite of news articles in the city newspaper, at the time of this study, reporting fighting on the rise at Brandon High School and a Time Warner news program, produced by a local media organization, about school violence in the city that focused in part on the schools, Brandon High has a publicly acclaimed peer mediation program. Among other honors the program won the JC Penny Golden Rule Award and was granted a New York State certificate of excellence from a state senator. These honors are proudly displayed in the trophy case in one hallway of the school.

During the 1991–1992 school year, the guidance counselors at Brandon High School developed the peer mediation program based on the belief that students themselves needed to resolve fellow student conflicts and that violence was best addressed when individuals learned from the conflict resolution process. A handbook distributed by the Brandon Mediation Team called "When We Listen, People Talk!" noted:

> Traditional interventions teach students that adult authority figures are needed to resolve conflicts. Adults are forced into the role of arbitrators, determining what is and is not acceptable behavior. Students are frequently disciplined (expulsion, suspension, time-out rooms, scolding) in an effort to control and manage their behavior. This approach does not empower students. While adults may become more skillful in controlling students, students do not learn the procedures, skills and attitudes required to resolve conflict constructively. With peer mediation, they do.

Fair Play, Inc., a conflict resolution service, provided the training for the peer mediation program at Brandon High School. Fair Play, Inc., founded in 1981, is part of the city court system and is used by the judicial branches as an alternative to small claims court. Alice Carver, a mediator with Fair Play and the trainer at Brandon High, said that "about five years ago, Fair Play got into the prevention side of conflict—that's how we ended up working here at Brandon." Alice Carver noted, during the first day of her training for the new mediators, that she had been doing the training since 1991 and that the incidence of violence had gone down 63 percent since then.

Student volunteers for the peer mediation program received twenty-two hours of training during the summer. The fourteen students taking part in the training during the 1997–1998 year were in the tenth and eleventh grades. Eight were girls, six boys; ten were White and four were African American. Students volunteered to be peer mediators; some were urged by their counselors or by teachers. Guidelines for the peer mediation program were many, though they were not always followed. They included: confidentiality, once a month in-service meetings, and maintenance of a 75 percent grade point average 90 percent of the time. Mediators were on-call one day out of every ten, but teachers had the discretion to forbid a student mediator from leaving class for a mediation, though this rarely happened. Most teachers in the school supported the peer mediation program, if for no other reason than that it gave them a venue to dismiss unruly students, whose conflicts could be dealt with elsewhere than in the classroom.

In general, the adult developers of the program tried to convey to students that being part of the peer mediation program was a privilege and a responsibility, and therefore required of them serious consideration and work. The school system coordinator of the program noted that there had been 900 mediation sessions at Brandon High since the program began, and only two fights. However, the statistics used by the adult developers of the program—that there had only been two fights in the school and that violent incidents had decreased 63 percent since the inception of the program—reflect artful play with numbers rather than reality. All teachers whom I interviewed complained of an increasing incidence of violence in the school; in the first four months of the school year alone, sixty students were suspended for fighting (see Table 9.1).

THE LIMITS OF DEFINING CONFLICT AS INDIVIDUAL DIFFERENCE: THE BEHAVIORIST MODEL

Students were taught in the peer mediation training that most disputes were a matter of "disagreements" and "misunderstandings" that could be resolved through purposeful talk. They were also taught that mediation existed to give disputants a channel for airing their grievances and working toward an agreement that all parties could feel good about. How a definition of conflict was created and influenced the mediation process depended on, first, teaching students that conflict was inevitable—inherent in our

TABLE 9.1
Statistics on Mediations From September 4, 1997
Through December 17, 1997

Total number of mediations: 66
Causes of Disputes
Threats: 30
Rumors: 10
Name-calling: 6
Physical fighting: 12
Verbal fighting: 8

Number of disputants involved:	136
Number of disputants who were African-American:	97
Number of disputants who were White:	31
Number of disputants who were "other" (mostly Latino):	5
Number of disputants who were female (including 1 teacher):	94
Number of disputants who were male:	40
Number of disputants whose race and gender were uncertain:	2
Number of repeat offenders:	18
Number of mediations that were between African-American and White disputants:	6
Number of mediations that were between African-American and Latino disputants:	2
Number of mediations that were between Latino and white disputants:	3
Number of mediations that were between African-American and African-American students:	45
Number of mediations that were between White and White students:	10
Number of students in the school (according to 1997–98 census):	1,309
Number of students who were African-American:	633
Number of students who were White:	598
Number of students who were "other" (mostly Latino):	77

There is about a 50–50 ratio of girls and boys

human natures. During training, for example, Alice Carver explained that "conflict is neither positive nor negative. It's a part of life. Everyone is going to have conflict," and she concluded that conflict, then, was "a signal for change."

Throughout the training a behaviorist model of conflict was taught, in that students learned that conflict was primarily caused by "mismanaged behavior" and that conflict resolution was a matter of having disputants change their behaviors, and therefore their life circumstances. The construction of conflict in this manner was made evident on the first day of training when students were asked to line up on either side of a line on the floor and to try to pull another person over the line using one hand. After the activity, the losers were asked how they felt about losing, and the winners, how they felt about winning. The lesson of the activity was that individuals should learn to "straddle the line" and to therefore create "win–win situations." Creating a win–win situation was a matter of having disputants "see from the other person's perspective" and then changing their behaviors to accommodate the other person.

Also central to defining conflict as a matter of individual difference based on a behaviorist model was the focus on techniques used in counseling, which, though appropriate for counseling, were not always sufficient for mediations (Apter & Goldstein, 1986; Goldstein, Harootunian, & Conoley, 1994). The executive director of Fair Play likened peer mediation to counseling and said that it was very much influenced by the literature surrounding "reflective listening," which, in the context of the mediations, meant listening carefully and trying to be reflective about each disputant's viewpoint of the problem (Fisher & Ury, 1981).

During the training, the notion of reflective listening was reiterated several times. During a role play exercise, for example, student mediators were urged to practice reflective listening as a way of "creating understandings," as one trainer explained. Students were urged to remain neutral during mediations and to envision conflicts as a matter of, again, misunderstandings that could be resolved through an objective assessment of the immediate dispute and by offering disputants suggestions for changing their behaviors. Later, another Fair Play trainer urged student mediators not to repeat or focus on any offending words that the disputants might say because "you want to take the sting out of words." According to the trainers, this, too, creates understanding, by "defusing" hostile situations. The importance of defusing hostile situations, remaining neutral, taking the sting out of words, and focusing on individual behavior were practices that many mediators remembered in interviews months after the training. After one new student mediator conducted a mediation in December 1997, she noted that the dispute was about one girl calling another girl "a whore" and that she worked to show the two disputants that they should not take such "words" seriously. She noted:

It's important to defuse the situation. In a he said/she said kind of thing [students calling each other names], the words really don't mean anything because they're just pretty much words. People shouldn't even worry about it because the words don't mean anything.

When asked, "But what if the words are very hurtful, even racist or sexist?" the student responded, "I'd just tell them you can talk it out with the person instead of saying 'Oh well, I'm just going to beat her up' or something like that." Students were guided through a means of dealing with conflict in a way that entailed a respectful engagement with people's feelings. Conflict was to be resolved by taking into account people's individual differences, which might, at times, be the result of cultural differences. Then, mediators were required to work to have disputants change their behaviors by, first, determining the relationship of the disputants; second, examining the issues that resulted in the conflict; and, finally, assessing the feelings of the disputants. Once these factors were clarified, student mediators were to work to change people's feelings—creating win-win situations—and to have disputants alter their behaviors in order to change the issues that had resulted in the conflict. Missing from this scenario were prolonged discussions about the complex issues of sexuality, race, and social class that were nearly always a part of actual mediations (Canada, 1995; Giroux, 1996; Soriano, Soriano, & Jimenez, 1994).

The student mediators, who were, for the most part, good students, learned the lessons of the training well. And students—both mediators and some disputants—benefited from the program. Sometimes conflicts between people can be resolved if disputants have a venue to air their grievances during a mediation process that takes seriously their differences in opinions, as the peer mediation program does. But many mediations involved issues that surpassed this nature of conflict; and in these, more complex conflicts, student mediators were often unprepared. Administrators in the school were not blind to this fact. As one adult mediator and special education teacher noted: "I think mediation is a good communication tool that we have here in the building. I think it works for some kids—it works for rational people, with people who have small, resolvable problems."

Unfortunately, many disputes are not small, resolvable problems, and the disputants can seem irrational. Often, then, student mediators grappled with issues that were not addressed in the training—for example, fights that went on between boys and girls that had sexual elements attached to them (Katz, 1995; Stein, 1995). While student mediators attempted to grapple seriously and effectively with girl/boy disputes, they were often incapable of doing so. The following is an example taken from an interview held with a mediator after she had conducted a mediation involving a boy and a girl. She explained:

> The girl who was fighting sat [at the mediation table]. She talked . . . but we kind of got stuck because these people were really so mad and their stories were so totally different that we were kind of stuck—like, things weren't coming together. The girl thought that the guy hit her—no, the guy thought that the girl hit him, but it wasn't really a hit, it was a smack, so he turned around and smacked her. Ms. Harding [the adult mediator] was there, which was good because they weren't agreeing on anything. The girl just said she was so mad and the boy was just like, "Yeah, okay," and there was nothing else to really do. Afterwards it was just like, "You should not have hit her." She [Ms. Harding] was saying that guys should not hit girls—she was trying to make him think that guys shouldn't hit girls. That's kind of like her opinion. I don't think they should either, but I don't think girls should hit guys either, so it's her opinion, and her focusing on the guy hitting the girl wasn't right. She should try to keep it to herself and stay neutral . . . I think, I'm not sure. I think the mediation settled that difference that they had, but I'm not sure if it's going to help in the future, really. He said he didn't do it. So you see why it's difficult. She is saying that he turned around and smacked me and he is saying that he didn't do it—didn't touch her. I kind of think that he probably did it, he just wants to get out of here [out of the mediation room], but I think that, personally, he probably didn't even hit her hard, just hit her like this [lightly]. And you know she was like, "he hit me closed hand," and he, actually, I think he said he did hit her, like, just like this [hitting lightly].

What constitutes sexual harassment? How does one categorize a dispute such as this one: as "harassment," as "assault," as a "fight," or as an example of "kids being kids"? When should mediators interject their "opinions"? Are students permitted to raise issues of sexuality and abuse? In the following examples, as in the previous one, students were at a loss for how to proceed with mediations that were certainly, as were most mediations, complex, entailing issues that were systemic, cultural, economic, and sexual. The disparity between the training and the reality reflected, not so much the shortcomings of the training, but the grand complexity of student disputes. The examples also point out the extent to which conflict resolution is based on a behaviorist model of conflict that aims to change the student, and not to address the context of the disagreement—the issues of poverty, race, and sexuality that are so often evoked, but not specifically addressed, in mediations.

In one mediation, a fight between two ninth grade African-American boys was discussed. During the free breakfast program at school, two students, from very poor families, Sam and John fought over a donut. John had tried to take Sam's donut and Sam had come close to striking John. In the mediation, the students refused to not fight. They only relented when they were threatened by the adult mediators with being sent to the city alternative school for students with "behavioral problems." Dennis Brossard was one of the adult mediators in the room, the other was Jane Harding. On this particular day, an available student mediator could not be found.

During the mediation, Dennis Brossard tried to get Sam to say that he could visualize a different way of acting, but Sam insisted that he could not have acted differently—that he had to fight. "If I could have acted differently, I would have done that," he said. "I was hungry." The fact that he was apparently hungry was not addressed further in the mediation. Sam insisted that he had to fight because John had "played" [teased and insulted] him. Dennis Brossard said, "You know the administration will send you to [the alternative school] if you continue this way." Sam looked up, became a bit agitated, but also tried to show no reaction, though he, like most students, obviously feared the alternative school.

Ultimately, Dennis Brossard adopted behaviorist models to achieve his goal: conflict was defined as an individual matter—related to the student's "locus of control"—and punishment with being sent to the alternative school was threatened.

Dennis Brossard turned to Jane Harding and asked her, "Where is Sam's locus of control?"

Harding said; "He has external motivation. His locus of control is external. He won't be played, that's all he knows, and he'll go down if he has to." She asked Sam, "Is it worth it to you, first to go to [the alternative school], then, probably, Homebound [a program that restricts the student to his or her house], then—what, jail?" Sam did not respond.

Jane Harding asked both the boys, "Do you feel like the issue is squashed [over] between you two?"

John said, "Yes."

Sam said, "No. If he [gets] smart it won't. If he plays me."

Jane asked Sam, "How are you going to respond if he's playing you?"

Sam said, "We are going to get into a fight."

So she told Sam, "You are going to end up in [the alternative school]."

Suddenly, Sam sat up a bit and said, "I can sit down and ignore it." Ultimately, though, the boys would not agree to not fight. At the end of the mediation they would not shake hands. The mediators saw the issue as a matter of "mismanaged behavior," but Sam understood it as a matter of defending his only meal. Several months later, Sam was placed in the alternative afternoon school program, which was, for students like Sam, a stepping stone to the alternative school.

In another instance, Dan, an African-American boy, and Mike, a White boy, went to mediation. They had fought the year before and one had broken the other's collar bone. In the mediation, it came out that Mike didn't like Dan "looking at" Mike's seven-year-old sister. Also, Mike complained that Dan called him insulting names. Dan turned to Mike and said that he wasn't the only person doing so. "I'm with a group of 18 to 20 people. I'm not the only one calling you 'bitch.'" The student mediator wanted to know, "Can you change your behavior in any way," ignoring for the moment the fact that "bitch" (a way of calling a boy homosexual) was used and that Dan was quite possibly a member of a gang. When an announcement came over the loud speaker, interrupting the mediation, the two boys took the opportunity to leave the room suddenly, in opposite directions, before signing the agreement not to fight again.

Other disputes that entailed complexities of poverty, race and sexuality included disputes between two African-American girls over a boy. The boy was the boyfriend of one of the girls and the lover of the other. In an interview following the mediation, the student mediator said he thought it was "funny" that two girls fought over a boy and that he wanted to get the girls to recognize how "stupid" it was. This was also an example of a White mediator failing to understand the cultural context of a conflict issue involving African Americans. In another case, an African-American girl who had gone to mediation explained that she and a White girl had fought in gym class. According to the African-American girl, the two didn't get along because the White girl looked down on her because she was Black. In another case, a fight in gym class was started when a White girl accidentally spilled water on an African-American girl and the African-American girl yelled in response, "I hate White bitches!" In all these disputes and others, issues involving sexuality, race, gangs (or at the very least, groups of friends), and perhaps racist and homophobic name-calling were raised, but not explicitly addressed, in the mediations.

In general, the training for the peer mediation program defined conflict according to personal and individual differences—differences that could be overcome through techniques of reflective listening, behavior modification techniques, and low-level counseling that would create understandings between people. In mediations, student mediators and adult mediators urged disputants to visualize different manners of acting in an effort to change their behaviors. A behaviorist model of conflict, combined with a philosophy of democratic humanism—based on unity, the importance of seeing from another's viewpoint, and respect for others—undergirded the training and had a lasting effect on student mediators and the philosophy of the program.

Unfortunately, many disputes entailed more serious issues than "individual" or "personal" differences. Throughout the year, forty-four students went through mediation more than once. Why were there such persistent problems? During one day, I sat through two mediations involving the same person with a different disputant each time. One student, whose father had died during the year, had gone to mediation eight times. In all these mediations, issues of conflict that arose due to discrimination, hostilities associated with sexuality and gender, depression, self-hatred, and problems associated with poverty, were left unspoken.

WORKING THE SYSTEM:
THE BENEFITS OF PEER MEDIATION

I think mediation is particularly good for the kids who are mediators because it puts them in a practice mode of carrying out the things they've learned where there's a lot of secondary learning going on that they can apply to their own life.

—Todd Jenks, Brandon school psychologist

In spite of the disparity between what mediators learn and what they face in mediations, the mediation training is still somewhat valuable. The problem is that those who have disputes do not take part in the training. Those who are mediated do not learn how to resolve conflicts, nor do they benefit from the résumé booster aspect of being a mediator. Being a mediator is highly valued in the school, and no doubt to some extent by employees and college admission personnel; being mediated is not. In the previous quotation, the school psychologist made evident the importance of the "secondary learning" (the learning that the mediators do) that takes place during the mediation process. The benefits that mediators gain from the program—from being trained, being certified, and conducting mediations—is, in many ways, the primary focus and purpose of the peer mediation program. The mediation training teaches students some important skills and ideas about conflict resolution, but to some extent it is teaching the wrong people.

The reason a training session for new mediators can be only twenty-two hours long is that the students who do volunteer already possess some conflict resolution skills. In interviews, student mediators expressed their bewilderment regarding school fights; they, in fact, never fought. The question, then, is why not teach the disputants what the mediators learn, with an additional focus on the cultural, structural and economic bases of conflict?

In an article, Louis Georgianna (1996, p. 5), the district coordinator of the peer mediation program, explained the benefits of the program. While he noted figures collected by the school demonstrating the overall success of the program in resolving conflicts, much of the focus was on the mediators themselves. He wrote:

> The role of the student mediator is one of tremendous personal responsibility. It provides a unique learning environment for the student mediator as well as the disputants while providing direct services to the school community. Several student mediators have commented on the impact that mediation sessions have had upon their perceptions of the world. This learning situation allows students to function in adult roles, learn excellent skills, and contribute significantly to their whole school environment while under the supervision of caring and concerned mentors. The student mediators learn the benefits of volunteering and providing a service that encourages their peers to problem solve constructively. In addition, each trained mediator learns the power of effective listening and the important role this serves in relating to and resolving problems with others.

He noted, too, that student mediators learn to arrange their schedules appropriately, to be available for mediation, and to be spokespeople for presenting their accomplishments and the program to other schools, parent associations, and the local university. In interviews, most student mediators mentioned as a benefit of the program their own development and the skills that they gained that could be used in their own lives with their families and friends. One student noted:

> I think [the mediation training] taught me a lot about not only mediation, but things about myself and how other people react to each other and behave. I thought it was really neat to learn all that stuff because there were some things

that I really didn't know, but now I can relate to other people. And my friendships are better now because I can talk to people and help them through their
problems. I learned how not to offend people with things I say and with my body
language . . . it will sort of help me out relationship-wise with friends. I know
how to talk with people now and not to get into business that I'm not supposed
to be getting into.

Another student explained, as well, that the training foremost would
help him in his own life. When asked about the training in general, he
responded:

About the training? It made me think a lot about arguing with my mother and my
brother. It made me stop and think, maybe think of how I'll word something and
how to be a lot more neutral instead of pointing fingers. I haven't gotten into
mediation. I hope that when it comes I'll be prepared. It's really helpful. I
haven't even really talked to anybody that's been to mediation because lots of us,
most of my friends think fighting people is not worth it.

Like most of the clubs and extracurricular activities in the school, the
peer mediation program was developed as a privileged and honored
school activity. It was a privilege to be on the team; likewise, privileged
students participated in the program. Peer mediation, then, while a successful program in addressing some conflicts in school, is also one of the
many clubs available to students with aspirations for college and professional occupations. When student mediators introduced themselves during
the first day of training, several mentioned that they had joined the mediation team partly because it looked good on their résumés. Overall, discussions of the benefits of the mediation program by students and adult
coordinators were multilayered, describing, sometimes simultaneously,
the benefits for disputants, the benefits for student mediators, and the program's attachment to school clubs. One student, when asked why he
decided to become a mediator, responded:

Because I was already in Peer Leadership [another extracurricular activity] and I
really liked it. I was even thinking about being a teacher. At the beginning of my
freshman year they had an orientation and a list of all the clubs. I really wanted
to do the mediation program and was looking forward to it because it can really
help me in the future.

Whether a student becomes a peer mediator because of a concern for
school conflicts or because of the program's benefits for him or herself

depends on the student, but most rightly noted the benefits it would provide them. Meanwhile, students also noted their concern for conflict in the school; they and the adult coordinators hoped and worked to make the program effective in reducing conflicts. But all participants involved, especially the students, viewed the mediation program as they would most extracurricular activities in the school—as an activity that could provide them with valued experiences.

That poor, White, and African-American students did not generally participate in the peer mediation program as mediators does not necessarily mean that they did not want to or that the school did not want them to join. Rather it reflected a schoolwide problem: almost everything in the school was divided along socioeconomic and racial lines. Ultimately, White students from professional and secure families worked the school system to their benefit by joining the appropriate clubs—the National Honor Society, the Yearbook Club, the Peer Mediation Program—while many poor White and African-American students did not.

While there were some poor African-American and White students at Brandon High School with ambitions for college, there were many who did not have such ambitions, and those who did wish to attend college often did not "work the system" in the way that those from middle-class and professional backgrounds did. For the African-American students, joining the peer mediation team was viewed, as one of them explained, "as sissy." Later, she referred to it as "being White, you know, Oreo." Researchers, such as Signithia Fordham (1996), are right to recognize how Black students sometimes avoid White dominated clubs and teams in fear of being perceived by their peers as "acting White." In addition, the mediation team, and perhaps other kinds of student clubs and organizations, did not appeal to students who were poor and outside the mainstream culture of the school. The focus on individual difference that undergirded the peer mediation program could not possibly engage youth whose complex conflicts existed all around them—in their neighborhoods, in their families, and in their relations with adults, friends, and the opposite sex.

RECOMMENDATIONS

Definitions of conflict need to be more inclusive of the global urgencies that arise when one considers the patterns that develop around peer mediation—specifically, that so many girls, people of color, and poorer students go to mediation at Brandon and other schools, and that the students who train as mediators in the mediation program, as in most extracurricular activities, are generally the most active and high-achieving students. Peer mediation programs need to prepare student mediators to address complex conflicts that arise due to systemic and cultural violence associated with deep prejudices and injustices in our society. Not engaging with the realities of, for example, homophobia makes the peer mediation program ineffective in many instances. For example, the focus on remaining neutral and "taking the sting out of words" must be reconsidered. While it is important that student and adult mediators remain consistent with all people, that they be understanding and open-minded, they must also name injustices and teach students the difference between, for example, sexual harassment and flirting. With regard to injustices, neutrality is beside the point; language should be at the center of the mediation process.

It is impossible to say that mediation is not the time or the place to deal with complex issues regarding sexuality, class, gangs, and race, since it is during mediations that these issues most often arise. Unfortunately, in mediations, conflict is constructed in psychological terms of individual difference, and hence, behaviorist models of conflict resolution are recommended and followed. In their place, however, a more global (perhaps sociological) model might enable mediators to recognize that conflict is sometimes best addressed through advocacy, by taking seriously people's words and stories and helping them through a conflict, not as neutral mediators, but as strong advocates and friends. Words must be tended to, especially when they may be deeply insulting—for example, calling a student who is in the special education program an "idiot"—as happened one time—is more than just a sting. In general, by their example, the trainers of the peer mediation team referred to prejudice and harassment but did not engage it seriously. In interviews, students, too, reiterated that "names" were not an issue. In short, then, though well prepared for "small, resolvable problems," student mediators were not prepared for the more complex issues that often came to the mediation table.

Peer mediation programs must attract students from low socioeconomic families of all races to the mediation team. This will benefit both those students and the mediation program. The students will acquire the résumé booster benefits of the program and may learn something important about conflict and their own lives during the mediation training and process. The peer mediation program would benefit, as well, from having the perspectives and energies of students whose lives are often full of the complicated cultural issues that the program should aim to address.

Ultimately, these two recommendations—that student mediators be better prepared for the complex cultural issues that arise in mediations and that the mediation program attract as team members students of low socio-economic status—complement one another. By bringing complexity to the process, the program will attract those students whose problems are complex. And by bringing students whose problems are complicated to the program, the program introduces "experts" in such conflicts to the team. While some would feel that the peer mediation program should only focus its attention on minor disputes in the school (which can nevertheless escalate), this underestimates the capabilities of both the program and of the students, thus shortchanging a valued, and ultimately effective, form of conflict resolution.

REFERENCES

Apter, S., & Goldstein, A. (1986). *Youth violence: program and prospects*. New York: Pergamon Press.

Bey, T. M. (1996). *Making school a place of peace*. Thousand Oaks, CA: Corwin Press.

Bogdan, R., & Biklen S. K. (1998). *Qualitative research in education: An introduction to theory and practice*. Boston: Allyn & Bacon.

Canada, G. (1995). *Fist stick knife gun*. Boston: Beacon Press.

Crary, D. R. (1992). Community benefits from mediation: A test of the "peace virus" hypothesis. *Mediation Quarterly, 9*, 241–252.

Erickson, F. (1973). What makes school ethnography "ethnographic"? *Anthropology and Education Quarterly, 4*(2), 10–19.

Fetterman, D. (1988). Ethnographic educational evaluation. In D. Fetterman (Ed.), *Qualitative approaches to evaluation in education*. New York: Praeger.

Fisher, R., & Ury, W. (1981). *Getting to yes: Negotiating agreement without giving in*. Boston: Houghton Mifflin.

Fordham, S. (1996). *Blacked out: Dilemmas of race, identity, and success at Capital High*. Chicago: University of Chicago Press.

Georgianna, L. (1996). The Brandon High School Mediation Team. *Journal of the School Administrators Association of New York State, 27*(1), 4–6.

Giroux, H. (1996). *Fugitive cultures: Race, violence, and youth*. New York: Routledge.

Goldstein, A., Harootunian, B., & Conoley, J. C. (1994). *Student aggression: Prevention, management, and replacement training*. New York: Guilford Press.

Harrington, C. B., & Merry, S. E. (1988). Ideological production: The making of community mediation. *Law and Society Review, 22,* 10–16.

Johnson, D. W. & Johnson, R. (1995a). Teaching students to be peacemakers: Results of five years of research. *Peace and Conflict: Journal of Peace Psychology, 1*(94), 417–438.

Johnson, D. W., & Johnson, R. (1995b). Why violence prevention programs don't work—And what does. *Educational Leadership, 52*(5), 63–68.

Johnson, D. W., Johnson, R., Dudley, B., Ward, M., & Magnuson, D. (1995). The impact of peer mediation training on the management of school and home conflicts. *American Educational Research Journal, 32*(4), 829–844.

Katz, J. (1995). Reconstructing masculinity in the locker room: The mentors in violence prevention project. *Harvard Educational Review, 65*(2), 163–174.

Levinson, B., & Holland, D. (1996). The cultural production of the educated person: An introduction. In B. Levinson, D. Foley, & D. Holland, (Eds.), *The cultural production of the educated person: Critical ethnographies of schooling and local practice.* Albany: State University of New York Press.

Lincoln, Y. (1988). Do inquiry paradigms imply inquiry methodologies? In D. Fetterman, (Ed.), *Qualitative approaches to evaluation in education.* New York: Praeger.

Payne, D. A. (1994). *Designing educational project and program evaluations: A practical overview based on research and experience.* Boston: Kluwer Academic.

Reiss, A. J., & Roth, J. A. (1993). *Understanding and preventing violence.* Washington, DC: National Academy Press.

Shook, V., & Milner, N. (1993). What mediation training says—Or doesn't say— About the ideology and culture of North American community justice programs. In S. Engle, & N. Milner, (Eds.), *The possibility of popular justice: A case study of community mediation in the United States.* Ann Arbor: University of Michigan Press.

Soriano, M., Soriano, F. I., & Jimenez, E. (1994). School violence among culturally diverse populations: sociocultural and institutional considerations. *School Psychology Review, 23*(2), 216–235.

Spindler, G. (Ed.). (1997). *Education and Cultural Process: Anthropological Approaches.* Prospect Heights, IL: Waveland.

Stein, N. (1995). Sexual harassment in school: The public performance of gendered violence. *Harvard Educational Review, 65*(2), 145–188.

Stevahn, L., Johnson, D. W., & O'Coin, I. (1996). Effects on high school students of integrating conflict resolution and peer mediation training into an academic unit. *Mediation Quarterly, 14*(1), 21–36.

Van Slyck, M., & Stern, M. (1991). Conflict resolution in educational settings: Assessing the impact of peer mediation programs. In K. Duffy, J. Grosch, & P. Olczak, (Eds.), *Community mediation: A handbook for practitioners and researchers*. New York: Guilford Press.

Webster, D. (1993). The unconvincing case for school-based conflict resolution programs for adolescents. *Health Affairs,* pp. 127–141.

10

Peer Mediation:
An Examination
of a School District's
Training Program for Educators

Rebecca Stevens

University of South Carolina Spartanburg

INTRODUCTION

Community problems that infiltrate the schools as violence particularly concern teachers, administrators, and other school staff. In Northeast City, where the research reported here was conducted, youth gangs engage in cross-town rivalries, gun violence among youths has increased, and many youths in the city's least affluent sections believe that schooling cannot improve their future job prospects. Multipart violence prevention efforts in the schools span all grade levels, starting with the youngest students. Programs include ones to enhance self-esteem, provide academic enrichment, and offer mentoring. Peer mediation is another widely used program.

School-based peer mediation programs depend upon the involvement of adults to serve as program coordinators, provide ongoing support for students' skills development, refer students to mediation, and practice mediation skills themselves. Consequently, in addition to mediation training programs for students, the Northeast City school district also provides programs for school teachers, administrators, and staff.

Mediation training for school teachers, administrators, and staff may be a critical link between the vision and the reality of a successful, school-based peer mediation program. When adult staff have mediation skills, they can infuse them into their daily practice with their colleagues and with students, and thus model the interpersonal skills and formal strategies needed for resolving conflicts constructively. This can impact the school's culture. In addition, the teachers and staff can provide support and guidance to individual students. With this support, students can fulfill the potential of the peer mediation program for solving their own conflicts, writing agreements, and seeing to the enforcement of them in as autonomous a manner as possible. Thus, youth can be assisted in becoming more responsible and independent.

However, as the chapter points out, this rationale for training school personnel in peer mediation is problematic. Teachers who have trained as mediators often want to practice their skills in the classroom. Thus, they assume the task of mediating students' disputes themselves, rather than referring those disputes to peer mediation. If a school adopts peer mediation as a policy, then teacher mediation in the classroom may be inappropriate because it undermines the policy. To prevent that, adult supporters need, not only to learn the steps used in peer mediation so that they may serve as facilitators in mediations, but also to receive training and practice for their roles as facilitators, and as mentors of student mediators.

My strategy in this study was to attend the mediation training program sessions provided for teachers and other school personnel, to interview the trainer, and then to interview a small sample of the school staff who attended the training to find out what they had learned and how they were using it in daily practice with students as well as in the peer mediation program. The research was formulated as part of a broader study of peer mediation in the city's high schools recounted elsewhere in this volume by Ronnie Casella (chap. 9) and Kim Williams (chap. 11). This research was designed to listen to the concerns and experiences of various adults who work daily with students and who had trained in peer mediation.

The perspectives of the adults in a school are important because they can teach students the skills of mediation and they can foster an environment that embodies the ideals of peer mediation. Interviewing these educators was important, also, because their views add valuable insights to the conceptualization of peer mediation in schools. There has to be a partnership between those within and those outside the public schools to make the most of what peer mediation has to offer students, schools, and the community. The close look at peer mediation provided by the several studies described in this book can help in developing appropriate youth violence intervention and prevention programs in communities as well as schools.

There are two parts to my study. One explores details of the training provided to teachers and other school professionals. For this, I participated in the training program and conducted follow up interviews with the trainer. The other examines what four educators told me they did with their training. This two-pronged research design allowed me to get an impression of the hopes, goals, and expectations of all involved.

THE TRAINING PROGRAM

Two types of sessions were offered to educators in the school district I studied. One type was the basic mediation skills training, which was similar to the peer mediation training provided to students. The other was a "turnkey" training for educators who had already received the first training session and wanted to be more involved in the ongoing support and refresher training provided to the students. This study examines only the basic mediation skills training.

The basic mediation training I observed took place the last full week of the summer. I interviewed Tracy Moody, the trainer, two months later. This time lapse allowed me to review my transcripts of the training and formulate research questions.

Tracy Moody had been training students and teachers in peer mediation for over ten years. Until six months prior to this training, she had been working with Fair Play, Inc., a community mediation agency, but she left there to join a small group of consultants. Despite the change, she still used the training manual from Fair Play, Inc., in her workshop.

The spring before the training was to take place, Tracy distributed flyers advertising the training. These flyers were given either to building peer mediation coordinators, so they might continue building schoolwide support, or to a contact person, usually the principal, at a school that had indicated an interest in starting a peer mediation program. Ninety educators signed up for the training. To keep the groups to less than thirty people each, two training sessions were run in August, after which thirty-five people remained on the waiting list for training at another time. Only 30 percent of those who attended the training sessions were teachers. (Mediation training had been available for six years to teachers in the district, which may explain the low proportion of teachers attending these sessions.) Fifty-four percent were teaching assistants. There were two nurses and one psychologist, library assistant, secretary, health aide, hall monitor, and counselor.

Despite the school district's support for peer mediation programs, not every school had such a program. However, the school district had a long-term contract with Tracy Moody to provide mediation training until all district schools had established a peer mediation program. At the time I interviewed her, Tracy expected this contract to be in place for a few more years.

As a participant observer, I looked at how the staff were trained, what knowledge and skills they were expected to learn, and what they were being trained to do. The training program was conducted all day for five days. Participants learned the terms of mediation and the causes of conflict. They learned the sequence of steps in mediation. At different points throughout the week, participants were given time in small groups to practice the mediation steps. The groups were arranged so that those from the same school, same academic area, or same role in schools were grouped together.

I asked Tracy, the workshop facilitator, about the training: "What are your approaches to conducting the training as a learning experience for the participants?" She responded that because it was a "training," she did not cover a lot of theory in the week:

> I start out with the vocabulary, teaching what we mean by these things, what we mean by the values and also building the ground work for the elements of conflict. Things they have to understand. And there's a table to add questions about relationships, assumptions, and perceptions, and that's the base. And then I teach the flow of mediation, the steps.

> Then, after I teach the flow of mediation, I teach step by step. First, is the opening statement so they work on that. Next, is: "You're going to have to ask questions, can we work on that?" Then, the listening. They [learn] piece by piece and then, before they do a form of mediation, they practice just the beginning of it so they don't have to get a hold of everything at once. They can focus on just the beginning of it. I guess the idea is they get it in bits and try to experience the steps of mediation.

From this description and my own observation of the week's activities, it was clear that most time was spent on how to conduct a mediation. However, Tracy did address ways to facilitate a mediation. She told me that there are two areas of difficulty for many educators involved with peer mediation programs. First, they want to give advice:

I think [educators] have a harder time not getting involved in giving advice. They have an idea what the solution should be so they steer it that way. There might be another solution brought up and they don't pay enough attention to it because it's not their idea of a solution.

Second, and critical to the ideals of youth peer mediation, is that educators have trouble trusting that a student can be a mediator. Tracy addressed the issue of trust in the training:

The thing is because when they are learning to do it the first couple [of] times they're nervous and go through that kind of process but it's hard to think of a sixth grader, or a seventh grader being able to do it. . . . I give them more techniques for asking questions like "What would you ask a disputant to do about this?" And [I] give them those kind of buzzwords, buzz questions on handling the situation.

Peer mediation is a strategy to get disputants to change their behavior towards another individual—the other disputant. As Tracy Moody told me:

If the root [to a conflict] is you and I have a personal problem in something you have done or something that has offended you . . . then the way I react to that, because I am programmed to react that way, to hurt you, to be violent, then mediation may be a way of dealing with that.

Peer mediation addresses specific issues between disputants. Any agreement reached concerns only the interactions between the disputants and does not intend to alter global behavior and reactions. However, as Moody pointed out:

Community violence challenges this mediation model of resolving conflicts. Many violence issues that come into the school come in from the community, and they may involve large groups of youths. These groups may not be just the students directly involved in confrontations but their network of friends.

As Ronnie Casella (in chap. 9 of this volume) makes clear, peer mediation programs do not address the broader issues students bring into the classroom from the community. They do not address issues of gender, race, and social class that often underlie eruptions of violence between youths. Tracy Moody described how she dealt obliquely with such issues as she trained student mediators:

> "What are you going to tell people when they ask you about this?" That has to be standard in school mediation. They will be asked about that and that means you have to talk about the whole idea of getting gangs of people and groups of kids—all my friends don't like all your friends—they have to agree together. Even if they agree to disagree and to stay away from each other, they have to agree together. "What are you going to tell people when you leave here? What are you going to say?" And, sometimes, "Who are you going to say it to?" But that's an important part of the agreement.

Tracy realized the limitations of this approach when she said that there were other ways of dealing with youth violence than through mediation. One of these, she said, was to "look at what's going on at the root of it." However, she did not elaborate on how to do that.

Instead, she offered another option, based upon her own education in conflict resolution as a one-on-one interaction, simple conflict resolution education at the elementary level:

> I think lots of time when we think of violence in the schools you're thinking about some of the stuff that's coming in from the outside and the mediation program is not going to stop. There have to be other avenues. That's why I believe so much in doing the early elementary conflict resolution education which isn't just mediation.

Last, Tracy explained that she and the district's staff development administrator met periodically with all the peer mediation coordinators from the schools. These meetings were intended to help solve any problems and difficulties peer mediation programs were having.

INTERVIEWS WITH TRAINEES

I went into the interview sessions wanting to find out from the educators what they did after they got back to their sites with the information they had learned. I interviewed four people. Three (Tamara Simpson, Amy Riemer, and Philip Melitta) had attended one of the weeks of basic mediation training, and one (Charlotte Meadows) had attended the turnkey training. The interviews were conducted two to three months after the basic mediation training session and one month after the turnkey training.

The four educators differed from each other in significant ways, reflecting the different jobs of those attending the mediation training. Three people whom I interviewed were support staff. Only one person was a classroom teacher, and he taught at Garfield alternative school, where students might be in and out of the program in as little as one marking period. For all four, peer mediation was a small part of their practice, and each was one of a number of adults involved in supporting the mediation program in a school. Each of these adults had a different idea of what peer mediation was and what it could offer students and the school community. The programs at each school were at different places in their development, the number of years they had been running, and the degree to which they had been institutionalized.

Tamara Simpson, Librarian Assistant

Tamara Simpson was a librarian assistant at Brandon High School. She had begun this job the previous school year (but had been in the building for less than a calendar year when I interviewed her). She had no training in education or teaching. As a librarian assistant, she assisted "students and teachers in whatever they need. Mostly research needs, but also the daily maintenance of the library, some clerical-type work." Tamara was also the multicultural trainer at the high school. This position developed from her involvement with a district program with different activities in each school. When I interviewed her, Tamara was working on "having community dialogues and trying to talk about some of the issues that are in our community and try to figure out how to stop them from filtering in[to] the building." Violence was of particular concern. The previous year, Tamara had participated in the Black History Month activities at the school, and she hoped to do so again. She got involved with the peer mediation program by approaching Len, the previous program coordinator. He told her about the summer training, so she signed up. She got involved because, she said, "I consider one of the gifts that I have and something that I really like in my job is my ability to interact with students."

The peer mediation program at Brandon had existed for several years. The mediation team was strong, and several adults served as supervisors. According to Tamara the conflicts that came to mediation were for the most part "he said she said" conflicts. Tamara said that the people who came to mediation wanted to solve their problems, so the issues were not too complex or broad in scope. Tamara saw her role in the peer mediation program as serving as a supervisor of the mediations carried out by the students.

> I truly believe that since it's called the peer mediation program that the effectiveness [is] of having your peers trying to come to a solution without necessarily having authority figures involved. If that can happen that's fine. For the most part, people take what's going on in mediation seriously because the other consequence is going back to the administration. I believe in empowering all of our students. That's very important. I worked for mediators as well as mediatees or whatever the people that are talking to each other are called. I believe that with most roles in the school that when students are able to do them our job is simply to back up. Be a supervisor.

Tamara perceived peer mediation to be about improving students' ability to communicate with one another. When she described her role as "simply to back up," I was struck by the similarity between that role and the one played by librarians, whose task it is to assist their clients to carry out their own agendas. Her perspective fitted well with that of the trainer whose workshop she had attended.

Charlotte Meadows, Special Education Teaching Assistant

Charlotte Meadows was a teaching assistant in a special education class of learning disabled students. She had no formal training in education or teaching, but she had a strong background in mediation. Her undergraduate major was Peace and Conflict Studies, and she had helped set up a mediation program at her college. When she interviewed for a teaching assistant job in Northeast City she mentioned her mediation background, which proved appealing.

When she arrived at Broadbent High School she introduced herself to Mr. Brook, the coordinator of the Safe Schools Program and the peer mediation program. At the time, Mr. Brook had no training in mediation. He merely performed the administrative functions and organized the schedules for peer mediation. Thus, Charlotte was assigned the task of conducting the refresher sessions at the weekly peer mediation meetings. There were about thirty students in the school who were trained as mediators, and attended weekly team meetings.

Charlotte said that many adults in the building who had attended the mediation training—and had received a stipend for doing so—did not participate in the school's mediation program. This was a problem that she was addressing through personal contacts:

> I have been trying to make personal contacts with all of them, saying I am here, we are having a mediation training, please come. But if they are not committed, you know, that is not something we can really force upon them. I guess we just really need to stress that when we choose adults or ask adults to be a part of this that we are asking people who have the flexibility and who are going to be committed to be a part of mediation.

According to Charlotte, many teachers in her school used specific mediation skills with their students and colleagues. They used active listening, strove to understand what the issues were in any dispute, and focused on making choices. Her concern was that teachers were more inclined to infuse the peer mediation skills into their own practice than to support the student peer mediation program. (Tamara had spoken to me of the importance of having the school staff infuse the ideals and practices of peer mediation into their daily practice, which was what she did with her training. She had not perceived any danger to the student peer mediation program from her doing so.)

However, Charlotte's comment raises several issues. What is the purpose of peer mediation? Is it to maintain a safe, calm environment in a school? If so, is it the best way to do that? Might safety and calm be better achieved by adults, rather than students, conducting mediations—or, by adults using the specific skills needed for mediation as part of their teaching repertoire? Or, might safety and calm not be more easily obtained by metal detectors, and corridor patrols than by peer mediations?

If peer mediation is not primarily to maintain a safe, calm environment in a school, but to teach students a way to settle their own disputes without adult intervention, is this the best way to teach them that? For instance, if the skills of negotiation, which are taught to mediators, are crucial for resolving conflicts, then shouldn't all students learn them? Why not teach negotiation skills directly to every child rather than to a few who have been identified as potential mediators? These and other questions remain to be considered.

Amy Riemer, School Counselor

Amy Riemer was the school counselor at Garfield, the alternative school in Northeast City for students found in possession of a weapon on school property. Amy's responsibilities at Garfield included making students' class schedules, record keeping, keeping track of the master schedules of all the programs operating within the school, making sure students took the Scholastic Aptitude Tests (SATs) and their final exams, and posting their credits. Amy also monitored students' transition to and from Garfield and was the liaison between Garfield and the other district schools. She also ran the career-planning program.

Counseling was a part of the Garfield program for students, and Amy located the mediation program within this counseling component. The mediation program at Garfield was not a peer mediation program because the students at the school were not trained to be mediators and they were not invited to mediate conflicts. Amy explained the reasons for this. First, the student population was very small, so it would be difficult to maintain the critical component of confidentiality. Second, students traveled in and out of the school every academic quarter. With such a transient population, it was impossible to train a cohort of students who would be able to serve the student population for any length of time. Amy planned to address the lack of student mediators by getting a copy of the Northeast City School District master list of peer mediators. This would allow her to identify any incoming students who had already received the training.

Students at Garfield were not aggressive, according to Amy. "They are really low social skills kids, not aggressive kids." She perceived that the students rarely had conflicts with each other; they had "conflicts with life . . . conflicts with rules."

> Many of the conflicts they incur or find themselves involved in are not mediat-
> able, so I think that we have caught pretty much the conflicts with each other. We
> don't have fights typically. Part of the main focus of this program, from my point
> of view, is to teach the kids that it is okay to go to adults for help because what
> got the kids here is that they are self sufficient in many aspects of their lives and
> therefore if they need that knife to get home from school, they don't see break-
> ing the rule as important. They need to learn how to identify with some societal
> rules, but also how to seek help when they are not in the same mold as every-
> body for whom the rule was decided.

Amy attended the August training program to receive the formal mediation training she needed to become a certified mediator. Prior to this training session she had attended Northeast University's school counselor program and district staff development programs. "From my work there, I did informal peer mediation since I've been here which is since the program opened in '94," Amy said. "What I did not have was actually the certification to say . . . [I] had the formalized training that the district offers."

Now, with the students, she could conduct formal mediation sessions that were more structured. Only she and the math teacher, whom I also interviewed, had received the district's mediation training. Informing the students and teachers about the mediation program at the school had been slowed down because the principal had been out on sick leave from September till November, so the school population knew about peer mediation only "in a general sense."

As of the end of November, only one student's conflict had been mediated, another mediation was scheduled, and one was pending. At the school, there was a cooling-off period between the time a conflict was referred to mediation and when the mediation actually occurred. This gave Amy time to meet with each student, explain mediation, and get everyone's agreement to participate:

> As the coordinator, I need to go through their rights and responsibilities, what this means, give them some information and make them aware of it and certainly to wait for their agreement.

Spotty attendance then became a complicator in having a mediation take place at Garfield:

> She [a student disputant who was going to go to mediation] was very willing but she was coming in real sporadically, and the day she came the other party wasn't here. Now, one of the other girls has completely dropped out of school and she's probably going to be dropped. So, sometimes attendance will take care of a lot of situations, unfortunately.

I asked Amy what she hoped students would learn from the mediation program. She replied:

> To generate their own solutions would be one hope. The other hope would be to learn how to stick to their word and the other hope would be to be aware, and I guess maybe this is the first thing, aware of what mediation has to offer as a vehicle for solving problems and to feel comfortable with using that process.

Amy's hopes reflected her belief that students at Garfield needed guidance from adults in how to resolve problems without resorting to violence and in how to keep to their agreements. She saw mediation as a way for the adults in the school to teach students these new skills.

Philip Melitta, Teacher

Philip Melitta had been teaching math at Garfield for three years, since the school was first set up. He taught all of the math classes.

> I teach a lot of different things. I teach all the mathematics in this building, which means it's seventh through twelfth grade. . . . I'm doing preparations for eight different courses.

Prior to going to Garfield, he taught through the district's homebound instruction program. He was a certified teacher, working on his master's degree. In addition to his daytime teaching, he taught after-school programs and was a trained mediator.

Philip became involved with mediation for two reasons, one personal and professional, the other pedagogical/instructional. Personally and professionally,

> I chose to do [so] because I thought it would be beneficial to me as a teacher. I want to be the best teacher I can overall, and first of all, I thought it would make me be better with my students, and second of all, I think it looks great on a résumé.

Philip's comment about his résumé echoes similar comments made to Ronnie Casella (as reported in chap. 9 of this volume), by student mediators about the importance of their being a peer mediator for their college applications.

The pedagogical/instructional reason given by Philip had to do with his students. Mediation would be an additional way to teach students:

> Dealing with our populations, we're an alternative education [and] conflict happened from day one. So conflict is something that has occurred since this program's been around. We've always dealt with it through adults' perspective. Adults pretty much said this is what is right and what is wrong. What the mediation offers is an opportunity for students to resolve their own conflicts with what knowledge they have.

So for Philip, mediation was a strategy or tool to make students more responsible for dealing with and resolving their conflicts. Even when the mediation session is facilitated by an adult, it is the disputing students who have to come to a mutually acceptable agreement. For him, that point was the essence of the program, and what was most valuable to the students.

As mentioned, Philip was one of two adults in the school trained as a mediator. Making the mediation program a part of the regular school program at Garfield had been difficult. He and Amy Riemer had to be trained. And then they had to inform the students and the teachers. There had been two mediations at the school by the time I talked with Philip. He described a mediation:

> I get the students to address how they feel about the situation. Once they say how they are feeling they have to obviously pretty much talk one at a time. Once you get the facts on the table, you try to dig as much as you can without actually putting words in their mouth. It's not my job to, even if I saw one of the students doing something, it's not my job to say, "You're lying. I saw you do this." It's my job to get them to say what they perceive. That's the most important thing, what they perceive to be the truth.

> Once each student hears each other's side of the story then I say: "Okay what can we do about this? Do you think there is something we can do?" So it's just coming up with different options. Teaching them survival skills, in the age where there is a lot of gun shootings going on—there are two people who [were] shot here yesterday right outside this school. It's not the safest thing and you have to ask these students at a young age: Do you have alternatives? Do you have to walk down that street that's not well lit? Can you make an alternative choice to take this route in life or do you have to fight? Do you think there is anything else you can do? You have to make the students think.

Philip repeatedly articulated a goal of the mediation, to give students the opportunity to generate their own solutions, to be creative, and responsible.

Philip pointed out that mediation is a conflict resolution strategy for specific conflicts involving specific disputants. Although some may think otherwise, he said, mediation is not intended to change a person's behavior in general:

The misconception, because some staff people say now that those two kids went to mediation they are going to be great in everybody else's class. I said "No. It has nothing to do with them acting up in your class or them swearing at you or this and that. It has to do between the two students." So that's another thing is it has to be reinforced amongst the staff that it's not behavior more or less in your classroom, it's a conflict between the two parties—three parties—and that's a totally different situation.

Thus, Philip perceived mediation as having limited influence on a student's overall behavior. On the other hand, he had found that learning the skills to supervise and support peer mediation had helped him improve his own practice of teaching, particularly classroom management, so that he was able to deescalate student conflicts that might previously have erupted into fights.

THEMES

I inquired about what the educators did with the information they had learned when they got back to their sites. Two themes emerged from these inquiries, both of which seem relevant for any school-based peer mediation program. Educators were taking on peer mediation skills in two ways. First, educators were operating as supporters for students in the formal peer mediation process. Second, these educators were absorbing the skills into their daily practice with students and colleagues, thus modeling the constructive conflict resolution and interpersonal interactions at the heart of peer mediation.

Support for the Formal Process of Peer Mediation

These interviews have raised questions concerning the extent to which peer mediation is conducted according to the formal process outlined in the training sessions. For example, Amy said that she had a background in counseling and had been doing mediation for years. She attended the August training to get the mediation certification. As a result, she felt she had obtained a certificate that said she was qualified to do what she had always done.

However, mediation is a formal process with steps to follow. The micro skills that are part of the process can be valuable in many situations. But until the disputants have been read the rules and procedures, until both open and closed questions have been used to get at the issues, and until solutions have been generated and an agreement written and signed, what is going on is problem solving or facilitating a discussion, not mediation. The question educators have to answer is: How important is it to students who are disputants that peer mediation be conducted to the letter, and not reformatted into an informal process?

At Garfield, the mediation program was run by Amy and Philip, both of whom had taken the training. Theirs was a mediation program run by faculty and staff, not a peer mediation program, since no students had been trained as mediators. The introduction of the program was in its initial stages; students and teachers knew a little about it. However, it was completely up to the teachers to refer the students to mediation, and so a great deal of responsibility for generating the number of mediations was on the shoulders of the teachers, as it is in many schools. If teachers have not all bought into the program, then mediation will not reach many students. Amy was not in the classrooms, so she could not refer students to mediation for disputes within the classroom.

Amy talked about very different reasons for having a mediation program at her school than the others mentioned. Tamara, for instance, said that a peer mediation program allows students to solve their own issues, it empowers them, gives them power and autonomy and independence from adults. But Amy said that her mediation program was to help kids learn to trust adults and come to adults when they had a conflict. These are different conceptualizations of peer mediation from which students may learn very different things.

Though an array of conflict resolution and self-esteem building programs were offered in the school system, there was no educator responsible for coordinating these efforts, and no K–12 curriculum to ensure that the general population of students in the city learned all the micro skills that are part of the peer mediation process.

The four adults I interviewed had varied perceptions of peer mediation. There are, I believe, both advantages and disadvantages to this. This irregularity of interpretation and understanding of peer mediation might be because the definitions and use have been adapted to fit each site, which could be an advantage. However, if peer mediation means something different at each school, and is practiced differently, then the continuity between schools, especially feeder and receiver schools, is lost. Can peer mediation be so many different things, and serve a variety of ends? Peer mediation is a formal structured process with a sequence of steps. The steps, infused informally or in a different sequence may be beneficial, but they become something other than peer mediation. The distinction should be made by trainer, adults, and students alike. The topic of school culture that embodies the skills and interpersonal relations of peer mediation is discussed in the next section.

Absorbing the Skills of Mediation into the School Culture

The second theme concerns the culture that evolves when adults in a school use the skills of peer mediation as part of their everyday interaction with students. Peer mediation had been introduced into the school district I studied several years earlier. The data I collected indicated that the district had begun a program to develop within school buildings a culture that embodied the ideals and practices of peer mediation. Staff development funds were available to nonclassroom educators to participate in the training sessions. It is commendable that the district and schools took action to foster a whole school approach to constructive conflict resolution by having the training available to all school staff. That allowed a wider range of adults to become involved in the formal peer mediation program. It also enabled more educators to infuse the skills of peer mediation into their daily practices with students and colleagues, thus cultivating a culture of prosocial interpersonal relations and constructive conflict resolution. Intentionally moving to a whole school approach as a model of conflict resolution education would be a reasonable evolution of the programs of the past years.

According to Charlotte, the teachers in her school used the mediation skills with students and colleagues. Tamara also emphasized the importance of school staff infusing the ideals and practices of peer mediation into their daily practice. She indicated that this was what she did with her training. Although Charlotte mentioned teachers using peer mediation skills with their colleagues, she did not elaborate on this. Yet, the training sessions had ostensibly been about peer mediation, and since the people attending were adults, the skills they had learned could have had positive consequences for their relationships with peers in the schools where they worked. Tensions in schools are often fostered by disagreements among the adults working there, even the adults working together in one classroom. Hence, training programs in peer mediation could help reduce disagreements among those employed in schools.

The educators I spoke with from Garfield school felt that there was a tremendous need to have more staff trained in mediation. They felt that the mediation program needed the support of teachers who were familiar with this model of conflict resolution education to support a school culture that was compatible with it. However, as educators in an alternative program to expulsion for weapons possession, they were hesitant to pass the control of the mediations to their students.

FUTURE RESEARCH AND CONCLUSION

More research needs to be done to understand how peer mediation gets implemented and how it is modified by those on-site so that it best serves their needs, yet still reflects the principles and practices of peer mediation. Another theme for a future research project is to explore what attracts educators to peer mediation training. Are the adult staff who attend limited to those who perceive themselves as having enough extra time or flexibility in their daily work schedule to take on this new program? Are most classroom teachers so overburdened that they cannot take on any new tasks or responsibilities including peer mediation? Is the presence of a diversity of school adults, like those in attendance at the two training sessions I studied, due to the fact that students with discipline and interpersonal problems get placed outside the classroom? There are many adults in a school who deal with disruptive students—those who supervise the in-school suspension, counselors, psychologists, social workers, and administrative interns to name a few. Which adults are personally, or professionally, attracted to peer mediation? Which adults can be most useful in facilitating the success of a peer mediation program, and why?

Tamara, Philip, Amy, and Charlotte were only four of a much larger number of educators in the Northeast City school district who had been trained in peer mediation. The goal of the training was to have school staff support a school based peer mediation program. The data collected from these four educators revealed that their use of the techniques they had learned took two forms: active support of the formal peer mediation process, and infusion of the ideals and practices of peer mediation into the educators' daily practice. Each was valuable, but each had a different impact on the students and on the schools where the educators worked.

11

What Derails Peer Mediation?

Kimberly M. Williams

State University of New York at Cortland

INTRODUCTION

Peer mediation is a popular strategy in many schools today. Although varied in its procedures and processes, peer mediation generally involves (in theory) trained peers, behaving in an unbiased and dispassionate way, helping other students resolve conflicts nonviolently.

The project described in this chapter involved participant observations at student and staff mediation training sessions, peer mediations, "hot spots" in the schools where fights tended to occur (the cafeteria and hallways), and mediation refresher courses. The project also included interviews and focus groups with disputants and mediators. In this chapter, I describe themes that emerged from the data, including the ways that peer mediation was socially constructed. I conclude with practical advice on ways to prevent peer mediation programs from being derailed.

Observations were conducted at two urban high schools in the same school district where the prevalence of violent fights and weapon carrying appeared to be on the rise. At Brandon High School, peer mediation had been in place for five years, and the administration boasted of a substantial reduction in fights. However, when we started asking more specifically about that reduction, we were unable to obtain any numerical data and we discovered that fighting was still perceived to be a major problem in the school. At London High School, the peer mediation program had begun after Christmas break the year before we started our observations. In this school, the culture of peer mediation was different from that at Brandon, where almost everyone in the school was aware of mediation, knew what it was, and knew what was appropriate for referral. As a result, several mediations a day took place there. In contrast, when I discussed mediation with students at London High School in the hallway during lunchtime, few knew that mediation took place in the school and most could not describe what mediation was. Only seventeen mediations took place between the start of school in September and the end of December, and most cases occurred after a physical fight or the threat of a physical fight.

The City School District had invested much in the peer mediation program. Rather than attempting to reinvent the wheel, we wanted to improve it by studying and informing the practice of mediation. In the school where I conducted the research, I examined the consistent problems that mediators had, provided constructive feedback to mediators and adult supervisors, and examined the situations in which mediation had positive outcomes (led to peaceful resolution with no fights resulting later). I also was interested in examining when mediation did not work (according to the disputants) and in rethinking some of the issues of gender, race, and social class issues that might prevent traditional forms of mediation from being successful in preventing violence.

Menkel-Meadow (1995) argued that "if we are to take seriously the notion of a transformative process in mediation (either at the individual or group level), we must unpack more critically the practices by which we get there" (p. 218). (For some suggestions about how to do this, see Baruch Bush & Folger, 1994; Kolb & Associates, 1994; and Merry & Milner, 1993). Through qualitative research, we will be able to unpack the "transformative process" of mediation and the "practices by which we get there."

Although some research has argued that peer mediation is ineffective at reducing violence, the City School District believed that it had statistics to the contrary. Some researchers, such as Kinasewitz (1996), found a reduced number of referrals for aggressive and violent behavior in one large, public high school after peer mediation was implemented. And McMahon (1995) reported a 42.2 percent decrease in harassment after the institution of peer mediation in a middle school. Heller (1996) argued that peer mediation was an important component of strategies to reduce school violence along with: staff and community involvement, sensitivity to students' racial and socioeconomic concerns, and effective intervention strategies such as the teaching of anger management skills. There have been no comprehensive studies that have looked at how peer mediation transforms the culture of the school in which it is located. This study began to do this.

QUESTIONS TO ASK
ABOUT PEER MEDIATION PROGRAMS

This chapter draws on ethnographic studies by myself and my colleague, Dr. Ronnie Casella, to describe some of the places where peer mediation gets derailed from its mission of preventing fights or other violent acts from occurring in school. Some questions that those instituting mediation programs face are: Who gets selected as mediators (staff and students)? Who decides who shall be selected? Who is responsible for the peer mediation program? What gets sent to mediation? Who decides what shall be sent? Do mediators receive feedback about their performance, and if so, how? Do policies and procedures reflect peer mediation as an educative device rather than a punishment for those sent to mediation? And finally, is peer mediation used as a preventive tool or an intervention?

Although schools may be able to answer the above questions, there are hidden problems inherent in them. For example, *Who gets selected as mediators?* Some schools choose the most academically able students or the most "responsible" school citizens. In some schools, these students may not be representative of the school as a whole. Also, other students may not view the students chosen to be mediators as their peers but more as mini-administrators. As a result, those other students may be less likely to take mediation seriously. At London High School, student mediators were fairly representative of the student body according to race and gender. However, mediators were all strong students and/or good athletes. Most of them had challenging curricula and a variety of cocurricular activities. Many aspired to go to college. Their courses and activities took up so much time that they found it difficult to schedule mediations. At Brandon High School, most of the student mediators performed very well academically. Most were White, despite the fairly equal ratio of Blacks to Whites in the school. As at London, mediators at Brandon had difficulty in finding time to conduct a mediation. However, because more trained mediators were available, the problem was less acute than at London.

Students have to be committed to the program to become mediators, but they have also to be available to conduct mediations. Often, coordinators do not consider the potential availability of students when selecting mediators. Also, because most programs select students through an application and sometimes an interview procedure, they tend not to be as impressed by weaker students who may not be involved in academic cocurricular activities. However, several of the best mediators in the schools we observed were involved with athletics and/or a variety of nontraditional activities inside and outside school. Involving these students, some of whom may even be leaders of neighborhood groups, has a great deal of potential for reaching students who have traditionally avoided mediation.

Another question is, *Who takes responsibility for the peer mediation program?* In some schools, the guidance office takes responsibility for it; in others, a particular guidance counselor, as was the case at Brandon High School. However, at London High School there was a designated Safe Schools Coordinator who was responsible for building security, suspensions, hall monitors, and peer mediation. Without someone clearly defined as "in charge" of peer mediation, the program is almost inevitably doomed to fail. Sometimes, the person in charge changes roles, is transferred to another school, or retires and is not replaced. Then, nobody is in charge of the program. This causes serious problems even for previously flourishing programs.

At Brandon High School during our study there was a transition of personnel and the new guidance counselor in charge of mediation was not as outwardly enthusiastic with the students. The previous counselor was known throughout the district for being very (perhaps overly) involved with peer mediation. With the changing of the guard, there were some difficulties, but because of the buy-in from the administration, the new counselor continued to devote time and energy to the mediation effort. At London High School, the Safe Schools Coordinator was constantly seeking support from the teachers through letters and discussions, but the teachers did not come to meetings and trained teachers would not sign up to help with mediations. The coordinator needed assistance and support from others in the school, but could not get it. This made it difficult to get appropriate referrals, and adults to facilitate the process. It is important, not only to have a person in charge, but also to have support from staff and administration.

What conflicts get sent to mediation? And who decides what should be sent? At Brandon High School, students referred themselves and teachers, administrators, and other staff also referred students for verbal threats, arguments, harassment, and fighting. At London High School, usually students were sent to mediation for fighting or threats of fighting. Mediation at each of these schools was therefore viewed differently. At Brandon, mediation was used mainly for violence prevention. At London, mediation was viewed as violence intervention.

Mediation was not developed to be an intervention to violence, yet in some schools it ends up serving this purpose. Those who advocate the use of peer mediation in schools believe that schools need to attempt to stop conflicts from escalating to violence by teaching those on the front lines (teachers, hall monitors, and assistants) how to identify conflicts and make referrals to mediation *before* violence happens. In addition, students need to view mediation as a way to resolve conflicts before they escalate. At London High School, students did not think they belonged in mediation unless they had been in a physical fight.

How do peer mediators receive feedback about their performance? Often in schools, the assumption is that the peer mediators are well trained and, with occasional refresher courses and meetings, they will be good mediators. However, our observations showed that student mediators frequently do not follow the steps they have learned, do not remain unbiased, do not use neutral language, have difficulty identifying issues and/or writing agreements, avoid underlying issues (because they don't have skills to handle strong emotions or challenging topics), and give advice to disputants about what they themselves would do. These are problems that if not addressed with immediate feedback from an adult, experienced mediator or trainer, continue until much of what makes peer mediation work is lost.

Do policies and procedures reflect peer mediation as an educative device rather than a punishment? When students view peer mediation as something they are forced to do, or something that is an add-on to their punishment, they become hostile to it. The perception that peer mediation can result in a disputant getting into more trouble if a written agreement is broken creates an environment where disputants are leery about making such agreements. At London High School, for example, students perceived they would be at greater risk of being suspended again after a fight if they attended mediation, made an agreement and then broke it, than if they did not attend mediation at all. In addition, they perceived that they would get the same punishment for a fight regardless of whether or not they went to peer mediation. Thus, mediation was seen as taking on more punishment.

Is peer mediation a tool for violence prevention or intervention? Peer mediation was designed as a violence prevention strategy. However, many schools use it as an intervention after violence, in the form of a fight or assault, has occurred. We have also seen it used after sexual harassment has taken place. Schools need to decide how they intend to use peer mediation and remain consistent in the way it is used. London High School tended to use mediation as an intervention after a fight. Students were confused when "little things," such as verbal threats, "ribbin'," or arguments, got sent to mediation. Brandon High School used mediation as a violence prevention tool and conducted several mediations per day for what students referred to as "little things." Students and staff accepted this because the administration had been consistent in sending the message that mediation was meant to deal with conflicts before they escalated into physical or verbal assaults. Consistency is important, and sending the message that mediation is meant to prevent violence from happening by helping students come to agreement about a conflict, is essential to a strong peer mediation program.

THE IMPORTANCE OF UNDERSTANDING STUDENT PERCEPTIONS OF MEDIATION

At London High School, I interviewed and conducted focus groups with students to better understand their perceptions of mediation at the school. Was it considered helpful or punitive? Was it viewed as useful? Did it make a difference? My approach was to ask students in a systematic way, something that had not been done before.

There were many contradictory messages that students reported. For example, administrators would tell students that they had to go to mediation, but when students arrived at mediation, they were told that the process was voluntary. At that point, students would sometimes opt to leave because as one student put it: "You can fight in the mediation room if you wanted to. You're still going to get three days kicked out of school. It don't make no difference." The three days out of school as a punishment was not seen as a very big deal by some students. However, most students said that they wanted to graduate, so they feared getting into any more trouble from breaking an agreement. As one girl disputant said, "We violated the agreement, that's why we got kicked out 'cause we signed the agreement and we broke it and so we got in more trouble for [fighting] than if you [had never] made an agreement and broke it." Her perception was that people got into more trouble for signing an agreement and breaking it than for not agreeing to go to mediation. This was another reason why students in trouble wanted to avoid mediation.

The difference between the actual practice and what was supposed to happen was significant. There was supposed to be a "cooling-off period" after a fight before a mediation took place, but sometimes disputants were asked to mediate right away. One disputant became very angry as she gave her opinion: "The mediation can cause more problems too. Because I know for me . . . if I just got done fighting with somebody and you're going to put me in the room with them trying to talk it out. Oh no! It's too hard to do that right then. It's going to cause more problems. You're just going to fight again. That just brings up old stuff that's going to make you mad."

The problems that occurred during the mediation process (and they occurred regularly according to my observations) had a strong impact on how the disputants felt about the process of mediation. My focus groups with these students were very telling. The general feeling was that mediation was a waste of time because students could simply put on an act to come to an agreement they'd never stick to because they'd just move their conflict out to the street. The conflict did not end with mediation. Students agreed that they put on an act to get out of the mediation room. As one girl put it: "We were still in the mediation room when the girl left and they were like . . . 'We could sense something is still going on. Do you think the problem is over?' I'm like 'No, I don't think the problem is over because it's not over for me, and I could tell by the way she was looking it wasn't over for her either.' But see the thing what it is about, if you've got someone in mediation you can't be like . . . 'Oh, stop rolling your eyes.' You can't tell somebody what they can and what they cannot do. You ain't their mama." So the eye rolling and body language continue, and the difficult issues are almost never addressed. Student mediators admitted to me that they did not know what to do in these situations when disputants were hostile, so, in their frustration, they usually let the disputants leave without giving both parties a chance to speak again. The goal for mediators and disputants was to get a written agreement in the shortest possible time so they could get to lunch, class, or back to the comfort of their friends. Mediators were very busy people, and taking time out of their classes or cocurricular activities to mediate was difficult for them. As a result, they frequently would rush to agreement, give advice, and sometimes even write the agreements for the disputants. Hence, the conflicts were far from resolved, and frequently a wound was opened further for the disputants.

I asked students what they thought the majority of fights were about. The answers supported what I had already thought from my observations. They said, almost in unison: "Over boys or over girls. Yeah, that's what it is. 'He said/she said.' 'Where you're from—she's from the east side, she's from the west side.'" When I asked what was at the root of the "he said/she said" talk, the answers were vague, "I heard she was talking about me. . . . She's come and say something like around me so I can go back and tell her and then." But as some said, "It could be over anything. I know there's a lot of girls in this school right now who are fighting over a stare. She just stared at her wrong. I was like, 'If you all want to fight why don't you just come around the corner and do it?' You know what I'm saying?" The unspoken subtext of the "stare" was usually a romantic relationship gone awry. Most of the "girl fights" were over boys and boyfriends.

Most students admitted that those who did not really want to fight, or students who were not "tough" or "good fighters" would fight in school because they knew administrators, hall monitors, or teachers would break up the fight quickly. Those who "really wanted to fight" would do it on the street. The street fights were usually about retaliation or over romantic relationships—the fights that were filled with passion.

Mediation concerns me as a culturally biased enterprise of Whites once again imposing cultural attitudes of calm, rationality, and impartiality (attributes that have been most often associated with being a good White male) onto a process that is filled with passionate emotion. At the center of almost every conflict we saw that made it to peer mediation, was a young person seeking love and acceptance—either in a romantic or a platonic relationship gone awry. Caring relationships cause many people to feel a range of very strong emotions that are frequently ignored in mediation because "impartial" peer mediators frequently feel uncomfortable addressing strong emotions. As one mediator put it (when speaking about why she did not invite the disputant to talk more about a relationship that was critical to understanding the root of the dispute), "It's none of my business."

In the schools we observed, mediators were more likely to be White and disputants more likely to be Black. This difference of ethnic identity causes cultural tensions about what are considered acceptable displays of emotion. Schools run by mostly White, middle class adults have the view that all fighting is bad. Students who fight should be punished. Some students come from homes that hold the view that fighting is a necessary part of relationships, and may, at times, be the best way to resolve conflicts. This is at least consistent with other societal beliefs, that boxing is okay, as are wrestling, and football, and war. In those situations, someone wins, and someone loses. It is no wonder that many students (and many adults) have difficulty accepting the view that win-win solutions are possible, particularly if they feel certain they can win a fight.

How do you survive in a room filled with "neutral talk" when you are filled with emotion? Can we only do mediations as a preventative measure before an issue has escalated to one that is filled with emotion? If so, how can we tell when the moment is appropriate for mediation? How do we deal with most conflicts that are emotional? There are no simple answers to these questions, but it does seem that schools (students and staff included) need to become better equipped to deal with intense emotions in ways that do not lead to violence. Conflict needs to be understood as something that need not always lead to violence, and all students need to be equipped with strategies for anger management, for ways to recognize when their anger has been triggered and how to reduce it before it escalates to violence. Students also need to learn realistic and culturally diverse ways of communicating with those whom they care about. Students also need schools that provide a caring environment, where caring relationships are a part of the culture, and where being in a caring relationship means resolving conflicts peacefully. Mediation alone is insufficient, but can be a welcome complement in a caring school culture where all students are learning how to handle their anger and conflicts nonviolently.

CONCLUSION

Peer mediation is a popular strategy in schools today. There are benefits to preventing violence through the peaceful resolution of conflict, if programs run well, paying careful attention to the potential pitfalls. This chapter has mentioned some of the pitfalls observed at two high schools. These pitfalls were not the same for each school. Careful observation of the entire process of mediation may help a school identify some of the areas where problems are likely to arise: the selection of students and personnel to work on the peer mediation program and direct it, the training of staff and students, the selection of staff and students to be mediated, what actually happens in a mediation session, the promotion of peer mediation in the school (including all messages about peer mediation sent to staff and students), in-service training for staff and students, and perceptions of staff and students about mediation. Examining each of these at regular intervals will give a good picture of the peer mediation program in a school, and help identify areas needing more attention. Peer mediation is a time-consuming project for a school to do well; regular evaluation of the program components, followed by action to provide improvement where needed, are essential to its success.

REFERENCES

Baruch Bush, R. A. & Folger, J. (1994). *The promise of mediation: Responding to conflict through empowerment and recognition.* San Francisco: Jossey-Bass.

Heller, G. S. (1996, April). Changing the school to reduce student violence: What works? *NASSP Bulletin, 80* (579), 1–10.

Kinasewitz, T. M. (1996). *Reducing aggression in a high school setting through a conflict resolution and peer mediation program.* (Research Practicum). Nova Southeastern University, Fort Lauderdale, FL.

Kolb, D. M., & Associates (1994). *When talk works: Profiles of mediators.* San Francisco: Jossey-Bass.

McMahon, P. P. (1995). Stemming harassment among middle school students through peer mediation group exercises. Research Practicum. Nova Southeastern University, Fort Lauderdale, FL.

Menkel-Meadow, C. (1995, July). The many ways of mediation: The transformation of traditions, ideologies, paradigms, and practices. *Negotiation Journal, 11*(3), 217–242.

Merry, S. E. & Milner, N. (Eds.) (1993). *The possibility of popular justice: A case study of American community justice.* Ann Arbor: University of Michigan Press.

12

Reaching Troubled Teens Through a Literacy Tutoring Project

Domingo P. Guerra

Syracuse University

Joan N. Burstyn

Syracuse University

THE PROJECT AND ITS OBJECTIVES

This chapter describes a pilot literacy project, from a northeastern city of the United States, that broke new ground by engaging as literacy tutors for young children a small group of high school students from Garfield School, a unique alternative school for students who were found on school property in possession of a weapon. As well as the high school students, the pilot involved first, second, and third grade students attending an after-school program at a community recreation center. The names of students have been changed in this chapter to protect their anonymity.

While the details of this project may seem straightforward to the reader, they were quite tortuous to those involved. Each day brought new hurdles to overcome, because one or two tutors absented themselves from school or the young tutees were more eager to play than to read. Sometimes the teens themselves wanted to play basketball rather than spend time tutoring. In addition, daily discussions took place between us, the project organizers, and the community center staff to insure that we worked together harmoniously. We came to the recreation center with a school-like project expecting to research its effectiveness. Thus, we needed the tutees to attend our tutorial sessions as regularly as possible.

The community center staff wanted to keep the children at the center happy and occupied with lively recreation activities. They had no objection to a tutee of ours playing outside one day instead of reading to a tutor. So, we had to spend time insuring that the expectations of both the project and the center could be met.

The four people supervising the project brought skills and experience of varying kinds: one was a teacher educator, with a focus on conflict resolution and the prevention of violence in schools, a former teacher of seventh through twelfth grade; another, a former counselor for college students and a qualitative researcher on drug education and violence prevention; another, a qualitative researcher and experienced teacher in all grades, especially kindergarten and first grade; and the fourth, an undergraduate and aspiring lawyer, who was an experienced literacy volunteer. Two were White, one African American, and one Hispanic.

One of our objectives was to offer high school students who had already become involved with violence an activity that would simultaneously increase their prosocial skills and their involvement with the community. We saw this as important because the teens participating in this project had already become alienated from the wider community in which they lived. Insofar as they were noticed by that community, they were noticed for doing something wrong. Tutoring, we surmised, would provide them with praise from their tutees and from those adults running the community center and the project, thus reinforcing a new image of themselves as enablers not disrupters.

Another objective was to improve the teens' basic literacy skills and thus make their academic success more likely. All the high school students in this project were average or less than average achievers academically. In "Frontin' It," chapter 6 of this book, Kimberly Williams, suggests why students with low academic achievement are more likely than students with higher academic achievement to engage in violence. Lack of reading ability, which may stem from a variety of sources, such as lack of access to books, poverty, and high pupil to teacher ratio in schools, seems closely related to low academic achievement (Gunn, Simmons, & Kameenui, 1998; McQuillan, 1998, chap. 7). Several studies have suggested that older students who are poor readers improve their own reading when they serve as tutors for younger students (Cohen, Kulik, & Kulik, 1982; Coleman, 1990; Labbo & Teale, 1990). Therefore, we expected that by reinforcing the students' basic literacy skills, we might also effect a change in their academic performance and indirectly make it less likely for them to engage in violence.

An important objective for our project was to improve the literacy skills of the six-to eight-year-olds who participated in it. In the 1990s, President Bill Clinton announced, as part of his national agenda, the goal of ensuring that every child can read by fourth grade. He asked people to volunteer to help first, second, and third grade students improve their reading skills. We were particularly interested in the president's initiative because early literacy makes it less likely that students will fail in school and engage in antisocial behavior.

We hoped, also, that the teens, who belonged to the same citywide community as the young children, would come to see themselves in their new role as tutors. We watched to see how their tutees responded to the teens, and whether they respected them as tutors.

A final and most crucial objective specific to this literacy project was to provide both the tutors and the tutees with reading material on conflict resolution, anger management, and positive interpersonal relations. This was done through the books we chose for them to use. By introducing this literature to both groups of participants, we expected to reinforce the positive effect of the project on their behavior, and encourage them to avoid violence both inside and outside school. We were particularly aware of the importance of this literature for the younger students, since research studies have suggested that the earlier in a student's life an intervention takes place, the more likely it is to be successful.

ORGANIZATION OF THE PROJECT

Five high school students, four boys and one girl, attending the alternative school were selected by the school counselor after discussion with the project director and colleagues. All students at the school participated, daily, in some community service project. However, the school had difficulty finding service projects for the students other than menial tasks, like cleaning floors or emptying waste baskets in service agencies or washing dishes in restaurants. Most service placements were despised by the students and many absented themselves from their obligations. This eight-week literacy project appeared to be an attractive alternative to the students. The selected students were contacted and agreed to participate in it. Permission for them to do so was obtained from their parents or guardians.

While this sample did not match the gender breakdown at the school at the time, which was nearly fifty–fifty, it did more closely match the racial breakdown of the school where a large majority of students (85%) were African American. One boy was White, and three of the four boys and the one girl on the project were African American. Approximately 15 first, second, and third grade students who attended the center's after-school program each day volunteered to take part in the project. All of them were African American. As will be described in more detail later, there was absenteeism among both tutors and tutees, so the numbers attending on any one day fluctuated.

During the first two weeks of the project, the five high school students and those running the project who planned to supervise them attended a daily two-hour workshop conducted by a literacy expert. That period was crucial for all the students in preparing them to change the way they saw themselves, from being people learning to read to being people who taught others how to do so, from being students to being tutors. They were encouraged to keep a journal while they were on the project specifically reflecting on teaching young children to read. Samples of children's books were distributed for them to look at and read aloud. The students discussed why it was important to have their tutees choose which book they wanted to read or have read to them. In pairs, and as a group, they practiced listening to one another, reading out loud with inflection to add interest to the story, and ways to affirm younger children and inquire about a story. They were encouraged to use the following scheme for their tutoring:

- Read to: tutor reads to the child.
- Read with: tutor and child discuss and read the story together.
- Read: child reads the same story or another one to the tutor.

As the site of the project we chose a local community center that ran after-school programs for neighborhood children. Most programs provided by the center were recreational, and so the place was seldom quiet, and the children there expected a lot of physical activity. We would have liked to have conducted the project in the quieter environment of an elementary school; however, we were unable to do so because the high school students attending the alternative school were all forbidden to enter any other school in the district.

Our first task was logistical. The first, second, and third grade tutees were committed to attending the community center prior to the introduction of this project, so we were not responsible for getting them there. The tutors, however, attended school some distance away and had to be accompanied to the site. After several days of taking the tutors by car to the center from school, we abandoned that procedure because of the potential danger to our driver from gang fights in the neighborhood. Instead, we arranged for the center to provide a minivan to pick up the tutors at school each day.

The staff at the community center took great pride in the after-school recreational programs they offered. They protected the wellbeing of each child attending the center by developing an understanding among them that the building was a "safe haven" from the disputes erupting often on nearby sidewalks, especially where the territories of various teenage groups, or gangs, intersected. After some discussions, during which we of the university group explained our plans, the staff agreed to allow us to carry out our project at the center and offered us a conference room with two sections divided by a folding screen wall to use for our activities. On one side of the room a row of windows was set, about five feet up. On the other side were two posters. One poster showed a youth on a bicycle riding on a street between tall buildings and triumphantly raising his hand in a victory gesture. He seemed to be riding out from the poster. Written on it were the words: YOU ARE MORE POWERFUL THAN PAIN! The other poster showed another youth jumping high and exultantly. In the far background was the outline of a city. The words printed on that poster were: YOU ARE THE UNIVERSE! The two posters enlivened the room and provided symbols of success for the young people at the center. Both of the posters depicted Black youths, which must have added to their impact since most of those attending the center were African American.

Each section of the room had a long table in the center with chairs to the sides. We used one section for tutoring and the other for drawing and coloring. Sometimes, several tutors and tutees seated around the long table distracted one another, so we sometimes separated pairs, allowing some to work together in the large hall adjoining the conference room.

The tutoring activities were supervised at all times by the adults running the project. At least two adults, and usually three, attended each session. The supervisors insured that tutors and tutees found a comfortable spot to work in, and that books were available when needed. They monitored what went on in each session, and debriefed the tutors about each day's sessions immediately after they had finished as described in more detail below. Sometimes the debriefing was conducted one-on-one and sometimes as a group.

The tutors found it easier, particularly at first, to work with the older children than with the first graders. It took time for the tutors to gain patience in listening and helping. The tutoring was conducted one-on-one, so there were often several young children awaiting their turn. Domingo Guerra, an author of this chapter, used his experience as a kindergarten and first grade teacher to devise drawing and coloring activities for young children to do while they waited. Those who had completed their time with the tutor sometimes chose to draw the story they had read; others chose to write and draw pictures of their own stories with Guerra's help. He, or another adult supervising the project, might also read a book to a small group. As an enticement for the young children to continue coming to tutoring sessions, they were told that at the end of the project they would each receive a package of crayons. We expected extrinsic motivation to be augmented by intrinsic motivation based on a new joy in reading, drawing and writing down their own stories and in interacting with caring tutors.

Each day, after the young children left, or sometimes while they were drawing, the adults took time to talk with the tutors about their work, encouraging them to reflect on what had gone well and what had not succeeded. The discussions dealt with the mechanics of reading and, also, with the interactions that had taken place between tutor and tutee. In the first weeks of the project, the tutors kept journals. They became less conscientious in keeping them as time went on, however, and as more incidents from their lives outside school began to impinge upon their work for the project.

At the end of the eight weeks, the tutors and tutees were given a choice of what they would like as an affirmation of their efforts. They chose a pizza party and an opportunity to have photographs taken of the tutors and tutees together.

REFLECTIONS ABOUT THE PROJECT

The attitudes of the teen tutors toward the first, second, and third grade students changed over the eight weeks. We coached the tutors in how to provide positive feedback and encouragement. We modeled that behavior ourselves in relation to the teen tutors because they needed considerable practice before they felt comfortable reading aloud to another person. They had no experience of "being a teacher" and so it was difficult for them to imagine how a teacher thought about his or her teaching. For instance, when discussing and reading the story with their tutees, the tutors found it difficult at first to understand what a discussion of the book might be and how to ask questions of another person that might encourage them to talk about the story. And, they had to be reminded about the ways that first, second, and third graders' reactions to the stories might differ from their own.

The teens brought with them their own experiences of relationships and learning. Some of those experiences had been extremely negative. When asked whether he enjoyed reading, one of the tutors responded: "They used to call me the stuttering king when I used to read." And another added: "Reading used to put the spotlight on me, and others would laugh at me." So, their initial response to tutees' inattention was often to say something negative or to yell at them to pay attention. The trainer had spoken to the tutors about the joy of reading, the need to praise their tutees for their work, and about ways to see some disappointing behavior by their tutee as a "teachable moment." However, these concepts were quite new to the tutors for whom reading had been a struggle and praise hard to come by. It took them a long while to understand what we were asking of them, and longer still for them to take the risk of using the new techniques they had learned.

As already mentioned, at first the tutors often seemed impatient with the young students' sassiness and inattention, tending to retort to their remarks with ones in like vein or with threats of coercion. However, at each session, we made time to praise the tutors for some aspect of their work, and to talk with them about what it felt like to be the teacher in such a situation, asking them how they would like a teacher to respond to them if they said something similar. As they got to know particular first and second graders, who in their turn would wait for one particular tutor to read to them, the tutors became more attentive to the tutees as individuals, patiently listening to them and prompting them only when needed. The tutees responded by becoming less sassy and more fluent in their reading.

The tutors told us that they polished their own reading skills by reading aloud to the young tutees. One asked why no one had ever taught him to read the way he was teaching others now. Another said: "It gave you a chance to work with little kids better. Like, if you want to be a teacher or something, it is helping you out. It's helping you out a lot; you do a lot of reading. For my education, it is beneficial."

The teen tutors also asked the adults in the project about themselves and their work. One member of the team, the undergraduate literacy volunteer who planned to attend law school, often found herself questioned in the informal time after the session about her work and her aspirations. The tutors may have found her particularly approachable as a young person not much older than themselves, and as a person of color. However, they questioned all of us and found our interest in themselves to be curious and exciting. The informality of the environment, both for the tutoring sessions and the debriefing sessions between the project members and the tutors, encouraged conversations that led the parties to a greater understanding of one another.

Within such a narrow window of time and experience, only a small amount of influence could be expected. Nevertheless, we surmised that while the teen tutors provided the first, second, and third grade students with a model of how they might tutor younger children when they became teens and told them what they had to learn in order to do that, the adult project members modeled for the teens how they might function as adults and explained to them how they might achieve their goals.

The three tutors who completed the eight-week pilot project all obtained and held down jobs that following summer. We cannot claim that the literacy volunteer work had a direct relationship to these facts, but we feel confident that the experience of persisting at a task over several weeks until it was finished, and the opportunity to practice interpersonal skills while on the project had some impact on their success during the summer immediately following the project.

Attendance was a problem among the tutors. Only three of them completed the eight weeks of tutoring. Some did not attend school regularly, and so were unavailable to tutor after school on the days they were absent. The only girl among the tutors disappeared from the neighborhood, having broken her probation, and one boy was sent to a detention center part way through because of the gang activities described later in this chapter.

We learned that merely to arrange for tutors from the alternative school to tutor at the community center was problematic for some because of the territoriality of the local gangs. To get to the center from the school, students had to cross the boundary between two gangs. This was dangerous for some of them, and so we arranged transportation for them all. By doing so, we helped to assure their attendance.

Gangs proved to be a problem for another reason. We had chosen tutors who, we soon learned, belonged to rival gangs. Although this choice was not intentional, we thought it might turn out to be fortuitous because, at first, they seemed to break through their rivalry. They began to help the process of building the group's *esprit de corps*. They would calmly share ideas in our discussions about their tutoring. However, they later fell out when members of their two gangs, playing basketball at the center, got into a fight. One of the tutors fought with a boy from a rival gang who was not a tutor. However, a tutor from the boy's gang watched the fight and then turned abruptly to walk away from the center with his fellow gang members. That move was perceived to be threatening and likely to mean that they were looking for reinforcements. Someone ran upstairs to the tutorial room with the news:

"Can you believe that TK goes off with them? His gang!"

"Yeah, we saw him go off with them," said another, excitedly.

"How do you know he's not calming them down?" asked our project coordinator.

"I don't care what they do," replied a tutor who was a friend of the one who had engaged in the fight. "They want trouble. I can call my brothers all the way from Georgia. I'm no-one's . . . !"

"No, don't, LM," responded the coordinator.

The fight destroyed the fragile "truce" the gang members had established while they did their tutoring. The fracas ended after some time, but the tutor who had engaged in the fight was sent to a detention center. He never returned to the project.

CONCLUSION

Benefits to the Tutors

The pilot project demonstrated that literacy tutoring has the following benefits to offer high school students at-risk of becoming engaged in violence. First, the bond with their community was strengthened by their efforts at helping the young students, some of whom were the siblings of their friends. They felt themselves to be useful, and those who knew about their work agreed. A second benefit was that the community service component of their alternative school curriculum became more meaningful to them. Previously, the jobs they were assigned appeared demeaning to them. This was highlighted in the following comments:

"Hey, LM," called JD when the project was suggested to him. "Come and try it [the literacy tutor program]. You won't have to clean toilets!" He went on to explain later: "The boys have to do clean up community service; the girls do office work, stuff like that."

The tutors' own literacy skills improved as they became teachers of those skills. We would have liked to have had the opportunity to follow up on the tutors' academic progress after their experience. Unfortunately, we were unable to do that because all three who completed the project left the alternative school once the semester ended to return to one of the regular high schools. Our belief is, however, that these high school students need greater improvement than could be gained from teaching basic literacy skills, and that for any significant improvement to take place, their tutoring experience would need to be followed up by sessions in which they became the tutees and someone else tutored them in the interpretive skills they needed to read high school textbooks. We will build this component into the design of the project for the future.

By the end of the project, the tutors understood that they had an influence on the young students. Small children would wait, patiently, until the tutor they knew from the last time was ready to work with them. Though we might like to interpret the tutors' awareness of their influence as their seeing themselves to be role models for the young students they tutored, they did not use such words to us. Thus, we can only infer from their behavior that they may have done so. Clearly, the experience of tutoring did provide the teens with an opportunity to see new ways to gain status in the eyes of adults, some of their peers, and those "coming up" behind them.

The task of breaking the hold of peer pressure for teens to conform to behaviors unacceptable to the adult society is enormously difficult, fraught with backsliding and even violence, but it is the task these students have to be persuaded to undertake. We believe that the praise of their tutees helped the teen tutors in this process.

Through the experience of being a teacher instead of a student, the tutors began to exercise some control over the way they reacted to others, and to the ways others saw them. That was a huge step. At the same time, their perception of themselves as readers and tutors improved as they engaged in reading to and working with the young students. There were, however, limits to these changes. The pressure of outside influences, including those of the recreation center itself, with its provision of opportunities to play basketball instead of participate in tutoring, made it difficult for the tutors to develop as "professional" an approach to their work as we would have liked. We saw the need to take the group to another setting, such as a public library, for a few tutoring sessions to emphasize their "professionalism." Although we could not do that at the time, we plan to do so in the future. We perceive a public library as an important place to locate such sessions because the students may not have previously frequented a public library, and, as McQuillan (1998) stated:

> Reading material is basic to all education, and providing a rich supply of reading matter to children of all ages, as well as a place and time to read, is the first step

to bridging the gap between poor and good readers. This means that school libraries must be stocked with interesting and appealing materials and appropriately staffed; students need to be given time to read silently books of their own choosing . . . and states and communities need to fund public libraries with reading material for people of all backgrounds and interests. This seems a reasonable place to start in our efforts to provide all students with equal opportunities to reach high levels of literacy. (p. 86)

A second pressure on the tutors was for them to remain, in the eyes of their peers, the same as they had always been. Any change might signal danger to their friendships inside and outside school. This pressure illustrates the complex interactions of the various systems influencing the teens. In light of the work of Pianta and Walsh (1996) on such interactions between systems, we would argue that to achieve the greatest likelihood of change among the tutors, we must help them develop camaraderie so that they become a support group for one another. We need, also, to reach out to the adults with whom they interact in their lives, to assist them by reinforcing the teens' new behaviors.

When we began the project, we anticipated that the tutors' exposure to the acts of teaching and learning would carry over into their schoolwork and beyond. We were not able to assess whether that was true. We know only that all three boys who completed the tutoring project obtained summer jobs and kept them for the whole summer. We were unable to follow up on their subsequent progress in school. However, we intend in a future iteration of the project to build in a follow-up study to track the students involved when they return to a regular high school or leave school to work. We hope that this type of intervention can be a catalyst to assist students who have spent time in an alternative school to re-integrate into the regular public schools.

We were also unable to follow up on the progress of the tutees, to assess their increase in reading skills either at school or at home. We would like, in the future, to establish some connections between the project and the schools and homes of the young children being tutored. We used children's books that reinforced creative conflict resolution and ways to handle passionate emotions without violence; we would, in the future, plan to send home with the children information about those books, and we would seek other ways to establish a stronger link with the adults in their families.

We note that any project with students already at-risk of engaging in violence will likely encounter problems similar to the ones we did. The logistics of carrying out such a project are difficult, but not insuperable. We also conclude that the high school students' difficulty in persisting with such a project makes it desirable to schedule the tutoring for a short, well-defined period, such as eight weeks, followed by an affirmation to them as a group for service well done.

Benefits to the Tutees

The pilot project, using teen tutors, offered some important benefits to first, second, and third grade students who were at risk of falling behind academically in school. Specifically, the one-on-one tutoring supported each child in developing his or her literacy skills. We observed that most of the young students felt at ease reading to the teen tutors. The teens shared many of the same cultural references as the young students, images and phrases from TV, for instance. Most of the time, the young students behaved as though they felt neither intimidated, nor judged in their discussions, as they might have done with an adult.

The model of skills development that the tutors used affirmed each child's worth and self-dignity. Each child got to listen to and discuss a book until he or she could "read" it without hesitation. Sometimes, an adult on the project joined in listening to the young person read and added his or her encouragement. We worked with the tutors to build their vocabulary of praise and encouragement and to discourage their use of chiding if a tutee appeared inattentive or became distracted. Although encouraged to continue until the tutorial session was completed, a tutee was free to leave a one-on-one session at any time to join the coloring group.

A third benefit offered to the first, second, and third graders was that they saw teenagers as helpers for themselves and others, and as positive, caring role models. This is important in a neighborhood where teens are often perceived as antisocial and dangerous. Parents of young children need to see the teens in their neighborhood—even those who, for one reason or another, have got into trouble with the law—helping the younger children in ways that are positive. The young children in our project often overheard the adults running the community center, and those running the project, praise the teen tutors about the good work they were doing. We added to this prosocial dimension of the project by providing appropriate grade-level books for the tutors and tutees that dealt with creative ways to resolve conflicts and ways to manage one's anger, such as those recommended by William Kreidler and Educators for Social Responsibility (Kreidler, 1984, 1994).

Last, the young students experienced continual positive reinforcement for their reading, explaining, and drawing. The literature shows that young children tend to grow into fluent readers if older children, and adults, both young and old, read to them, and discuss with them the meaning of the words on cans and boxes at home, on advertisements and notices in stores, at school, and on TV (Neuman & Roskos, 1993). Also, adults who discuss the books and newspapers they read with young children encourage them to become fluent readers who find it easier to do well in school than those who lack such fluency. And though it is not always the case, those who do well in school are less likely to engage in violent behavior than those who fail. Hence, we believe that literacy work with young students, such as that described in this chapter, will help prevent them from becoming the next generation of students banished from regular school for bringing in a weapon.

We plan to expand the project in the future by increasing the emphasis on developing professional skills for the literacy tutors, and improving the literacy training for the tutees. We also want to change the location from the community center to a school. The tutors told us they would feel safer traveling to a school that did not mean crossing the lines of rival street crews, and, at the same time, we feel that the atmosphere of a school rather than a recreational center would better fit the project. (On the other hand, we realize that the change of location might end the informal exchanges that seemed integral to the success of the pilot project. We may, therefore choose to run two comparable projects in separate settings to assess the value of a quiet, controlled school environment and a relaxed, uncontrolled one upon literacy acquisition, and upon the growth of interpersonal skills.)

To help build a relationship with a local elementary school, after the pilot project finished, Domingo Guerra worked at a local school for five weeks with a first grade teacher as a literacy tutor for five students there. He worked out an expanded scheme of tutoring, and ways to guarantee success for the tutees and the tutors. In addition to the activities used in the pilot project, he had the first grade students make a brightly colored book with drawings from their reading or their imagination, and with sentences repeated three times on a page. These books enabled the children to write a little story as well as read one. The first sentence was written by the tutor as the child spoke the sentence to him; then, below, the child stuck on the page a printed copy of each word and read them, and finally, below that sentence, the child copied each word and read them. By the time the book, with its sentences and colored pictures, was finished, the child could read it all, and, if he or she wished, could take it home to read to family and friends.

Guerra also planned for each young child to be taped twice while reading: the first time at the beginning of the tutorial sessions, and then again at the end of them, so that every child could listen and discern his or her own progress. We believe the tape recordings would also serve as an encouragement for the teens who would be able assess their own effectiveness as tutors through listening to their tutees' progress.

To introduce these changes into our literacy project in the future would mean more training for the tutors, providing them with additional skills for facilitating the work of the young tutees. In addition, we would like to take the tutors, sometime during the eight week tutoring session, to a school in a different neighborhood so that they could see how children learned to read in a different setting from the one in which they worked, and as mentioned earlier, we would like to organize some of the tutorial sessions at a public library. Each of these changes for the tutors would add to their understanding of the roles of teacher and mentor. We would provide some guided exercises to help them use their experiences to reflect back on their own behavior as students, and to understand better what their teachers were expecting of them.

Since the time the pilot project was undertaken, the authors have been part of a team working with an alternative school to institute a whole school approach to violence prevention, along the lines suggested by Burstyn and Stevens in chapter 8 of this volume. All students at the school take a year-long prosocial skills course and some students, but not all, explore the skills they have learned through laboratory experiences in art and radio program production. We believe that a literacy project, such as the one described in this chapter, would be particularly effective if provided as a laboratory experience for alienated teens who have undertaken a prosocial skills course in addition to their training in literacy tutoring.

REFERENCES

Cohen, P., Kulik, J. A., & Kulik C. (1982). Educational outcomes of tutoring: A meta-analysis of findings. *American Educational Research Journal, 19*, 237–248.

Coleman, S. (1990, March). Middle school remedial readers serve as cross-grade tutors. *The Reading Teacher*, pp. 524–525.

Gunn, B. K., Simmons, D. C., & Kameenui, E. J. (1998). Emergent literacy: Instructional and curricular basics and implications. In D. C. Simmons, & E.

J. Kameenui, (Eds.), *What reading research tells us about children with diverse learning needs: Bases and basics.* Mahwah, NJ: Lawrence Erlbaum Associates.

Kreidler, W. J. (1984). *Creative conflict resolution.* Glenview, IL: Scott Foresman.

Kreidler, W. J. (1994). *Teaching conflict resolution through children's literature.* New York: Scholastic Professional Books.

Labbo, L. D., & Teale, W. H. (1990, February). Cross-age reading: A strategy for helping poor readers. *The Reading Teacher,* pp. 362–369.

McQuillan, J. (1998). *The literacy crisis: False claims, real solutions.* Portsmouth, NH: Heinemann.

Neuman, S. B., & Roskos, K. (1993, Spring). Access to print for children of poverty: Differential effects of adult mediation and literacy-enriched play settings on environmental and functional print tasks. *American Educational Research Journal,* 30 (1), 95–122.

Pianta, R. C., & Walsh, D. J. (1996). *High-risk children in schools: Constructing sustaining relationships.* New York: Routledge.

13

The Challenge for Schools: To Prevent Violence While Nurturing Democracy

Joan N. Burstyn

Syracuse University

This book began with the claim that violence in schools mirrors the violence in society and is exacerbated by the availability of guns, urban and rural poverty, drug and alcohol abuse, suburban anomie, and the media's celebration of violence. Each of these must be addressed if people want to end violence.

The effects of guns, poverty, drug and alcohol abuse, anomie, and the media's celebration of violence are dealt with daily by educators. They search students for weapons at school doors, confiscate knives and box cutters, break up simulated intergalactic warfare on playgrounds, stop injurious fights in corridors, provide needy students breakfast, lunch, after-school programs, drug and alcohol counseling, and give comfort to those whose mother or father is in jail.

Poverty is an overwhelming issue in some schools, especially those in cities or rural areas. The problems associated with poverty are not new. They have been with our society for decades. In *Ribbin', jivin', and playin' the dozens: The unrecognized dilemma of inner city schools* (1974), Herbert L. Foster discussed the "street corner" lifestyle and behavior of inner city Black children (Foster, 1974, pp. 27–31). His description is strikingly similar to Elijah Anderson's recent "code of the street" (Anderson, 1999). Foster was alarmed that street corner behavior was misunderstood:

> It is behavior that many white school personnel consider to be symptomatic of emotional disturbance and/or social maladjustment, often resulting in the improper placement of these youngsters in programs for the emotionally disturbed or sometimes the retarded. It can also be argued that these school personnel act out of guilt, racism, or ignorance. (Foster, 1974, pp. 29–30)

Now, in the first years of the twenty-first century, Foster's (1974) "street corner" lifestyle, or Anderson's (1999) "code of the street," is perceived—rightly or wrongly—as more dangerous and more pervasive than before. Its danger has become greater as handguns have proliferated; its pervasiveness has been amplified by its valorization in film, music, TV, and on the Internet. In addition, "the code of the street" thrives on poverty, which has deepened in some places since the 1980s, as the loss of traditional manufacturing jobs has accelerated and the income differential between wealthy and poor in American society has become greater than at any time since the beginning of the twentieth century.

Educators have reacted to the spread of "the code of the street" by enacting zero tolerance policies and developing renewed enthusiasm for alternative schools. Foster's remarks of 1974 remind us that we need to examine who is punished by zero tolerance policies and who is sent to alternative schools. Are we creating new forms of discrimination? In Northeast City, where the research for several chapters of this book was done, African-American students make up a larger proportion of the students in alternative schools than in the school population overall. Many students in alternative schools, of all ethnic groups, come from low-income families.

Income disparities in society help foster "the code of the street" by making life there seem financially attractive to middle school and high school students, even those who expect to graduate from high school. The service sector now employs over sixty percent of the labor force and is projected to employ a larger percentage in the future. So, service jobs are easy for high school graduates to find, but they are mostly low-paying, low-skilled, and with low expectations: "fast-food workers, cashiers, waitresses, child care providers, retail sellers, house cleaners, and general laborers. . . . The working high school graduate is not likely to earn enough to live independently, much less support a family" (Schneider & Stevenson, 1999, p. 62).

Most disturbing about the proliferation of jobs that pay too little for a person to live independently, is the lack of hope engendered in young students, particularly those doing badly in school. Anderson writes that the quality of life taken for granted by many is not available to those in some urban communities. Hence, in order to survive, parents may encourage their children to act in "indecent ways" and thus contribute to the "streeting down" of the community (Anderson, 1999, p. 312).

"Streeting down," wherever it occurs, threatens the civility of society. The code of the street is confrontational and violent. It thrives on loyalties that demand defense of territory, and retribution for physical attacks and insults. It relies upon force to maintain personal dignity, and pride.

Yet, as Anderson points out, many people who live on a low income do not participate in "the code of the street." They struggle to maintain a different code of ethics, a life of "decency." Their struggle has been made more difficult since the influx of drugs, particularly crack cocaine, and the proliferation of hand guns in American cities. The authors of this book found that the young people they interviewed and observed accepted American values of individual initiative and the search for material well-being. They did not reject consumerism. On the contrary, they wanted to acquire the latest fashions, the best sound equipment, or the most attractive jewelry. When they had the money, students spent lavishly on gifts for their parents, boyfriends, or girlfriends. Their biggest problem seemed to be how to get the money for what they wanted to buy. Since many students could look forward only to low-paying service jobs, even with a high school diploma, they felt the draw of dealing in drugs, despite the danger from doing so. A student attending an alternative school in Northeast City, who was caught dealing drugs in spring 2000, told a teacher he had earned $1,000 at the job in less than eight weeks. The lure of such riches is difficult for some students to resist, although the likelihood that their drug dealing will lead them to carry and use weapons—if only for their own protection—is high.

Only rarely, in many suburban schools, does violence involving weapons erupt, though, as the incidents of gun violence in small town, suburban, and rural schools during the last few years have made clear, these eruptions can become lethal. However, as Bender notes (chap. 4 in this volume) more subtle forms of violence are well known in suburban schools (as they are in urban and rural schools). These subtle forms need to be dealt with as promptly as more lethal forms of violence.

Indeed, most violence—in most schools—is subtle and often unnoted by adults. Casella (chap. 2) commented on the deleterious effect on counseling programs at Brandon High School—for students coping with the suicides of two peers, and with family tensions, academic stress, sexual harassment, or bullying by peers—by the decision to divert time and energy from those programs to preparing the school to respond to an unlikely gun attack such as occurred at Columbine High School. The danger from such high profile incidents of school violence is that they divert the public's attention away from investigating the social context of violence, the history of a person's life and the social systems in which that life has been embedded. Instead, they focus the attention of parents and educators, nationwide, upon the need for tangible protective measures for all students in all school buildings. I, and other authors in this volume, believe that such a focus is misguided and may lead to actions that prevent public schools from carrying out an important task: to help every student become a member of a democratic community.

A possible motivation for a person to act violently is frustration at the complexity of his or her life. Complexity is often compounded for the poor who contend with lack of public transportation, lack of affordable child care, instability of jobs, housing, and medical coverage, and frequent changes in public assistance policies over which they have no control. A more affluent person may face the same insecurities of job and housing, and different, but perhaps equally frustrating, complexities: the time demands of professional versus family life; the need to arrange for child care each day after school, on school vacations, and on special occasions when parents travel; and the endless details of credit payments, medical and life insurance, and mortgages.

Consumer choice, loudly trumpeted by business interests, has run amok. Each person now must decide, and then reconsider each week or month, the best among a plethora of choices: phone, television, and computer access, electricity supply, credit cards, lawyers, doctors, and hospitals. All tout their virtues in newspapers, and on radio and TV. Viewers are urged by drug manufacturers, masquerading as customers relieved of arthritis pain, allergies, or chronic constipation, to press their physicians to prescribe their products at the first sign of a symptom.

How do people learn ways to prioritize these choices? Indeed, do they know that one choice might influence their ability or necessity to make other choices? On election day, does it make a difference whether I take the time to vote for president, or purchase a new car? Should I sign up for a cable company today, before the bargain offer expires, or keep an appointment for a new job? How do I learn to prioritize among these items?

Not many schools provide courses that address issues such as these. Nor do schools encourage students to question society's insistence that we make them. Why need I choose between two competing insurance companies in order to acquire medical coverage? Why do people in other countries not have to make that choice? Are they less free than I? If they are less free, what effect does that have on their lives compared to mine? Robert Kegan (1994) argued that these questions, and others in postindustrial society, call for a new level of thinking. He expects us to educate people to that new level. Though Kegan might disagree that statewide tests for school students encourage the level of thinking he advocates, those tests do place students under increased pressure. Some find the pressure unbearable. There is no evidence at the moment to suggest that the high profile incidents of gun violence in schools have been connected with increased academic pressures. However, in 1996, I argued that a society. such as the one Kegan claimed we were creating, could so complicate the lives of adults that they would revolt in frustration with the complexity:

> How will those who cannot cope respond to the growing frustrations they feel in their lives? One response might be increased acts of violence throughout society. A reaction to those acts of violence might be that those with power would abrogate the rights of their fellow citizens who seem unable to cope. In doing so, the powerful would abandon the values of pluralism and equity we have striven to maintain. They might thereby destroy all possibility of a true participatory democracy. (Burstyn, 1996, p. 201)

If we respond to school violence by abandoning our dedication to pluralism and equity, which there are signs we may do, we will endanger our democracy.

From the discussions of violence in the lives of teenage boys and girls in Part I of this book, the reader will have gained a picture of the role that cultural expectations play in their lives. These expectations change over time, and vary among ethnic communities. Janie V. Ward (1995) suggested that over the last thirty years, the African-American community has suffered an erosion of its traditional values of care and connectedness as a result of:

> economic oppression; a national preoccupation with consumption, excessive autonomy, and individualism at the expense of connectedness to the group; and the increasing cynicism of many Black teenagers toward a social system that

professes an ideology of social justice, yet offers little more than illusions of equality. (Ward, 1995, p. 177)

Ward calls for a concerted effort to teach young people of color a "sense of belonging and pride in one's heritage" (Ward, 1995, p. 185) to develop a healthy sense of self. The complexity of that task, especially for African-American men is highlighted by Thomas Parham (1993) who claims that the negative self-image of some African Americans comes from overidentification with Eurocentric values such as "controlling people and resources at all costs, individual centeredness, intense competition, and developing a sense of worth which is externally derived through the acquisition of material wealth" (Parham, 1993, p. 57). LeAlan Jones and Lloyd Newman, two boys from the south side of Chicago who reported on life and death there, saw a direct link between low self-image and the violent quality of life in the Ida B. Wells development in their neighborhood:

> Violence breeds violence in The Wells. . . . When young people around here are touched by violence, it changes their whole persona. And if there's no reform, there's going to be more and more violence.

> Kids around here have got to have more things to do. They need counseling. Get the teachers to put more emphasis on teaching them how to love and respect one another before they start teaching them how to add and subtract—because if the kids are violent and show no respect, how can they learn anything? (Jones, Newman, & Isay, 1997, pp. 153, 155)

Their words remind me that, in the last decade, scholars have searched for the etiology of violence, along the lines used for the prevention of disease (Reiss, Richters, Radke-Yarrow, & Scharff, 1993). Their research suggests that children living with chronic violence, such as reported in The Wells, develop psychological stress symptoms (Martinez & Richters, 1993). Martinez and Richters comment that these symptoms may be adaptive responses to abnormal events, or they may be "maladaptive reactions with longterm negative consequences for normal social, emotional, and cognitive development" (Martinez & Richters, 1993, p. 33). The impact of chronic violence on children's images of themselves; "their beliefs in a just and benevolent world; their beliefs about the likelihood of surviving into adulthood; . . . [and] the value they place on human life:" all these, Martinez and Richters suggest, are issues for further research (pp. 33).

Researchers also perform the meta-analysis of large data sets from studies of school students. Arguing that while the incidence of youth violence may have declined, its gravity has increased in recent years, Kingery, Coggeshall, & Alford (1999) show, by analyzing the findings of several studies, that certain items can be spoken of as risk factors for weapons carrying by youth. However, they caution educators who wish to use risk factors to guide their decision-making that "most research on risk factors does not establish whether a particular risk factor is the *cause* [emphasis in original] of a problem behavior" (Kingery et al. 1999, p. 310). And, they state that if risk factors are used in making policy, they should be used to establish special assistance for students at risk, not to punish or label them. Of interest in relation to the previous discussion of the effects of chronic violence on children, was the finding that, among 18,000 students who had answered the National Longitudinal Study of Adolescent Health, conducted by the Carolina Population Center at the University of North Carolina:

> Students who were victims of extreme violence or who witnessed extreme violence were also more likely to carry weapons at school. Students who had been stabbed in the past 12 months were 6.3 times more likely to carry a weapon at school. Weapon carrying was more likely among those who had had a gun or knife pulled on them, . . . had been shot, . . . had been involved in a physical fight, . . . or had witnessed a shooting or stabbing. (Kingery et al., 1999, p. 319)

That violence in schools cannot be dissociated from violence on the streets and in people's homes becomes obvious from these data. Attempts to end school violence have to be augmented by changes in other systems that impinge upon students' lives—child–family, socioeconomic, legal, media, and the political system.

As a small step, a longitudinal study of outcomes from the Syracuse University Family Development Research Program, which provided education, nutrition, health, safety, and human resources for five years to 108 families recruited in the first trimester of a teen mother's pregnancy—the teen mothers having less than a high school education and no work or semiskilled work experience—showed that intervention and support for children from before birth to the age of five positively affected their relations with adults, and "their ability to get their needs met with adults" (Honig, Lally, & Mathieson, 1982 as cited in Honig, 1999). When the children were teenagers they expressed more positive views of themselves than a contrast group, and were more likely to say that they would be involved with some form of education five years later. The follow up questions relating to juvenile delinquency showed a most profound difference between the intervention and contrast groups. As teenagers, only six percent of the intervention group (four of 4 cases) but 22 percent (12 of 54 cases) of the contrast group were processed as probation cases by the County Probation Department. "For the program group, the estimated juvenile court costs per child was $186 compared with $1985 per child for the control group [in 1988 dollars]. Thus, FDRP program participation resulted in juvenile delinquency savings to the community" (Lally, Mangione, & Honig, 1988, as cited in Honig, 1999, p. 3). From the perspective of cost effectiveness, early support of families to prevent delinquency and violence in children would appear to be a most effective expenditure of the nation's resources.

In this book, we have suggested that schools need to respond to violence by instituting a whole school approach to violence prevention. We have identified forms of violence in schools to which some educators may not have paid attention in the past, but which need their attention now. We suggest that a whole school approach be instituted as a democratic undertaking, part of a learning process in which adults engage as well as students.

Since the research for this book began I, Kim Williams (until 1999), Domingo Guerra, and others have introduced a whole school approach to preventing violence at Garfield alternative school under a subcontract from the Hamilton Fish National Institute on School and Community Violence, supported through the United States Office of Juvenile Justice and Delinquency Prevention. Our work at Garfield school has convinced us that a whole school approach has to be a multi-year effort that changes the school environment, and the behaviors of faculty and staff as well as students. Schools have to prevent systemic violence, insure the safety of all, not just some, students, and prepare all of them to become productive citizens in postmodern society. To ensure that our public schools remain places where individuals learn not only academic skills, but how to live together peaceably in a pluralistic democracy, is the intention of this book.

REFERENCES

Anderson, E. (1999). *Code of the street: Decency, violence, and the moral life of the inner city.* New York: W. W. Norton.

Burstyn, J. N. (1996). Meeting the demands of postmodern society. In J. N. Burstyn, (Ed.), *Educating tomorrow's valuable citizen*. Albany: State University of New York Press.

Foster, H. L. (1974). *Ribbin', jivin', and playin' the dozens: The unrecognized dilemma of inner city schools*. Cambridge, MA: Ballinger.

Honig, A. S. (1999, April 16). *Longitudinal outcomes from the Family Development Research Program*. Unpublished paper presented at the biennial meetings of the Society for Research in Child Development, Albuquerque, New Mexico.

Jones, L., & Newman, L., with Isay, D. (1997). *Our America: Life and death on the South Side of Chicago*. New York: Washington Square Press.

Kegan, R. (1994). *In over our heads: The mental demands of modern life*. Cambridge, MA: Harvard University Press.

Kingery, P. M., Coggeshall, M. B., & Alford, A. A. (1999, May). Weapon carrying by youth: Risk factors and prevention. *Education and Urban Society, 31,* 309–333.

Lally, J. R., Mangione, P. L., & Honig, A. S. (1988). The Syracuse University Family Development Research Program: Long-range impact of an early intervention with low income children and their families. In D. Powell, (ed.), *Parent education as early childhood intervention: Emerging directions in theory, research, and practice*. Norwood, NJ: Ablex.

Martinez, P., & Richters, J. E. (1993). The NIMH community violence project: II. children's distress symptoms associated with violence exposure. In D. Reiss, J. E. Richters, M. Radke-Yarrow, D. Scharff, (Eds.), *Children and Violence*. New York: Guilford Press.

Parham, T. A. (1993). *Psychological storms: The African American struggle for identity*. Chicago: African American Images.

Reiss, D., Richters, J. E., Radke-Yarrow, M., & Scharff, D. (1993). *Children and violence*. New York: Guilford Press.

Schneider, B., & Stevenson, D. (1999). *The ambitious generation: America's teenagers, motivated but directionless*. New Haven, CT: Yale University Press.

Ward, J. V. (1995, Summer). Cultivating a morality of care in African American adolescents: A culture-based model of violence prevention. *Harvard Educational Review, 65,* 175–188.

Authors

Geoff Bender holds adjunct teaching appointments from Syracuse University in both the English department and the writing program. His professional interests include the construction of masculinities in social and literary contexts. Also a poet, he is completing his first collection of poems. He has taught English at the secondary level for seven years.

Joan N. Burstyn is professor of cultural foundations of education and of history at Syracuse University. She is principal investigator of the Syracuse University Violence Prevention Project, a consortium member of the Hamilton Fish National Institute on School and Community Violence, which is funded by the U.S. Office of Juvenile Justice and Delinquency Prevention. Her last book was an edited volume titled, *Educating tomorrow's valuable citizen* (Albany: SUNY Press, 1996).

Ronnie Casella is assistant professor of education at Central Connecticut State University. He is the author of several articles and a forthcoming book on the policy of zero tolerance for disruptive behavior in schools. His research, reported in this volume, at Brandon High School was completed while he was a research associate with the Syracuse University Violence Prevention Project.

Domingo P. Guerra, a research assistant with the Syracuse University Violence Prevention Project, is completing his doctorate in the philosophy of education at Syracuse University. His research addresses the philosophy of violence in violence prevention/intervention programs. For over twenty years a teacher and administrator, from kindergarten to university, he has a special interest in brain compatible education and the philosophical issues it raises for notions of self, consciousness, and race.

Howard W. Gordon is executive assistant to the president of the State University of New York at Oswego. An accomplished creative writer, he has published an acclaimed book of short stories. He is completing his doctorate in cultural foundations of education at Syracuse University.

Kristen V. Luschen is visiting assistant professor of education studies at Hampshire College in Amherst, Massachusetts. The research described in this volume is part of a larger study she has conducted on adolescent female sexuality.

Rebecca Stevens is assistant professor of education at the University of South Carolina Spartanburg. A sociologist of education, she specializes in conflict resolution in schools and issues of multiculturalism. The research on mediation she describes in this volume was conducted while she was a research assistant with the Syracuse University Violence Prevention Project.

Kimberly M. Williams is assistant professor of education at the State University of New York at Cortland. She has a special interest in the effect of drugs on adolescents in schools and youths in college, and is the author of *Learning limits: College women, drugs, and relationships* (Westport, CT: Bergin & Garvey, 1998). She served as assistant director of the Syracuse University Violence Prevention Project in 1997–98 and as director in 1998–99 during which time she conducted the research reported in this volume.

Author Index

Subject Index